LCAAM

The Re-Emergence of Global Finance

The Re-Emergence of Global Finance

Gary Burn

First published in 2006 by
PALGRAVE MACMILLAN
Houndmills, Basingstoke, Hampshire RG21 6XS and
175 Fifth Avenue, New York, N.Y. 10010
Companies and representatives throughout the world.

PALGRAVE MACMILLAN is the global academic imprint of the Palgrave
Macmillan division of St. Martin's Press, LLC and of Palgrave Macmillan Ltd.
Macmillan® is a registered trademark in the United States, United Kingdom
and other countries. Palgrave is a registered trademark in the European
Union and other countries.

ISBN-13: 978–0–230–00198–5 hardback
ISBN-10: 0–230–00198–X hardback

This book is printed on paper suitable for recycling and made from fully
managed and sustained forest sources.

A catalogue record for this book is available from the British Library.

Library of Congress Cataloging-in-Publication Data

Burn, Gary, 1952–
    The re-Emergence of global finance / by Gary Burn.
        p. cm.
    Includes bibliographical references and index.
    ISBN 0–230–00198–X
    1. Euro-dollar market. 2. International finance. 3. Monetary policy –
Great Britain. 4. Monetary policy – United States. 5. Great Britain –
Economic policy. I. Title.

HG925.B87 2006
332'.042—dc22   2005058548

10 9 8 7 6 5 4 3 2 1
15 14 13 12 11 10 09 08 07 06

Printed and bound in Great Britain by
Antony Rowe Ltd, Chippenham and Eastbourne

This book is dedicated with love and thanks to my parents Ilse and Roy

In the living world there are no individuals entirely sealed off by themselves; all individual enterprise is rooted in a more complex reality, an 'intermeshed reality', as sociology calls it. The question is not to deny the individual on the grounds that he is the prey of contingency, but somehow to transcend him, to distinguish him from the forces separate from him ...

Fernand Braudel (*On History:* p. 10)

In truth, the historian can never get away from the question of time in history: time sticks to his thinking like soil to a gardener's spade.

Fernand Braudel (*On History:* p. 47)

Contents

List of Figures

List of Abbreviations

ABA	American Bankers Association
AIBD	Association of International Bond Dealers
BCEN	Banque Commerciale pour L'Europe du Nord
BEQB	Bank of England Quarterly Bulletin
BIS	Bank for International Settlements
BoE	Bank of England; Bank of England Archive
BOLSA	Bank of London & South America
CD	Certificate of Deposit
CMC	Commission on Money and Credit
DEA	Department for Economic Affairs
ECSC	European Coal and Steel Community
EEA	Exchange Equalisation Account
EFTA	European Free Trade Association
EPU	European Payments Union
FDI	Foreign Direct Investment
FDIP	Foreign Direct Investment Programme
FRBNY	Federal Reserve Bank of New York
FT	Financial Times
HMG	Her Majesty's Government
IBRD	International Bank for Reconstruction & Development
IDB	International Development Bank
IET	Interest Equalization Tax
IMF	International Monetary Fund
IRI	Instituto per la Rivostruzione Industriale
JFKL	President's Office Files, Department & Agencies (Treasury), John F. Kennedy Presidential Library
LIBOR	London Inter-Bank Offer Rate
MNC	Multinational Corporation
NSA	Non-Sterling Area
OECD	Organization of Economic Cooperation and Development
PFC	Principal Financial Centre
RUSIMA	Records of the Under Secretary for International Monetary Affairs, National Archives at College Park, MD, US.
SEC	Securities and Exchange Commission
TFEB	Traditional Foreign Exchange Banking System
VFCR	Voluntary Foreign Credit Restraint Programme

Preface

Some years ago I wrote an essay entitled 'Casino Capitalism: Another British Invention' in which I located the birth of the post-war rise of global capitalism in the decisions taken by the City of London financial community in the late 1950s. This evolved into an MA dissertation, which in turn became a PhD thesis and is now this book. During this long and somewhat tortuous journey, I have acquired debts to numerous people and institutions, beginning with the Economic Social Research Council (ESRC). They had turned down my application for a studentship twice already and I was back working for money, doing the thesis on a part-time basis and getting nowhere fast. I decided life was too short to spend all my free time thinking about global finance. I would apply a third time and if the ESRC did not come through I would go off to Italy and make furniture or something. They did come through. I went to Sussex University instead. I would therefore first like to acknowledge my gratitude and debt to the ESRC for their financial support and say that without it this book would never have seen the proverbial light of day. I presented my early research findings to the 1997 Annual Conference of the British International Studies Association and this became the basis for an article published in the *Review of International Political Economy*, which was awarded the Robert Cox Prize, and I thank the ISA for this and in particular, Robert Cox for his kind remarks.

I am equally indebted to those who, in different ways, helped me gather the empirical material which stands at the heart of this book. In no special order they are: William Keegan, Richard Fry, Charles Goodhart, Henry Grunfeld, Peter Spira, Douglas Dillon, Tony Coleby, John Fforde, Peter Gowan, Sir George Blunden, David (Lord) Cobbold, Doris Wasserman at SBC Warburg, John Booker, Chief Archivist at Lloyd's Bank International; Rosemary Lazenby and Jennifer Esposito at the FRBNY Archive, Henry Gillet and Sarah Millard at the Bank of England Archive, David Kynaston for unearthing Sir George Bolton's diaries and pointing me in their direction, Eva Ristl for helping me sort through the many boxes of US Treasury files at the National Archive in Washington DC.

This book has also benefited from numerous conversations and debates and from invaluable advice, encouragement and support going back over the years. I should therefore also like to acknowledge my debt to: Kees Van der Pijl, David Kynaston, E. H. H. Green, Richard Phillips, Angus Cameron, Sandra Halperin, Susan Strange, Peter Burnham, Libby Assassi, Justin Rosenberg, Randall Germain, Jon Moran, Barry Gills and Tim Gray. But above all to Ronen Palan. I thank him for his advice, support and for believing I had something worth saying. His unerring ability to clearly see the wood while I got repeatedly lost among the trees is a skill I could not have done without. I learned, but not quickly enough, that I ignored his advice at my peril. Finally, this book would not have been possible without the love and support of my friend and partner, Eve Belvain, who, while occasionally wondering why it was taking me so long to complete, never doubted that I would. Thanks too to Chloe and Charlie for their instinctive brand of spiritual guidance.

1
Introduction

The end of a Golden Age

The Long Boom, or, to put it more poetically, the Golden Age of Capitalism began around 1950 and continued for almost a quarter of a century, delivering to the developed world unprecedented growth and industrial development, virtual full employment, rapidly rising living standards and much greater social justice. So that by January 1969, as the US celebrated its 95th month of continuous economic growth, it appeared that the problems previously thought inherent in capitalism had been solved and the key to perpetual prosperity found.[1] Yet within three years unemployment and inflation began to rise simultaneously, the Dollar–Gold Standard collapsed, followed soon after by the Bretton Woods System itself; the fixed currency exchange system that had underpinned the Golden Age.

As global economic conditions worsened, Keynesianism and the Keynesian settlement came increasingly into disrepute and began to be assailed by the doctrine of monetarism, as corporate liberalism was by neo-liberalism. Inevitably the post-war consensus came under threat, as did the belief that achieving and maintaining full employment should be the overriding aim of every nation-state's economic policy. Eradicating the evil of inflation became the new all-consuming goal of governments across the globe, and the inherently contradictory nostrums of de-regulating financial markets and controlling money supply began to be applied. As counter-cyclical demand management made way for orthodox monetary policy and the wonders of deflationary medicine, unemployment began to rise to levels not experienced since the Great Depression, and the hegemony of the international financial market over national economic sovereignty, broken by the international crisis of 1931, became firmly re-established, further eroding political legitimacy, as democratically elected governments were ever less able, or willing, to pursue nationally defined economic programmes, in accordance with the wishes and interests of their electorates.

Global finance v. national capitalism

So what went wrong? It can be persuasively argued that even to begin to answer this difficult question involves examining discontinuity within a complex set of interlocking and interacting institutions – the international political order, the international financial structure, the systems of production, the macroeconomic structure, the rules of co-ordination and so on. Yet, going back to the capitalist crisis of the inter-war years, John Maynard Keynes and Harry Dexter White, the architects of Bretton Woods, saw the effect of massive disequilibrating international capital flows in precipitating systemic collapse in 1931, as having made a major contribution to the problem.

Did then the collapse of the Bretton Woods System and the end of the Golden Age signal a return to the unregulated international financial structure of today, or was the reverse true? That the gradual loosening of controls restricting the international movement of capital and the re-emergence of the power of global finance, beginning in the late 1950s, had provided the means of detaching financial capital from its subordination to productive capital, locked into national compartments constructed around the Fordist-Welfare-State concept. In this analysis the renaissance of global finance ultimately undermined embedded liberalism and its variation of 'national capitalism' that Keynes and White had thought so essential for the successful restoration of a multilateral international trading system after 1945.

Capital controls had originally been applied to counter the deflationary bias of an international trading system, where national interest rates and capital flows were determined more by international finance than domestic macroeconomic priorities. Keynes and White had designed the Bretton Woods system as a way of recreating an open multilateral world economy based on a new, quasi-public international financial order that was not prone to the systemic weaknesses which had so manifestly brought about the crisis of 1931. This meant, by definition, as Keynes wrote, that the 'massive sweeping and highly capricious transfers of short-term funds' that had had such a disequilibrating impact on the international monetary system would have to be prevented from re-occurring. Keynes and White believed, in fact, that a liberal order in international trade *and* finance were incompatible. If instead of countries in deficit having to rely on attracting 'hot money' to act as an adjustment mechanism, a supra-national agency existed to provide public international liquidity when required, such short-term speculative capital flows would be superfluous to requirements (De Cecco, 1976: 382). A distinction could then be made between 'virtuous' and 'vicious' capital movements, with controls placed on the latter, thereby preventing speculative hot money flows from, as Keynes put it, 'strangling' international trade, instead of playing 'their proper auxiliary role of facilitating trade'. While Keynes and White had different ideas on how to control such capital movements, they were agreed that states should have the right to apply such controls, and, in doing so, the right to apply exchange controls in order to screen current account transactions for illegal capital movements.[2]

In short, in place of the discredited liberal internationalism and *laissez-faire* ideology that dominated economic policy until the 1931 international financial crisis, Keynes and White wished to create at Bretton Woods, a regulated, restrictive international financial system. Naturally, opposition to this came from the American international banking community. They were hostile to the Keynesian emphasis on creating extra public international liquidity to ensure global economic expansion, which they considered to be inflationary and detrimental to the interests of foreign investment. They objected to the suppression of short-term capital movements which, when they facilitated the flow of capital into the US, as it had so often done in the inter-war years, had provided them with extra liquidity to augment their deposits. They feared a continuation of the cheap money policies of the 1930s and 1940s which had kept interest rates too low and stifled the US money market. They opposed government intervention which they felt would eliminate the need for private international banking and with it the profits accruing to such activities. And they feared, not only that IMF resources would provide governments with an alternative source of finance to that made so onerously available by private bankers, but also, that capital controls would allow member countries to 'insulate themselves from the threat of capital withdrawals'. They preferred the automatic control mechanism of the gold standard and required any supra-national institution which might be created at Bretton Woods to function in a similar way, so as to re-enforce the gold standard discipline rather than to 'subvert it' (Block, 1977: 53).

However, to what extent were, what Gill (1993b: 249) describes as 'financial interests associated with Wall Street and their counterparts in

Europe', able to resist the imposition of stricter state controls and a more rigorous system of international economic co-operation? Gill claims they were very successful, to the extent that the changes made to the Bretton Woods agreement on their behalf opened the door for the re-emergence of a *free* international capital regime after the return to convertibility in 1958. Certainly, the final Bretton Woods Agreement which was signed in July 1944 was, to a large extent, shorn of the controlling mechanisms Keynes and White had wished to set in place. In fact, De Cecco (1976: 382) sees in this agreement their 'almost complete defeat' at the hands of the US 'financial community'. Instead of the Keynes Plan for a powerful international central bank able to enforce counter-cyclical measures, what emerged after many changes was the IMF; a much weaker institution than even White envisaged, without the authority to penalise surplus countries. In that way the US bankers were certainly successful in countering the more radical parts of Keynes' and White's designs, and in so doing prevented a much more restrictive international financial system from being created. Yet, while they had managed to block the *obligatory* and mutually enforceable arrangement to control international capital flows, that had been planned, they were unable to alter the fact that Bretton Woods did *permit* states to control capital movements across their borders if they so wished.

Yet, the finer details of the Bretton Woods agreement are, effectively, irrelevant, as even before the Bretton Woods system proper came into operation in 1958, it had already been circumvented by an event that had taken place in Britain. To be precise, by the creation of a new, some would say 'natural', international money market: the Eurodollar market. An unregulated, international 'offshore' money market trading in US dollars, created, apparently spontaneously by merchant and overseas bankers based in London. For this parochial event led not only to the restoration of the City as the world's leading international financial centre, but much more significantly, to a restructuring of the global economy. It marked the beginning of a fundamental shift in how international financial relations were carried out, allowing (1) international finance to be gradually uncoupled from the international trade flows, and (2) an international monetary order that had been, essentially public, to evolve into one that was effectively private. The provision of equilibrating international liquidity that had formerly been the responsibility of the IMF came, once again, under the control of the market. In the process, a multilateral trading system that was almost wholly regulated and directed towards the development of distinct national regimes of accumulation was undermined and replaced by one that is today almost wholly unregulated and mostly responsive to the demands of global speculation.

The advent of the Euromarkets was then, as Durham (1992: 146) describes, the 'dress rehearsal for the full deregulation of international markets that finally took place twenty years later'. The nascent Eurodollar market of 1957 was the foundation stone of today's international financial system, where global foreign exchange markets presently trade an excess of $1 trillion a day – over ninety times the daily value of international trade.[3] Its creation, therefore, also marks the beginning of a return to the liberal internationalism of the private and central bankers that ended in ignominy in 1931, when the collapse of the gold standard, and with it the international financial system, brought about what Helleiner (1993: 22) calls a 'socio-ideological break' in financial affairs. With the Eurodollar market providing capital with a means of escaping from the official control, the period of restriction that began in 1931 and was formalised in the Bretton Woods Agreement, was at an end. In the neo-liberal view, this was a positive development, allowing for a more efficient economic order to evolve, where capital flows are determined by a competitive market rather than by political decree, designed to keep lenders and borrowers apart. Or as former Citibank chairman Walter Wriston put it, by 'national attempts to allocate credit and capital'.[4]

Yet the activity of combining the currency of one country with the banking regulation of another was not, in itself, a new innovation. For example, until the first half of the nineteenth century sterling was the accepted method of clearing between Philadelphia and Boston in the US. Also, a foreign market in dollars existed in London, Berlin and Vienna in the 1920s. And, of course, sterling was traded throughout the world in this way up until 1931. However, what happened in London in the late 1950s with the advent of the Eurodollar market, was not simply the creation of a new market trading in a foreign currency. What, in fact, the City bankers had done by creating this market, was to puncture a hole in the regulated international banking system, enabling capital to escape *offshore*. But what began as a trickle eventually became a deluge. Until the City 'came to resemble an "offshore island" much like the Cayman Islands or Curacao'. Although, unlike those islands, where there is an obvious coincidence of territorial and judicial sovereignty, for the City of London, offshore is a '*de-territorialized* economic phenomenon' (Overbeek, 1990: 151; Leyshon and Thrift, 1997: 76).

Here, it is generally argued, the Eurodollar was able to operate as a contraband currency, not only held and used outside the country where it had the status of legal tender, but, more significantly, traded in a market which exists and operates outside the system of state[s] sovereignty and, consequently, outside any national banking jurisdiction. And yet, as the City and its banks must, by definition, operate inside of British sovereignty, how can they operate – at the same time and in the same place – offshore? How can the City exist both inside and outside of British sovereignty? Ronen Palan (1998: 625) explains the creation of offshore as the result of deliberate state action taken to create a 'legally defined realm' in which regulation can be applied on a less intensive level. Given that the growth of the Eurodollar market would lead directly to the restoration of the City's fortunes a decade later, with all the benefits that accrued to the British state, it would be difficult to disagree with him that offshore, far from being the result of a diminution of sovereignty, as is often thought, should be regarded in Britain's case, as flowing from 'a radical redrawing of sovereignty' that has, on the face if it at least, re-inforced the power of the state. But if this true, how was it achieved?

Redrawing sovereignty in the City

The creation of the Eurodollar market is explained by Palan (1998: 634) as the result of an 'accounting device'. Because, what a number of merchant and overseas banks in the City had began to do when dealing in these ex-patriate dollars, was to run two 'books': one for 'domestic', the other for 'international' operations. They were responding to the legal restraints imposed by the Defence (Finance) Regulation of 1939 (reaffirmed by the 1947 Exchange Control Act), designed to protect Britain's currency reserves by controlling the short-term movement of capital out of the Sterling Area. This had the effect of compartmentalising the British banking system into a highly regulated domestic market and an unregulated international market, giving '*de facto* offshore status to all international banking and financial transactions ... isolated in a separate realm' (Versluysen, 1981: 93).

But how is this innovation to be understood? Can it be, as Palan claims, both the product of creative City accounting and the consequence of a radical redrawing of British state sovereignty? For this is to suggest that it can be explained by reference to two apparently dichotomously opposed theses: (1) that it is the spontaneous creation of seemingly anonymous international currency traders working in the City in the 1950s and looking for an international currency with which to replace sterling, and (2) that it was created as a result of intentional state policy. Yet explanations of the origins of the Euromarkets have, hitherto, tended to fall on one side or the other of this state v. market dichotomy.

The first thesis, the 'market explanation', is one generally put forward by economic liberals who would most probably concur with Forsyth (1987: 141), who explains that '[f]inancial innovation is a process by which the financial system adapts itself to new conditions'. Or as Loriaux (1997b: 7) describes it, it is 'a relentless transformative process driven primarily by the development of new technologies and more sophisticated financial instruments'. Based on this analysis, with regulation viewed, paradoxically, as a 'stimulate to', rather than a 'brake on' innovation, the creation of the Eurodollar was driven by the market seeking to overcome official obstruction, or 'friction', in the international financial system (Strange, 1976: 59; Johns, 1983: 2; Hampton, 1996: 38). Even the Bank of England adheres to this thesis, at least it did in 1972, when Governor O'Brien wrote 'restrictions which bite at all severely on financial intermediaries lead quickly to disintermediation or to the rapid growth of new intermediaries not subject to the same strictness of regulation' (BEQB, June 1972: 237).

Clearly, once the Eurodollar market had been established and the restrictive economic order breached, competition between major banking centres for shares in the Eurocurrency business was inevitable, driving a process of de-regulation and re-regulation in national banking law, in relation to reserve and capital requirements, lending quotas, the taxing and reporting of interest payments, profits, dividends and capital gains (Grabbe, 1996: 222). Yet, is this enough to fully explain the creation of the Euromarkets in the first place? The adherents of the second thesis, the 'state explanation', believe it is not.[5] While not denying the importance of market pressure, they see the Eurodollar market as having relied heavily upon state support from the start, primarily the support of the US and Britain. Thus the US has been deemed to have supported the market, either, by virtue of the fact that it neglected its role as the benign hegemon to regulate the international financial market effectively, or more actively, as Henry Nau (1990) claims, because it deliberately used its hegemonic power to promote deregulation. Britain too, although to a lesser extent, has been regarded as having actively encouraged and supported development of the Eurodollar market, taking various 'legal initiatives' and making certain 'legal changes' to smooth its way. But as the evolution of the Euromarkets – and especially that of the Eurodollar market – remains, for the most part, un-researched in terms of 'genuine historical sources', neither thesis is well informed. Debate with respect to their origins, thus, often tends to be reduced, too readily, to a simple state/market dichotomy, largely unsupported by fact.[6]

If Palan is correct a different understanding of the Eurocurrency phenomenon is required, one that transcends the simple, discreet, state v. market, public v. private division. This book seeks to do this and challenges this debate on three counts. First, that it is misinformed, due to a tendency to collapse the origins and development of the Eurodollar [Eurocurrency] market and the Eurobond market into a single history. For these are two distinct markets, dealing in distinct financial products that evolved at different times, so that supposed British state support for the creation of the Eurodollar market in 1957, and the subsequent evolution of an unregulated global financial structure, is predicated upon evidence of the Bank of England's involvement in the setting up, six years later, of the Eurobond market for the provision of long-term capital through the issuing of foreign currency bonds.

Second, that it has been unable to identify precisely the nature of the historical actors responsible for the constitution of the Euromarkets, due to a predilection, among many writers, to use the terms: 'Britain', the 'British financial authorities' and the 'Bank of England' interchangeably, or worse, as synonyms for the 'British state'. It is this neglect of the institutional specificity of the British state that has led to much confusion and masked the complexity of the processes that brought about the estab-lishment of the Euromarkets For example, while Paul Einzig (1964a: 9), one of the first to write about the Eurodollar market, claims that it 'received much encouragement from the British official attitude in favour of the system', Reid (1988: 8) and Moran (1991: 55) identify this more pre-cisely as the 'Bank of England'; Strange (1971: 209), the 'British monetary authorities'; Coakley and Harris (1983: 48), the 'British government'; and Hampton (1996: 73), the 'UK government', although 'indirectly, via the Bank'. Helleiner (1994a: 84, 196; 1994b: 169) is able to claim that the Eurodollar market was 'actively encouraged by British financial authorities'; was supported by 'Britain', and then again by 'the British government'; and that the Bank of England was its 'most active proponent'. He chooses, for the most part, not to make a distinction between these terms, ignoring the complex relationship between the state and civil society that charac-terised the governance of the City. But it was this unique institutional structure which gave birth to the Euromarkets, especially the role and character of the Bank of England, an institution originally established in 1694 to stand between the Crown and the Puritan market.

Finally, and following on from the second point, that development of the Euromarkets in the City of London is not then the result of the actions of protagonists who can be separated into the distinct and discrete categories of either 'market operators' or 'state officials', because the institutional structure is a direct consequence of the inter-penetration of 'state' and 'market', in the shape of what Ingham (1984: 134) calls the City-Bank of England–Treasury nexus,[7] where a coterie of powerful institutions, instrumental in defining state economic policy – the Treasury and the Bank of England – are themselves 'deeply embedded' within a network of ancillary institutions rooted in civil society and the economic system located in the City (Hall, 1986b: 17). Hence, it can be argued that the Euromarkets evolved out of actions taken after the Second World War to re-constitute the City as a pre-industrial financial centre, for what German economist Friedrich List regarded as 'cosmopolitan mercantile capitalism', operating outside the encroachment and control of the British state – a state that in its post-war Keynesian democratic form, had assumed responsibility for the national economy for the first time. Especially the development of Britain's industrial base and maintenance of full employment.[8]

More specifically, the creation of the Eurodollar market in the City in the late 1950s, was a direct consequence of decisions taken by Britain's financial elites to *re-establish* a regulatory order that was, essentially, largely independent of the state (Moran, 1991: 16), because 'banking regulation', which initially evolved out of the policy requirements of a private bank controlled by a City elite had remained almost entirely – until the crisis of 1931 – the 'private concern of the Bank [of England] and the City, not the public concern of Parliament and government' (Moran, 1984: 18, 22). It suggests that the concept of 'governance' or the 'governance of regulatory space', whether by the state or the market, is a more realistic model of a societal/state structure to explain financial innovation in the City, one which moves beyond the artificial divisions of 'state/market' or 'public/private', to locate where real power lies within the financial structure – power which waxes and wanes as it infects and is infected by socio-economic conditions and is caught up in the conjunctural dance of history. So, for example, the Great Depression of the inter-war years, the collapse of the gold standard and the international financial order, and the advent of the Second World War, which put the country on a financial war footing, brought the Bank, the City and the financial markets under the protection and the 'governance' of the British state. Without this, many of the City's merchant banks would not have survived. Yet, although the completion of this process was symbolised by nationalisation in 1946, because the Bank was able to maintain its essential 'institutional independence', it remained in many way the private institution of old, its relations with government continuing to be 'regulated by custom rather than law' (Hanham, 1959: 17). So the Bank was able to operate in much the same way it had done since the First World War – as a 'Praetorian Guard' for a City elite threatened by a 'potentially democratic state' (Moran, 1991: 66). In this way, when economic conditions improved in the early 1950s, the City was in a strong position to begin to recover its historic and hegemonic role.

Bank of England policy should not therefore be interpreted purely as a reflex action stemming from a hegemonic 'lag', whereby it irrationally promoted the City's role as an international financial centre 'long after Britain's days of financial predominance were over', as argued by Helleiner (1994b: 169). Nor should it be viewed as simply emanating out of a desire to re-establish for Britain the prestige associated with possessing an international financial centre, which for the Bank of England and state elites of a declining power, was the only opportunity that remained to play a leading international role, as suggested by Moran (1991: 6) and Dufey and Giddy (1978: 196). Rather, it should be seen as a strategy primarily designed to ensure that *financial capital*, and the financial aristocracy that controlled this capital – what Davenport (1964: 178) refers to as 'Old Etonian finance-capitalism' – could regain a position relatively independent from the state, which it had lost in 1931. Something that it was ultimately only able to achieve through the advent of the Eurodollar market (McRae and Cairncross, 1973: 17–18; Little, 1985: 53). More prosaically, of course, this market also allowed the City's financiers to issue dollar liabilities and thereby share in the denomination rents and the privileges of seigniorage that had that previously accrued exclusively to the US; something which became particularly important with the decline of sterling as an international currency (Swoboda, 1968: 14).

Accumulation and institutional change

States, markets, governance, sovereignty – the advent of the Eurodollar cut through these constructs like the metaphorical knife through butter, restructuring international financial relations and global capitalism in the process. All the more surprising then that the creation and early development of this most momentous financial innovation since the bank note is still largely unresearched. Instead, existing theories of the Euromarket phenomenon seemingly unhampered by the lack of supportive, hard, verifiable, historical data, rest comfortably on the deductive approach of both the, essentially, metaphysical historicism of

Hegel and Marx and the neoclassical anti-historicism of Popper, which, as Snooks points out, 'owed little to the systematic study of historical change'. Ironically, it was the assault of the latter on the former in the 1950s which had the effect of damaging historicism *per se*, to the extent that the descendents of those economists working in that tradition were most often diverted into economic history (Snooks, 1998: 55, 179). Which is why the inductive approach, with some important exceptions, became mostly associated with the production of a traditional history of events and 'great' personages, with its emphasis on dates and other historical facts.

Yet while an extensive examination of the relevant archival material might provide for a more comprehensive and verifiable historical narrative of the evolution of the Euromarkets, establishing a chronology of events and the names and identities of the significant personalities that had brought about these financial innovations, it is in itself not enough. For while – notwithstanding the impact of nature and natural phenomena – history can only be made by the actions or non-actions taken by men and women, such activity does not occur within a vacuum. More often a complex set of institutions 'fix the confines of and impose form upon the activities of human beings' (cited in Tuma, 1971: 20), institutions that both define, and are in turn re-defined, by our actions. For that reason purely *descriptive-qualitative* accounts that are the fabric of traditional history are in themselves unable to adequately explain change.

To account for historical continuity/discontinuity it is perhaps useful to adopt a methodology which can be described as *institutional-analytical*. Those institutions which informed the early development of the Euromarkets, 1957–65, were clearly those that were traditionally regarded as being part of the Inner City – the merchant and overseas banks, the merchant banking community and the Bank of England. When the City began using the dollar as a surrogate for sterling, it utilised part of the same institutional framework. A framework which itself was rooted in a structure that had evolved in Victorian England to create and distribute global credit. Institutional analysis therefore needed to move back to examining sterling and those 'historical mechanisms' for the organisation of global credit in the nineteenth century.[9]

So, at this third level, the methodology can be described as broadly *structural-institutional* and tipping the hat towards Braudel, in that it follows 'the path of transcending the individual' and 'the daily booty of microsociology', as well as the belief that 'documentary authenticity was the repository of the whole truth' (Braudel, 1981: 28). It is concerned with the 'plurality of historical time' and operates on three scales of levels: (1) *l'historie événementialle*, the traditional narrative history of individuals and events, concerned with the short-time span, relating to the early development of the Euromarkets between 1948 and 1964; (2) the intermediate scale of 'conjectures' which is concerned to elaborate a period of years between ten and fifty, taking the story back to the heyday of *Pax Britannica* that ended in 1914 and the liberal internationalism of the inter-war years centred around sterling and the return to the gold standard;[10] and (3) *la longue durée*, 'the quasi-immobile time of structures and traditions', which in this history goes back to, not just the early part of the nineteenth century and the beginning of modern cosmopolitan mercantilism and internationalism, but further back to the Glorious Revolution of 1688 and the rise of Whiggish money power, the beginning of the modern capital market for public and private finance and the establishment of a quasi-offshore, self-regulatory enclave, within the geo-political boundaries of the City of London.

The history of the Euromarkets forms then a useful test-case for elaborating a dynamic theory of how institutions are created and maintained, how they evolve and change. Coates (2000: 176) points the way when he writes that 'behind' the institutional uniqueness of each capitalist model 'lie different relationships between financial and industrial fractions of each national capitalism class'. But this analysis needs to be taken further, to show that these 'institutional differences' originate in the realm of the accumulation process itself through which capital expands. The creation of the Euromarkets and the re-establishment of the power of global capital that this made possible, can then be understood as necessary to allow Britain's dominant capital fraction to re-impose a form of accumulation which is both tangential and abstract, in that it does not rely on production to acquire a surplus, but, through commercial and financial intermediation, is able to 'absorb' a share of the surplus, in the form of interest, fees, commissions and arbitrage profit (Harvey, 1982: 257). To do this effectively the City needed to break free from any responsibility for, and reliance on, domestic production that had been acquired after 1931. It needed to move away from state control and the burden of national capitalism imposed by the Attleeite settlement. It needed to move governance back to the market. It could do all this only by re-opening and keeping open the international realm (Burn, 2002). But in 1945 this was easier said than done.

After the Great War, the City had embarked on an immediate 'return to normalcy': to an open unregulated international monetary system based on gold, with London at its centre. Nothing was allowed to stand in the way of this project. It was a pipedream and ended in disaster. But in 1945 even this was not possible. Britain was bankrupt, the dollar was king, the Bretton Woods System was in place and a socialist government was in power. Nevertheless, the City was determined to recover its historic role, and with the help of the Bank of England the re-establishment of sterling as an international currency became – although perhaps without the politicians' full understanding – the definitive economic policy of the post-war era. Gradually, the City reopened – the gold market, foreign exchange market, commodities markets and so on. The institutional framework that had originally evolved around the London bill market in the nineteenth century and had made England the 'clearing house' of the world, was dusted off and put to work again by the City's merchant banking community to carry out its international acceptance business. There was only one problem: sterling. Full convertibility was restored in 1958 and it was hoped that sterling could 'look the dollar in the face' once again. But exchange controls remained and sterling continued to pose a problem to the point where its increasing dysfunctionality threatened the survival of the institutional framework itself and with it, merchant banking profitability. Until, that is, sterling was replaced with a more robust global currency that would become the City's salvation: the Eurodollar.

That is the story encapsulated in this book. A story beginning in austere, late-fifties London, when a few City bankers, like the legendary Sir George Bolton, set about recapturing their world. A world that had passed away on the battlefields of Flanders and France, on the hunger marches and in the soup kitchens of the Great Depression and during the systematic barbarism and destruction of war-torn Europe. A world controlled by the interests of international finance and speculative capital. They did it under the nose of the British Government, inventing a new form of money and a market in which to trade it, that lay beyond the jurisdiction and control of any monetary authority. The advent of the Eurodollar heralded a return to the future: a first shot in the neo-liberal counter-revolution against the social market and the Keynesian welfare state; re-asserting institutions reaching back across Helleiner's 'socio-ideological break' in financial affairs, to the liberal internationalism and the disastrous *laissez-faire* order of the inter-war years, and beyond, to the heyday of *Pax Britannica*; drawing governance back to the market, until once again the City of London became the base for what was essentially, the 'private exercise of monetary authority' (Germain, 1997: 50). This is the story of the Eurodollar and the re-emergence of global finance. And how the City discarded sterling and reclaimed its historic role as the world's foremost financial centre.

2
The Evolution of the Euromarkets

Because of the unique contribution the Euromarkets have made, both to the post-war recovery of the City of London as an international financial centre and, more significantly, to the development and transformation of the global economy, it is not surprising that the literature dealing with both the recovery of the City and the operation and history of the international financial system during this period, is studded with references to Eurodollars, Eurosterling, Euromarks, Eurocurrencies, Eurobonds, Eurobanks, Euromarkets and Euromoney. These texts, in turn, can be divided into distinct – if naturally overlapping – sub-texts. Thus, literature on the recovery of the City emanates largely from two separate, if interconnected, debates revolving around the apparent contradictory relationship between Britain's manufacturing and financial sectors, the so-called City–industry divide, or, as Plender and Wallace (1985: 15–16) describe it, the phenomenon of the 'two Cities': (1) the broader Decline of Britain debate, and (2) a narrower Marxist/neo-Marxist debate on the conflict between capital fractions (financial/commercial v. manufacturing) in Britain, and how this impacts on Marxist state theory and the development of global capitalism.[1] Euromarkets also feature prominently in the literature on the post-war political economy of sterling, on the history of the City, the Bank of England and particular merchant and overseas banks.[2]

Literature on the operation, history and political economy of the post-war international financial system and international banking, meanwhile, feeds into debates concerned with explaining and understanding the problematic of the Euro-currency market, in terms of (1) its role in creating and supplying private international liquidity and credit necessary for the functioning of international trade; (2) how it contributed to US post-war foreign and domestic policy problems which led to the collapse of the Bretton Woods System and the replacement of the Dollar–Gold Standard with a pure Dollar Standard; and (3) its significance as an international unregulated market for *offshore* finance that has led to a re-structuring of the international financial system and US financial hegemony.[3] In addition, there is a large and comprehensive literature dedicated to the phenomenon of the Euromarkets in relation to financial innovation and financial liberalisation.[4]

Defining Euromoney

But what exactly is Euromoney? It is certainly not, the 'single European currency' the Euro, that was established in 2000 to be the common currency of the European Union. Euromoney as described in this book, pre-dates its namesake by more than fifty years. A Eurocurrency, as it evolved in the 1950s, is a form of currency held and traded outside the jurisdiction of the issuing state; for example Euro-dollars, Euro-sterling and, formerly, Euro-francs and Euro-marks and so on. Hence, the term Eurodollar denotes any dollar held and traded outside the control of the US money market and thus not subject to domestic US banking regulations and its interest rate structure, although, technically Eurodollars do remain in the US banking system, ensuring that ultimate control over foreign-owned dollars remains vested with the US monetary authorities.[5] Nevertheless, the *raison d'etre* for the birth of the Eurodollar was to supply the international realm with a sufficiency of international liquidity that was not being provided under the restrictive Bretton Woods System and a US still tied up in New Deal legislation. As Paul Einzig (1964: 35) saw it, 'There was a distinct gap in the international financial machinery. In the circumstances the appearance of the Eurodollar system was well-timed and providential.' The Eurodollar market is then, the name given to the unofficial, unregulated and unrestricted international money market, dealing in ex-patriate dollar deposits held in a very liquid, short-term form, in *parallel* to the official, regulated and restrictive market.

The Eurobond market, however, is an international capital market issuing and trading in foreign currency bearer bonds. That is, trading in bonds denominated in a currency other than that of the country in which the issue is made.[6] Because the term Eurobond was given to what had formerly been called a 'foreign dollar bond', it is sometimes referred to as a Eurodollar bond (Einzig and Quinn, 1977: 6). This has led to some confusion, as the term Eurodollar market is sometimes mistakenly used to describe both markets. To avoid any confusion, when I use the terms Eurodollar and the Eurodollar market I refer only to the former (1). When I refer to the terms Euro-bond and the Euro-bond market I refer only to the latter. It took time for the term Eurodollar to become widely accepted. Legend has it that it was originally coined by Einzig himself, sometime after the summer of 1959. William Clarke then used it in an article in *The Times* on 24 October 1960, entitled 'London – Centre of the Euro-Dollar Market' (Evans, 1992: 42; Kynaston, 2002: 269). But in its early years the market was also known variously as the 'Merchant Bankers' Market', 'Continental Dollar Market', 'London Dollar Market', 'Foreign Market for Dollars', 'Foreign Dollar Market' and the 'International Dollar Market'. More recently it has been referred to as the 'offshore financial market'.

The first Eurodollars began as ordinary dollar deposits with US banks, acquired by non-resident holders in one of a number of ways. For example: as export earnings from trading with the US and by selling assets in the US. But these dollars only became Eurodollars when instead of being exchanged for indigenous currency as was traditional, they were held on deposit outside the US. Accruing interest adjustable within a fixed term period from overnight to one year or more for deposits and overnight to seven years for loans, though most loans and deposits being for months rather than years, interest rates are calculated in accordance with the London inter-bank offer rate (LIBOR).

Providing verifiable statistical information regarding the growth of the Eurodollar market is problematic. First it was not collected by the Bank of International Settlements (BIS) until 1963, all figures for the years from 1957 to 1963 are therefore estimates.[7] Second, the difficulty of quantifying the percentage of the total Eurodollar deposits that are, in fact, re-deposits, makes it difficult to calculate the net size of the market. Third, they do not include positions *vis-à-vis* residents' holdings, nor the net balance after swap activities have taken place. Fourth, the Eurodollar is very often regarded as just one type of Euro-currency and statistics showing the growth of the Eurodollar market are not distinguished within statistics showing the growth of the Euro-currency market in total. Total Euro-deposits, net of inter-bank re-deposits, are thought to have grown from about $1 billion in 1960 to $19 billion in 1967, $57 billion in 1970, $215 billion in 1975 and $1050 billion in 1983. According to the BIS, between 1965 and 1978 the market grew by 30 per cent per annum, three times the growth rate of the world money supply. The BIS *34th Annual Report* suggests that, given that the core of the Eurocurrency market was to be found in the City, a 'useful indicator' of its growth for the years 1957 to 1963 is the total volume of liabilities and claims on non-residents of the overseas and foreign banks and accepting houses in London. These are shown in Figure 2.1. Statistics showing the growth of the Eurodollar (1963–68) and the Eurobond markets (1963–69) are reproduced in Figures 2.2 and 2.3 respectively. Statistics showing the growth of Eurocurrencies in relation to world reserves are reproduced in Figure 2.4.

The origins of the Eurodollar market

Given the voluminous and eclectic body of literature detailed above, it is somewhat surprising that very little research has been done on the evolution of the Euromarkets. In fact, it would seem that the majority of writers and commentators have been primarily concerned with expounding their various theses and to have relied, too readily, on

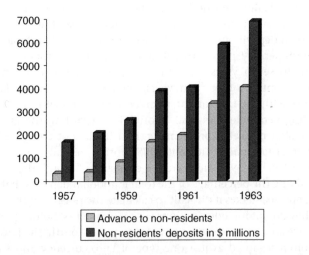

Figure 2.1   Total liabilities and claims on non-residents of the Overseas, Foreign and Merchant Banks in London, 1957–63

1964	1965	1966	1967	1968
9	11.5	14.5	17.5	25

Figure 2.2   Eurodollar market size 1963–68 ($ billion)

Source: BIS, *39th Annual Report* (Basle: BIS, 1969).

Country of borrower	1963	1964	1965	1966	1967	1968	1969
United States	—	—	331	439	527	2059	1032
Continental Europe	88	408	456	426	886	658	1082
United Kingdom	—	—	25	40	51	134	235
Japan	20	162	25	—	—	180	246
Canada	—	—	—	—	—	38	228
Rest of world	25	5	83	101	305	259	247
International institutions	5	121	128	101	—	40	40

Figure 2.3 Eurobond issues 1963–69 ($ millions)
Source: BIS, *Annual Reports*.

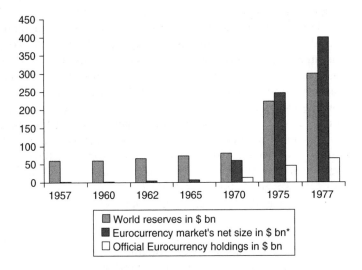

Figure 2.4 Eurocurrencies and world reserves
Notes: 1957–60 estimated; * Europe only to 1969; worldwide thereafter.

explanations which have been handed down from one writer to another. Often, membership of a particular profession or faculty appears to predetermine, to some extent, interpretation: with those operating in the market, for example, financiers, bankers, financial journalists and economists, tending to explain the advent of the Euromarkets as the direct consequence of unstoppable technological and market forces overcoming state erected barriers; sociologists and political economists seeing state action [or non-action] as vitally important, and economic historians, while recording the parts played by state and market actors alike, often appearing unconcerned with such a distinction, and with the nature of the forces and the concept of power, underlying the events they chronicle. Thus, while there is an abundance of references, from an array of academic disciplines already existing on the Euromarkets, most of them are derivative rather than definitive.

For example, Geoffrey Jones (1998: 138), in a more recent chapter entitled 'Banking after the Second World War' explains how and why the Euromarkets evolved as they did. He does this very succinctly, so that in a few sentences he sums up very much all that is known about the origins of the Eurodollar market. Yet, his account is virtually the same as that of Shaw's (1975: 114), written 23 years earlier. In fact, very little evidence appears to have been added to that which existed in 1960, when Holmes and Klopstock (1960a), in one of the earliest surveys on the Eurodollar phenomenon, pointed out that the history of the market is largely anecdotal and cannot, therefore, be 'exactly pinpointed'.

This evidence, as Jones informs us, adds up to, first, that dollars originally began to be deposited outside the US by communist countries. Second, that dollars began to be traded in Europe because of restrictive banking regulation in the US. Third, that British government restrictions on the use of sterling as an international vehicle currency drove British merchant banks to look for an alternative form of funding for their international financial business. This brief history is most often embellished with reference to one or more of five facts which have been reiterated down through the years. Facts which are largely unsubstantiated and form the superstructure of a body of anecdotal but conflicting evidence which has almost taken on the character of folklore. The five facts are as follows:

1. Communist-owned dollars were originally deposited with the Banque Commerciale pour L'Europe du Nord (BCEN) in Paris.
2. Communist-owned dollars were originally deposited with the Moscow Narodny Bank in London.

3. The Bank of England encouraged the Euro-markets to develop in London.
4. Sir George Bolton, formerly of the Bank of England and later chairman of the Bank of London and South America (BOLSA), pioneered the development of the Euromarkets in the late 1950s.
5. Sir Siegmund Warburg of Warburgs Bank invented the Euromarkets in the early 1960s.

What is certainly not disputed is that a 'very discrete' and embryonic Eurodollar market originated in the early years of the Cold War, after communist governments transferred their dollar holdings from New York to banks in Paris and London and in doing so created a new form of dollar holding, in ex-patriate dollars. There are, however, many different, conflicting and muddled versions of 'why', 'where' and 'when' this activity began, although, again, there is very little, if any, supporting evidence. This is confirmed by C. Gordon Tether, who wrote in the *Banker* in June 1961, that the market 'would seem' to have begun because some East European banks feared their dollar deposits held in the US were in danger of being 'immobilised'. Other writers, however, have been more specific in their claims. Thus, Sampson (1981: 109) believes that the market began in 1949, when the Chinese government deposited their dollars with the BCEN, a Soviet-owned bank situated in Paris. The name 'Eurodollar' is said to have been originally taken from the bank's telex address: EURBANK [hence the term Eurbank dollars and finally Eurodollars].

While Van Dormael (1997: 91), Mendolsohn (1980; 19), Wachtel (1990: 94) and Susan Strange (1976: 181) agree that the Chinese started the Eurodollar market, that is all they do agree upon. Van Dormael claims this did not happen until June 1950, when fearful the Korean War would prompt the US into confiscating their dollar assets, the Chinese deposited $5 million with the BCEN in the name of the Hungarian National Bank. Mendolsohn says that it began in 1949, when they began depositing their dollars in Paris. Although he adds that the Chinese still kept dollar balances in New York, and that it was these funds that were blocked by the US in 1950 at the onset of the Korean War, under legislation prohibiting trade with the enemy. Wachtel argues that it began after the Chinese Revolution prompted the US to begin freezing Chinese accounts in US banks. Strange attributes the beginning to the time when the Chinese and Russian governments became alarmed by the US government's sequestration of Yugoslav gold held in New York, in the late 1940s.

Mayer (1976: 454) agrees that it began out of a fear of sequestration, but by the Russians, not the Chinese, and later, in 1956. After the US invoked 'the spirit of the Neutrality Act of the 1930s' to freeze the assets of all belligerents in the war in Suez. Versluysen (1981: 22) agrees that it was the danger of US sequestration that persuaded the Russians to move their dollar holdings to Europe, but sequestration prompted in response to the Bolshevik government's 1917 revocation of all foreign debts contracted by the Czarist government. Sarver (1988: 18) offers yet another variation on this theme, believing that the Soviet Union feared the US would seize their assets because they were in arrears with respect to lend-lease loan repayments after the Second World War. Smith (1982: 122), also believes it was the Russians who invented the Eurodollar. He maintains, however, that they did this after the 1956 Hungarian uprising, when a Russian bureaucrat named 'Dregasovitch' moved his country's dollar balances to the Moscow Narodny Bank in London. Intriguingly Smith, as he goes on to explain, 'once pursued this faceless bureaucrat. ... The pursuit looked promising when a Russian banker said, "Dregasovitch didn't invent the Eurodollar, the people under him did; he just took all the credit", but the trail grew cold after that'. Yet despite Smith's investigating activities, Mayer (1976: 454) has a different view, placing the action as having occurred at the Narodny Bank in Paris, with '[t]echnical assistance ... from the Chase Bank'. Sarver (1988: 18) agrees that it was the work of the Russians at the Narodny Bank in Paris, but on the advice of a British merchant bank in London. Versluysen (1981: 22) however believes that it originated when the Russians began using 'friendly' European banks to place their dollars in New York. Only after opportunities for using offshore dollar deposits developed, he claims, did they stop routing their deposits through intermediaries and placed them directly with large European banks and the Vneshtorgbank's (Soviet Bank of Foreign Trade) own European affiliates in Paris, London and Zurich. Then, Holmes and Klopstock (1960a: 5), while qualifying their claims as resting 'on somewhat tenuous and circumstantial evidence', write that the market began when the Gosbank (the State Bank of the USSR), concerned to both 'employ dollar accruals profitably outside the confines of the United States' and to pre-empt 'attachment suits and blocking' by the US authorities, began searching Europe for surplus dollars, 'either directly or through their European correspondents' in particular their agents in London and Paris – the Moscow Narodny Bank and the BCEN. Finally, Born (1983: 306), who traces operations in Eurodollar credits as beginning no earlier than 1953, claims that Eastern bloc countries removed their dollar deposits from the US simply because they could get better rates in Europe, and that their actions had nothing to do with the Cold War.[8]

Where all these conflicting stories originated is unclear. Certainly most come free of any corroborating evidence whatsoever. Nevertheless, interesting as this subject may be from a purely historical view, especially with regard to the propagation of the Cold War, it is largely irrelevant from the purview of this book. So while it is true that Paris and other international financial centres, vied with London in the 1950s as a home for these early dollar deposits, and Canadian Banks also had large US dollar deposits which they traded in the so-called Cano-dollar market – a variant of the Eurodollar market – what is important is the fact that sometime during the early post-war period, the activity of holding dollar deposits outside the jurisdiction of the US regulatory authorities took hold. What reasons communist countries had for doing this and which banks they chose to further this end is, almost, immaterial. Nor is there any disagreement that the communist bloc was the original source of non-resident dollars. This is particularly significant, as Paul Bareau (1979: 59) points out, because it was the communist governments that began to supply a free, open market in non-resident dollars, and in doing so revealed that this was a market in which dealers could operate within the margins defined by the US domestic money market and make a profit. However, it was not the only source of non-resident dollars. The others being Marshall Aid and Korean War dollars. And this supply was then fuelled by the growing US payments deficit in the late 1950s and early 1960s.

In addition, the easing of rules requiring both banks and companies to surrender their excess dollar balances to their respective central banks, the introduction of non-resident convertibility in Western Europe in 1958 and the relaxation of exchange controls, all contributed to a broadening of the supply stream, so that by 1959 Dutch, West German (for a brief period), Scandinavian and Swiss banks, and banks in the oil-producing countries of the Near East were also feeding the market, through banks in Beirut and London. The banning by West German, Swiss and, later, French monetary authorities, of the payment of interest on foreign-owned balances also made sure that this supply stream was directed to London, as opposed to other European financial capitals, such as Frankfurt, Zurich and Paris.[9]

Central banks and the BIS were probably the most important source of funds while the market was developing (Scott-Quinn, 1975). For as the European recovery gained ground, the central banks of those countries running surplus balance of payments positions began to supply the market with their excess dollars, in order to maintain their currency parities within the Bretton Woods System and to control domestic money supply. They did this by placing these dollars directly onto the market, or via the BIS, or through 'swap' arrangements with their commercial banks.[10] Central banks also began to borrow dollars on the Eurodollar market to build up their reserves and defend their parities (Attali, 1986: 227). Thus, in 1963 it was estimated that at least two-thirds of the total Eurodollar market funds had emanated from central banks' offsetting balance of payments surpluses and deficits (Shaw, 1975: 128). This activity ended in 1971, at least by the Group of Ten major industrialised countries, fearful of the dangers of a multiple expansion of the market resulting from the habit which private dealers had of converting their Eurodollar holdings back into those domestic currencies they expected would be revalued.[11]

Developing a foreign market for dollars

It was not, however, the initial acceptance of foreign currency deposits that was the 'originating innovation' which defined the Eurodollar market, but rather, 'their placement outside the US money market and banking system' (Clendenning, 1970: 22). Again, this activity appears to have begun with the Communists, who had soon graduated to using the proto-Eurodollar market they had created, as a means of attracting other dollar deposits, which they then used to finance their hard-currency imports, quickly becoming, in the process, net borrowers in the market. Italian banks also began borrowing Eurodollars as early as 1950/51, to lend on to local businessmen. Up until the late 1950s the bulk of these non-resident dollars were re-invested back in the US, by Canadian, Swiss or other European banks, and thus became, as Johnson (1964: 6) describes, an 'appendage' of the US money market.[12] However, this began to change when the post-war boom took off and interest rates began to rise. In fact, as Robbie (1975/76: 26) claims, 'interest rate developments were crucial to the establishment of the market'. Because, unlike British and French banks, US banks were constrained by the Federal Reserve's Regulation Q, which placed an interest rate ceiling on time deposits in US banks, from following rates up.[13] Hence, the higher the interest rose, the more attractive alternative investment opportunities became to holders of dollar deposits. They began, instead, to supply a new market in the City of London, a type of market that did not exist in the US – the *wholesale inter-bank market*, which had been established in the mid-1950s.

The creation of this market was very significant for two reasons. First, it lay outside of British banking jurisdiction, and hence, for the first time, it allowed banks to go against a major precept of national banking regulation and borrow from one another, rather than through the discount houses. Second, because it was established within the foreign exchange market – with the innovatory difference being that instead of the dollar supplies being exchanged for other currencies, that is bought and sold, now they were lent and borrowed – it lay outside the official system for controlling capital movements. In this way, the inter-bank market, operating, as it was, outside both the traditional international capital market and the traditional foreign exchange market (TFEB), became the prototypical escape route *offshore*, which, very gradually, evolved into a parallel international capital market available to non-bank users dealing in Eurocurrencies (Versluysen, 1981: 21; Davies, 2002: 416). In fact, the inter-bank market began, as Steinberg (1976: 150) describes, as 'an international telephone market', after European bankers, with surplus dollar deposits in their New York accounts, started looking for better earning opportunities. Because in the US, not only were banks unable to pay out competitive interest to their customers, but US Treasury bill yields were also unattractive to the potential investor. However, it was only when UK local authorities were prevented from raising money through the Public Loans Board in 1955, and began to look for another source of funding that an alternative, more profitable, use for these ex-patriate dollars was found outside of the US banking system; subsequent, of course, to them being exchanged for sterling and moving into Britain's domestic money market.[14] Catherine Schenk (1998: 225) traces these dollar swap transactions to June 1955, when the Bank of England became aware that the Midland Bank were 'seeking foreign currency deposits unrelated to their commercial transactions'. The Midland, she claims, had originated the idea of switching these deposits into sterling, to take advantage of opportunities that existed for profitable interest rate arbitrage (as UK rates rose above the maximum rate payable in the US under Regulation Q), and to provide an alternative source of investment funding, at a time when the British Government's tight monetary policy was placing liquidity constraints on the domestic money market. Schenk sees these exchange deals as the beginning of a process of financial innovation that ultimately created the Eurodollar market. Certainly, Bank of England records show that the Banker's Sub-Committee made a decision in 1955 to allow banks to pay interest on non-resident dollar deposits, if they so wished.[15]

Yet, for the Eurodollar market to become a true *offshore* market, dollars had to be deposited and re-lent outside the jurisdiction of, not only the US banking system, but of all national banking systems. Hampton (1996: 45) believes that this activity began at the beginning of the 1950s, when the London dollar balances of British insurance companies operating in the US were transferred to merchant banks, who then lent them on to international borrowers. Smith (1982: 122) disagrees, maintaining that it did not take place until 28 February 1957, when the Moscow Norodny Bank in London, issued a loan of $800,000 through a London merchant bank. Once again, not one of these writers provides any supporting evidence for their claims. What is certain, however, is that by September of 1957 the Eurodollar market proper had begun to take off, after a sterling crisis created what Clendenning (1970: 23) describes as the 'first major incentive from the demand side'.

The British Government's response was to encourage the market to hold on to sterling by increasing Bank Rate from 5 to 7 per cent. It also attempted to reduce demand for sterling, by restricting its use as a means of financing non-Sterling Area trade, and re-financing, and reducing the maximum time credit period for other sterling credits. Ostensibly, this latter measure had the direct effect of cutting off the source of funding by which British merchant and overseas banks conducted a considerable amount of international business. This posed a problem for these banks, as they had traditionally relied on acceptance bills of exchange in sterling (the London bill) to provide credit for the financing of international trade,[16] Bearing in mind that in 1957, London not only remained the primary centre for foreign trade finance, but the pound was still a major international trading currency, financing around 40 per cent of world trade.[17]

Because the merchant banks were small, under-capitalized and unable to call directly on the cheap deposit base of the clearing banks, they traditionally had had to live on their 'wits', as Lord Brand of Lazards put it.[18] Forced to look for a new source of finance, they now found their 'salvation' in the pool of non-resident dollars collecting in the Eurodollar market. City merchant banks began bidding for these, which they then lent on in the course of their international business, creating in the process, what came to be known as the 'merchant banks' market', but what was the nascent Eurodollar market proper. This lead to a quadrupling of deposits taken in by the accepting houses between 1958 and 1963 (Mason, 1976: 115). These, in turn, were used to provide dollar credits to West European and Canadian firms through the intermediary of their own domestic banks, and also, in the case of the BOLSA, to firms in Latin America (Einzig, 1960: 25). The creation of the Eurodollar market had, in effect, provided the City with a way of acting as a centre for international finance without imposing a strain on Britain's depleted gold and currency reserves. Yet with these dollar deposits not needing, necessarily, to be swapped into sterling (or any other currency), before being traded, and, hence, not coming under exchange control regulations, what marked the start of the City's role as an entrepôt centre, also heralded the beginning of the *offshore* Eurodollar market.

The restriction on the use of sterling [together with the bank rate increase] is generally accepted then, as having precipitated the great expansion of the Eurodollar market which took place towards the end of 1957, and really the beginning of offshore proper. This is the explanation put forward by the Bank of England (BoE, 1964: 101–2). It is also a view supported by Sir George Bolton, perhaps, if anyone, the market's founding father (1967a: 1). Nevertheless, Higonnet (1985: 39) disagrees, claiming that the 1957 sterling crisis was 'more symbolic than practical'. As does Schenk (1998: 223), who believes that because these credit restrictions did not apply to the Sterling Area they affected only a small volume of transactions. She cites T. L. Rowan at H M Treasury, who wrote that such controls were 'not of major importance'. In addition, archival records show that, in any case, within one week of this ban being implemented it was being evaded by London merchant banks acting as nominees for their non-resident clients.[19] Certainly these facts would suggest, although for conflicting reasons, that the sterling restrictions were not the spur to the development of the Eurodollar market that has been commonly thought. However, this is to ignore the fact that it was during the period that immediately followed the ban, that demand for international trade credit rocketed. This is a far more important factor, suggesting even, that in the process of switching from sterling to dollar credits, the merchant banks were tapping into a much larger pool of capital with which to fund their business, which in itself was a stimulant to an expansion of international trade.

Another aspect of the argument being ignored by Higonnet and Schenk is one made by the Bank of England, that while it acknowledged the volume of transactions was small at the time of the ban, it considered this international credit facility a traditional service provided by the City, and one that had 'considerable prestige value'.[20] A loss of both prestige and confidence in sterling could then be expected to follow any ban. This is important, for given, as the *Banker* pointed out in 1958, merchant banks were extremely vulnerable 'at times of a general ebbing of foreign confidence in sterling', then the 1957 restrictions could be expected to have had a detrimental effect on all trade financed in sterling, not just that of the non-Sterling Area. Certainly, the merchant banking community (through the Accepting House Committee and the Foreign Bond Market Committee), mounted a vigorous campaign to win Bank of England support to have the restrictions on sterling rescinded, and the Bank was equally energetic in trying to persuade the Government to that end.

In fact, while eventually the Eurodollar market evolved to become the saviour of the City, in 1957 there were many members of the merchant banking community hostile to its development; seeing the dollar as a dangerous competitor to sterling and the London bill, which they still wished to see returned to its pre-1914 glory.[21] This, in part, explains why, well after the rise of the Eurodollar, the City continued to regard maintaining a strong pound as a pre-requisite for the preservation of Britain's stature in international finance. It also implies that the City's merchant and overseas bankers might have been a little ambivalent about using the Eurodollar to finance their international trade business instead of sterling. Yet if the accepting houses did not get their substantial extra deposits from the Eurodollar market, what was the source of these funds after September 1957? It was not until 1959 that the sterling restrictions were eased. In addition, discussion into the problems associated with sterling's role as an international vehicle currency would itself have awakened those sections of the City and the international financial community, who were not already aware of this alternative finance facility, to the existence of the Eurodollar market and it availability for use.

US banks take over the London Eurodollar market

The Eurodollar market grew steadily throughout 1958 and was largely established even before the return to convertibility of that year. Eurobusiness increased threefold in 1959 and doubled again in 1960, as the return to convertibility and a relaxation of exchange controls, not only stimulated a greater demand for international liquidity, consequent to a rapid expansion of international trade and investment, but also fed the nascent Eurocurrency market with a supply of dollars, attracted away from, and out of, the US by more competitive interest rate margins (Davis, 1976: 23). For, towards the end of 1958 interest paid abroad on dollar deposits rose well above US domestic rates. In addition, Eurocurrency banking was not affected by minimum reserve requirements or maturity constraints, which helped the Euro-banks to undercut the American banks and narrow the spread between their borrowing and lending rates. In fact, as Einzig (1972: 14) points out, the US Federal Reserve required that banks in the US maintain 'excessive minimum balances' on their foreign banks' accounts which were held with them, which had the effect of deterring foreign banks from opening accounts in New York. Nor was the Eurodollar market affected by the Glass–Steagall Act that separated commercial and investment banking. Consequently, both US banks and MNCs, expanding with the post-war boom, began supplying and demanding ex-patriate dollars, augmented by the large-scale arrival of more US companies into Western Europe.

In 1959 only seven US banks had offices in London, exactly the same number as in 1890. In little more than a decade, however, with the Eurobond market – a market issuing and dealing in foreign currency bonds – well established, another 29 had joined them, increasing their deposits in Britain seventy-fold and for the first time, exceeding those held by the London clearing banks. By 1970 the English merchant banks were on their way out and the US banks were the most powerful operators in the City's Eurodollar market. To the point where it had become, in practice, almost an extension of the New York money market (Einzig, 1971: 143; Mikesell and Furth, 1974: 24).[22] The Americans had begun by setting up international consortia banking and developing more innovative financial instruments, notably the internationally transferable Certificate of Deposit (CD), the sale of which the Bank of England first authorized on 23 June 1966.[23] It was a rather surprising decision, given sterling's weakness at that time. But the thought of the City having to turn away a spanking new international market, must have been just too much for the Bank to bear (Einzig and Quinn, 1977: 27; Attali, 1986: 238). It meant that banks based in the City could now issue and offer short- and medium-term Eurodollar securities (in multiples of $1000, in a minimum purchase of, normally, $25,000), to small savers for the first time, without having to go through the traditional securities intermediaries as before.[24] This was a very important development, because by making the offshore Euromarkets more attractive to non-bank funds, and extending the maturity of deposits to match the increasing length of credits being demanded, the market was opened to a wider public. This, in turn, had the effect of dramatically extending the process by which national capital markets were being homogenised. For the first time since Weimar Germany small European savers had the opportunity to invest in dollar instruments.

The establishment of the Eurobond market

In 1963, the issuing of bearer securities, prohibited in Britain since 1939, was allowed again, but only so long as they were not designated in sterling. Consequently a new type of securities market was established, one financed in Eurodollars: the Eurobond market. Such was the phenomenal success of this market that $33 billion worth of Eurobond issues were made in the first ten years (1963–73), and by 1984/85 this had grown to an annual rate of $58 billion (Struthers and Speight, 1986: 123). Unlike the Eurodollar market, which is a short-term wholesale dollar market, the Eurobond market dealt in foreign currency bonds, primarily dollar bonds, and, as such, is a market for long-term capital. Also, unlike the Eurodollar market, the history of the Eurobond is well documented, if nevertheless, contentious.

The bulk of literature maintains that the first Eurobond issue was put together and underwritten by S.G. Warburgs, the London merchant bank, and signed on 1 July 1963.[25] This issue amounted to $15 million of 5.5 per cent bearer bonds due in 15 years on behalf of the Italian motor-way operator Autostrade (Concessioni e Costruzioni Autostrade), and guaranteed by the Instituto per la Rivostruzione Industriale (IRI), an Italian state-owned industrial and financial holding company, although, the actual recipient of the money was FINSIDER, another of IRI's sub-sidiaries. The subscription agreement had been originally made on 14 January, signed on 1 July, in Holland, and the bonds were delivered to the purchasers at the *Banque Internationale* in Luxembourg after payment, on 17 July. Ian Kerr (1984), in his *A History of the Eurobond*, claims that the idea of a bond issue had immediately found favour with the IRI, when put to them by Warburg's Ronald Grierson, as a means of funding one of their subsidiary companies not creditworthy enough to come to the market in its own right. However, much of the groundwork for the first issue had been done with the European Coal and Steel Community (ECSC) in mind, rather than Autostrade. The ECSC wanted to create a 'financial structure which might bypass the US domestic market and avoid attracting further criticism from the US Treasury', concerned as it was by the outflow of dollars from America. But, according to Siegmund Warburg, this issue was delayed because conditions were unsuitable.

Whatever the reasons, the ECSC issue was replaced by the IRI issue, after which it took a further six months to draft a prospectus, obtain legal approval and comply with stock-exchange listing requirements, because of the obstacles put up by the London Stock Exchange, the Bank of England, the Inland Revenue and the Stamp Office. Chernow (1993: 674) claims that Siegmund Warburg consulted the Bank of England and the Bundesbank about 'creating a new global market in London to supplant New York', and once 'the British and German central banks expressed support for such a move, Warburg quickly formed an in-house team to explore ways to accomplish it'. According to Kerr (1984: 14), Siegmund Warburg, Gert Whitman and Eric Korner (directors of SG Warburg) invented the 'Eurobond concept' and Julius Strauss of Strauss, Turnbull & Co., invented the term Eurobond to reflect the Europeanization of the 'foreign dollar bond' market. Ronald Grierson was awarded the first ever Eurodollar bond mandate by IRI. Ian Fraser of SG Warburg and Geoffrey Sammons and Robin Broadly of Allen & Overy worked on the basic practical details of the issue. Robert Genillard of White Weld & Co. placed a part of the issue using White Weld's European sales network and Whitman, Strauss and Eric Korner placed another part with their Swiss clients. Peter Spira, also of SG Warburg & Co. 'is credited with running the books on the Autostrade issue'.

Although the Eurobond is considered to have been a financial innovation of the City, it was, as Attali (1986: 225) put it, a very 'strange contract', because, despite being drawn up in accordance with British law, due to the legal and technical difficulties associated with the issue, it was signed in Schophol Airport, Holland and quoted in Luxembourg. It was issued in dollars but the proceeds were used to finance investment paid in lire by an Italian company that was not the borrower. Even the printing could not be completed without the help of 'two aged Czech engravers' who were pulled out of retirement to do the job. Finally, although these bonds were 'the first negotiable bank instruments introduced under British law since 1896', the bulk of the funding for them came, via Swiss banks, from Continental Europe (Powell, 1988: 120; Fraser, 1999: 260).

Also, as Hinton (1987: 57) points out, the Eurobond market can be considered a 'British invention' only 'if German born Siegmund Warburg can be counted British'. This is an important proviso, as the British had almost forgotten how to issue foreign bonds (Powell, 1988: 119). Rolf Hallberg, the first chairman of the Association of International Bond Dealers explained: 'When we started on the internationalisation of the securities markets, there was little experience at raising money. ... We turned to people like Siegmund Warburg and Julius Strauss, who had experience before World War II' (cited in Powell, 1988: 119). However, far more important than Strauss, and possibly even Warburg himself, was Gert Whitman, who is generally credited with having been the technical expert behind the idea of making a foreign dollar issue in Europe sold by a European syndicate to Europeans. Whitman, like Warburg had raised money in this way in Germany before the Second World War.

While the Autostrade issue is generally regarded as the first Eurobond, not everyone agrees with this view.[26] City historian David Kynaston

(2002: 279) writes, that 'in a sense Warburg and the others were pipped at the post' when, in May 1963, Samuel Montagu arranged a $20 million three-year placement in 5 per cent bonds, for the Kingdom of Belgium, bought and paid for by a consortium of banks that included Kleinwort Benson and Schroders, as the *Banker* explained, 'out of their substantial holdings of Eurodollars'. *The Times* was certainly impressed and proclaimed that 'the first non-sterling foreign loan to be organized by the City since the war ... signals the resurgance of London as an international capital market'. But technically, this was not the beginning of the Eurobond market, because it was a private placement and not for re-sale on a secondary market (cited in Kynaston, 2002: 279). Perhaps the strongest claim to the title of the first Eurobond, after the Autostrade issue, is the 1957 Petrofina issue. It is one made by, amongst many others, Maurice Armand of Credit Lyonnais, and Chairman of the Primary Market Committee for the Association of International Bond Dealers (AIBD), and confirmed by the World Bank, who maintain that in 1957 a $5 million 20-year Eurobond issue was made on behalf of the Belgium oil company Petrofina SA. That this event took place in the same year as the Eurodollar market started has led to much confusion, helping to entangle the histories of the Eurodollar and the Eurobond markets in such a way that a great deal of misunderstanding has since ensued. Hence, Wachtel (1990: 95), who agrees with Armand, writes:

> Towards the end of the 1950s ... Eurodollar growth began to exceed the demand for US products. This development led to the start of the Eurodollar lending market. In 1957, the first large Eurobond issue occurred, a new issue of bonds for a Belgium oil company, Petrofina, worth $5 million and bought with Eurodollars.

But, although this may indeed have been the first post-war 'foreign currency bond', it was not the first 'foreign dollar bond' issue. For, according to Kerr (1984: 11), this issue had been made as a multiple currency issue. It is also possible that it was paid for with Eurodollars, although, given that the Eurodollar market was a very liquid bankers' market and one that was hardly organised at that time, it is more likely that the issue was bought with dollars in Europe, that is, dollars in the hands of wealthy European citizens, rather than from dollars circulating in the nascent Eurodollar market. Nor, it would seem, did the Petrofina issue come about as a result of any of the supposed 'legal changes' or 'legal initiatives' made to British law by the British monetary authorities.

The state v. market dichotomy

While the minutia of the origins of the Euro-markets remain under some dispute these arguments do not generally involve great conceptual, political or philosophical disagreement. This is somewhat surprising, given that explanations as to the nature and source of the underlying forces which could be considered to have determined their development tend to fall on either side of a state v. market, public v. private dichotomy. Yet this dichotomy goes largely unchallenged, if not unnoticed. There is little indication that those writing about the Euromarkets view the 'market' and the 'state' as anything more than discreet institutions and ahistorical universals. Consequently, these institutions are, for the most part, loosely defined in the abstract, with little thought given to the complexity of the relationship that exist between them in historical reality.

Those arguing in favour of a 'state explanation' have a tendency to freely interchange the terms 'Britain', the 'British state', the 'British monetary authorities' and the 'Bank of England'. In addition, the state explanation is, for the most part, devoid of supporting evidence and is based almost entirely on such bald observations as that the Bank of England 'encouraged', or 'welcomed' or 'fostered' the Eurodollar market.[27] Or, that the market had been 'created' by the Bank's 'quiet policy in favour of this type of transactions' (Savona and Sutija, 1985: 30). Or, that it was created with the 'blessing' of the Bank (Van Dormael, 1997: 145). Or, that it was the result of 'the liberal policy of the Bank ... in the regulation of overseas banks' (Holmes and Green, 1986: 252). Or, in the case of Moran (1991: 55), that it was the result of a 'conscious act' of Bank policy. But, again, not one of these commentators gives details of what the Bank actually did. Neither does McMahon (1964: 17), who claims that 'the striking increase in international flows of private capital of all kinds – long and short – was due, in part, to the "desire" of the Governor of the Bank of England to re-establish the City as an international financial centre'.

Strange (1971: 213) believes that the Eurodollar market developed in London because of a 'deliberate policy of the British monetary authorities' but the evidence she provides is open to interpretation.[28] Both Dufey and Giddy (1978: 42) and Hayes and Hubbard (1990: 29) claim that the Bank encouraged City banks to use dollars to finance third-country trade, as a substitute for sterling, after the 1957 sterling crisis led to the tightening of exchange restrictions, but none of these writers provides evidence to support this view. Other writers refer to 'legal changes', or 'legal initiatives', which brought about the Eurodollar market. Strange (1971: 204) says that, 'the breakthrough came with the decision of the Bank of England in 1962 to allow the issue in London of foreign securities denominated in foreign currencies – usually dollars', but gives no details of what the Bank did, or who instigated the action, although it is clear Strange is referring to the Eurobond, rather than the Eurodollar market.

Plender and Wallace (1985: 32–3) make no mention of legal changes, but say they were told, by 'many foreign bankers', that 'the Bank played a vital part in fostering the new offshore markets in London'; combining 'a light regulatory touch with an open door policy to foreign banks'. Unfortunately they omit to name the bankers in question. Roberts (1995: 183) also mentions the 'light regulatory touch' and adds that dollar deposits were 'welcomed and encouraged by the Bank', but not the form that this 'welcome' and 'encouragement' took. However, having said this, a few writers have defined particular measures that could be considered as having *encouraged* the Eurodollar market. Thus, that the Bank applied neither reserve requirements on Eurodollar banking, nor minimum capital requirements on the London branches of foreign banks, added to the fact that Britain did not impose withholding taxes to the interest banks paid to non-resident depositors, are seen as coming under the definition of encouragement, by Stigum (1978: 139, 175), who quotes an anonymous Bank official as noting: 'If the British interfered with the payout of Eurodollars, nationalized foreign branches, or whatever, that would kill more than the Euromarket, it would kill London.' Hence, 'non-action', as opposed to 'action' by the Bank of England and Britain is considered as evidence of state support for the market; what Geddes (1987: 133) describes as the Bank's 'benign neglect'. Taking this concept a step further, claims by Durham (1992: 147) that the Bank 'chose not to interfere' and by Mendolsohn (1980: 21) that it did not 'stifle' the market by 'a fussy application of its authority' can also be defined as state support. Yet, would it not be more accurate to describe this as *passive encouragement*, as Chalmers (1969: 92) does when he explains that the Bank's habit of intervening in the foreign exchange market to keep the cost of forward cover down had 'passively encouraged' the switching of Eurodollars into sterling.[29] Clearly then the veracity of fact (4) of the five facts outlined above as those that are commonly believed to inform the history of the Euromarkets, that they were encouraged by the Bank of England, is directly dependent upon establishing, first, what defines 'encouragement', and second providing evidence that this encouragement did, in fact, take place. Kelly (1977: 45), however, goes a step further, and makes an altogether grander claim, arguing that support for the market came, not simply from the Bank of England, but from government – a Labour Government, which in the 1960s, she claims, changed laws that had been restricting the development of the market. Dosso (1992: 10) agrees, believing that the UK government supported the development of the market, as a way 'of maintaining London's role as an international entrepôt for capital without the difficulties associated with the use of sterling'. However, while both writers argue that the Euromarkets were created in the City as a result of intentional government policy, neither provide any supporting evidence for these claims. Clearly, again they are both referring to the Eurobond market.

An insight into how a theory of intentional state policy could be constructed on the basis of a misreading of rather tenuous, or inconclusive, evidence can be seen by referring to Gowan (1999: 22), who argues that the 'Britain's government had allowed the City of London to operate as an "off-shore" centre for international private financial operations of all sorts almost entirely unregulated'. As supporting evidence he explains that 'this decision, pushed through by Harold Wilson in 1950 when he was President of the Board of Trade in the Attlee government, was undoubtedly Wilson's major contribution to the history of the world and indeed to the subsequent evolution of British capitalism'. Gowan, however, was unable to provide any details of this 'decision' and perhaps he is simply alluding to Wilson's decision to allow the reopening of London's commodity markets which subsequently took place in 1951.[30] For this led to the foreign exchange market being reopened which automatically re-established facilities for 'authorised banks' to deal in foreign currencies. Strange (1986: 37) also sees Wilson's decision as very significant, but more so as a 'somewhat symbolic step', giving 'the blessing of a Labour government to the revival of the City of London as a financial market place ...'. In which case, Gowan, in the absence of any other evidence, is relying entirely on the argument that by re-opening the City after the Second World War the Labour Government was, by definition, paving the way for the eventual reconvening of the unregulated international private financial system that collapsed in 1931, in the form of an *offshore* financial centre. Certainly, if the City had not been re-opened in the 1950s, it could not have become home to the Euromarkets in the 1960s. But this does not prove intent.

The point that needs to be stressed at this stage, is not that these observations are necessarily wrong, but because they rely on very little verifiable evidence, that the thesis which they support, the 'state explanation', remains, for the most part, inconclusive. Given that there is a second thesis, the 'market explanation', which tends to be presented as dichotomously opposed to the first, and seeks to explain the advent of the Eurodollar and the Eurobond as having been driven by the market, it is even more pertinent that evidence is found to establish the validity, or lack of it, of this explanation. Yet, advocates of the 'market' interpretation fare little better when supporting their claims, where, aside from Schenk's (1998) recent contribution, real evidence is, again, scarce. Einzig (1964a: 11; 1965a: p. vi), who came upon the existence of the market by accident in an article in the *Economist* on 11 July 1959, claims he was asked not to write about it by the London bankers he first spoke to, bankers who 'deliberately avoided discussing it' in the 1950s so as to keep it secret. Perhaps this was why Einzig kept quiet about most of what he was told. Although Lord David Cobbold, son of former Bank of England Governor, Cameron Cobbold, who worked for Sir George Bolton in the early 1960s, canvassing European banks for their dollar deposits, told me he was mystified by Einzig's reference to secrecy and could not explain it. Either way, Einzig does not name the merchant banks, nor the merchant bankers who were dealing in it – neither then, nor subsequently. The article, however, headed 'Dollar Deposits in London', details both the activity of converting dollars into sterling, in order to provide finance to British local authorities and hire purchase finance houses, and, more importantly, the borrowing and re-lending of dollars by London banks. For only the latter activity could possibly refer to dealing in offshore finance. Yet, while it goes into great detail of how the market operated, once again, it omits to identify the banks or the bankers operating in it, as does Gordon Richardson (1966: 7), a future Governor of the Bank, who explained that the 'London merchant banks have played a major part in this development'.

Grady and Weale (1986: 132) also claim that the accepting houses played 'a leading role' in the creation of the new markets, as does Geddes (1987: 133). Kellett (1967: 68) goes further. He maintains that Eurodollars 'were thought up by the London merchant bankers', and Steinberg (1976: 150) and Channon (1988: 6–7) assert much the same. Scott-Quinn (1975: 34–5) identifies 'commercial banks situated in a number of European countries'. And Bell (1973: 8) describes how after the Second World War 'a number of European banks (particularly UK banks) revived the practice' that had existed during the inter-war years, while Davis (1976: 23), argues that the market developed from the late 1950s onwards, 'in response to the rapid and sustained expansion of inter-national trade and investment'. But none of these writers provide supporting evidence. Tether (1961: 400), however, does name names. Explaining to the *Banker* that the merchant banks Kleinwort Benson and

Brown Shipley regard themselves as being the 'originators of the market'. He also lists the Bank of London and South America [BOLSA], Schroders, the Societe Generale and the Australia and New Zealand Bank as mayor players in the market in 1961. Unfortunately, again, no evidence is provided to support these claims. Alan Holmes and Fred Klopstock (1960a: 17), in a 1960 report on the 'Continental Dollar Market', commissioned by the Federal Reserve Bank of New York (FRBNY), also single out Brown Shipley as 'having been very active in the market'. They also give honourable mention to Samuel Montegu and again to BOLSA.

The name of BOLSA crops up repeatedly, as does that of its chairman, Sir George Bolton, who has been portrayed by one and all as a hero of the market. Yet no verifiable evidence has been supplied by anyone as to what he actually did. Siegmund Warburg, who describes Bolton as having the 'attitude of a merchant adventurer', writes that it 'was the merit of a few leaders, among whom George Bolton was one of the foremost, that London regained and maintained this leading position'. Kerr (1984: 15) concurs, writing that Bolton 'personally helped to remove some of the hurdles and to explain to the relevant UK authorities the benefits which might accrue if the new concept was a success'. Welsh (1986: 44) has a slightly different version of events. As do Plender and Wallace (1985: 32) who claim that Bolton 'sooth[ed] the Bank's concern about the implications for the regime of exchange controls', and Roberts (1993a: 27) who writes that 'the cause was taken up and won by Sir George Bolton'. Again there is no evidence to show what he actually did; *how* he 'won the cause', or *how* he 'helped', 'persuaded' or 'soothed' the Bank. There is, however, one important fact to be gleaned from all these references to Bolton's heroic activities. Without exception, they are concerned with the creation of the 1963 Eurobond market and not the 1957 Eurodollar market, because, significantly, Bolton was involved in the creation of both. Roberts alone takes the trouble to mention this. Once again, it appears that the inability of writers to distinguish between the discreet histories of the Eurodollar and Eurobond has led to some confusion. A confusion that is further clouded by the fact that while Bolton might have been a pioneer of both markets, he was also, until the spring of 1957, an Executive Director of the Bank of England, and remained a member of the Bank Court and their executive cabinet, the Committee of Treasury until 1968. It was he more than anyone at the Bank, who worked to free the City from state regulation so that it could re-establish its role as an international financial market. This is an important point, suggesting again, that to understand the development of the Euromarkets it is necessary to transcend the 'state v. market' dichotomy.

Historic mechanisms

That the City of London became the centre of the Eurodollar market in the 1960s is an indisputable fact. In providing an explanation for this it is not enough to ask why it occurred in London, but also, why it did not become centred in Paris, Zurich, Frankfurt or, most importantly, given the post-war economic dominance of the US, in New York.[31] In fact, London's success is often presented, as less the result of deliberate action taken in Britain to foster this new market, and more as a consequence of a more restrictive banking regulation applying in the other major financial centres. Hence, according to Mayer (1976: 463), the inter-bank market out of which the Eurodollar market emerged, was itself fuelled by 'restrictions placed by governments' in continental Europe. Then, as Young (1966: 49) points out, the Swiss Government restricted the use of the Swiss franc as an international currency, so as to discourage its use as a medium for organising international credit. It also kept deposit rates low and bank charges high, So as to deter the inflow of 'hot money', short-term capital that can be withdrawn on demand.

However, the rationale which determined that these restrictions be applied, cannot be understood in isolation, rather they tend to flow from state-specific institutional arrangements and structures which have themselves evolved as a consequence of how capital has been historically controlled and organised. Hence the fact, for example, that Swiss capital had been prioritised for national accumulation, meant that an effective Swiss money market through which short-term funds could be mobilised for external purposes, had not evolved in Zurich, and so was not available to be put into service for the mobilisation of Eurodollars. For Paris and Frankfurt similar conditions applied, as the French and West German banking systems, each in their own way, were both geared to providing long-term credit to their domestic industry. So that the French and German authorities put obstacles in the way of dealing in these new markets. The French hesitating to authorise a foreign currency bond until November 1963 by which time the Eurobond had already been born. The Germans, attaching a 25 per cent coupon tax to interest payments on fixed interest non-resident securities in 1965. Even the US banking system was created to meet the capital requirements of the domestic, rather than the international economy, so that, as Young (1966: 49) points out, the New York money market, 'geared to serve the New York Stock Exchange and, through it the American home industry, could not offer London's money market services'.[32] It was, again, not designed to effect a rapid mobilisation of surplus funds for external purposes. In fact, the US had never even had a centralised money market, defined as it was by its federal state structure. Following from that, New York did not have the need for a particularly well-developed acceptance bill market either. What it did have was then further restricted by the damage that followed the 1929–31 crisis, while London at least was able to retain its international business with Sterling Area countries.

New York was also regulated to a far greater extent than London, putting US acceptance banks at a disadvantage *vis-à-vis* City banks, as their customers were required to produce far greater documentation than their London rivals, for example, bills of lading, warehouse receipts, insurance policies and so on. In addition the US had a more de-centralised and fragmented banking system than the English, with other regional centres competing with New York in the provision of capital for FDI (Foreign Direct Investment). This had the effect of both weakening the power of New York to control the global credit system and complicating regulatory control of the international movement of capital (Germain, 1997: 82).

However, although the conditions might not have existed in New York, or any of the other major international financial centres, to take up the position as the world's international financial market that had formerly belonged unquestionably to the City of London in the heyday of the *Pax Britannica*, could it have been expected, given the economic conditions which prevailed in Britain in the immediate post-war period, that the City would resume this role? Yet, recovery did come in the late 1960s, as a direct consequence of the international banking business generated from the Euromarkets. And this, in turn, had evolved out of actions taken by the City's merchant and overseas bankers in the 1950s to fashion a world money medium to act in place of sterling, with which they could finance their acceptance activities, as described above.

If the origins of the offshore Eurodollar market can, then, be located in the 'merchant bank's market' of the 1950s then, how are we to understand this development? Is it enough to explain that the merchant banks, spurred on by the Bank of England's active encouragement or even its benign neglect, began to use non-resident dollar deposits as an alternative to sterling. Alternatively, did it happen, as Helleiner (1994a: 84) explains, because the City's merchant banks 'stumbled upon' supplies of ex-patriate dollars during the 1957-sterling crisis. Schenk

(1998: 225) does not believe so, as she has shown that banks had been using these dollars since 1955 and switching them into sterling, an activity which she sees as particularly innovative. Yet, it appears, this was the only aspect of the activity that was new. For according to Young (1966: 53), with the bill of exchange acquiring 'new popularity' in the immediate post-war period, as a financial instrument that could provide lines of acceptance credit to British industry, the syndication techniques used to put together these loans were precisely those which had previously been applied to providing finance for international trade, an activity which had largely ended in 1931. Then, in turn, because the companies that organised acceptance credits were those whose business was in the international sector, the 'routine business of discounting and collecting was in itself an important factor in restarting the world-wide machinery of trade credit, as the money market in turn needed short-term funds to deal in bills'. Given, in addition, as De Cecco (1974: 85) claims, that it was precisely the development of the usage of the bill of exchange in the nineteenth century, that was 'responsible for stimulating the development of merchant banks as a component of the British financial structure' in the first place, it is not surprising that Young concludes 'the openings to [London] merchant banks in the post-war world seem less a matter of chance than the natural consequence of their history'. This also accords with how Scammell (1968: 48) explained the recovery of the London Discount Market, in the late 1950s, as the result of it having 'carrie[d] into the new conditions and the new functions much of the paraphernalia of the old'.

In other words, the internationalisation of Britain's economy in the nineteenth century determined the evolution of 'historical mechanisms' necessary for the organisation of the international distribution of credit, that were reconvened when the international economy revived in the 1950s. However, if the re-assertion of a Victorian institutional frame-work for organising credit, resulted in the emergence of a new money market that breached the regulated and restricted international capital market on which the Bretton Woods system was constructed, how is this to be understood? Did the re-assertion of this institutional structure bring about the re-assertion of a *free* international financial structure? Does the causal relationship run this way? Or, as Michie (1992: 145) suggests, did the 'world economy's need for a financial centre which could act as a bridge between short- and long-term funds and as a conduit for international lending', call forth an institutional structure which only 'London's historic position as the credit capital of the world, with its links, facilities, expertise and attitudes' could provide?

It seems then that before understanding the political economic forces which drove the evolution of the Euromarkets and the re-emergence of global finance after the Second World War, it is necessary to first examine this 'paraphernalia' – the 'historic mechanisms' on which these markets were apparently predicated. The institutional structure that supported and drove the Victorian bill market and the international financial system on which the *Pax Britannica* operated and the extent to which it survived into the post-Second World War era.

3
Sterling and the City–Bank–Treasury Nexus

For the City of London to become the world's clearing house, a means of providing international liquidity had to have evolved, without which the explosion in international trade that accompanied the quickening of the industrial revolution and its expansion around the world, in the second half of the nineteenth century, could not have taken place. In providing this, by definition, the City became a market for global credit, which to operate efficiently, in turn, depended on the smooth mobilisation of 'savings' – not only British domestic savings, but also savings made available from the rest of the world. In other words, the City needed institutions to provide, as Leys (1986: 114) puts it, 'a trustworthy world currency and an efficient way of settling international accounts, insuring international trade, arranging international shipments, extending credit and the like'. In the nineteenth century sterling took on the role of this dependable universal currency, the London Discount Market became the international clearing mechanism and the Bill on London was utilised as an instrument for the provision of international credit. Together they allowed the City to function as a *transmission belt*, aggregating, first, small domestic sterling deposits and then deposits from all over the world, and utilising them to provide credit for the financing of international trade and speculative currency flows. Overseeing this process was the Bank of England, which, as a private institution owned and controlled by the City's merchant bankers, ensured what Germain (1997: 50) describes as the 'private exercise of monetary authority'. In this way, the Bank's unquestionable authority over the City prevented any encroachment from outside, allowing its institutions to operate within the sovereignty and protection of the British state but, at the same time, largely outside its regulatory reach, in fact, just like the Eurodollar market itself. Yet, the Bank, in carrying out its duel function as regulator and as a commercial bank in competition with other commercial banks, created a conflict of interest that De Cecco (1974: 83) refers to as its 'institutional schizophrenia'. This led it into conflict with both the market and the state, especially as the Bank took greater responsibility for Britain's monetary policy. This schizophrenia intensified at times of international financial crisis, especially with the collapse of the gold standard and the international financial system on which it was based in 1914 and the ultimately futile attempt to reconstitute the City's power and prestige in the inter-war years, by returning to gold in 1925.[1] Nevertheless, as this chapter will attempt to demonstrate, the institutional structure, which defined and defended the City's nineteenth-century role, both as a centre for the organising of global credit and as an institution for the private exercise of monetary authority, was able to survive Helleiner's (1993: 22) 'socio-ideological break' in financial affairs which began in 1931 and the collapse of the international realm. And it was there, ready to re-emerge, when international trade recovered in the late 1950s. But it managed to do this, only with the protection and help of the British state and by respite to Imperial Preference and creation of the Sterling Bloc.

Sterling, the discount market and the bill on London

The second half of the nineteenth century saw the rise of the City as the clearing house of the world, sterling as the world's reserve and vehicle currency and the adoption of the Bill on London as a mechanism for financing international trade. At the centre of this mechanism was a large capital fund, which, in the beginning, was made available out of the small deposits of the provincial joint-stock banks, now mostly head-quartered in London. This capital was used by bill brokers to discount bills of exchange, some of which had been accepted – by the merchant banks – on behalf of clients whose business was completely external to Britain. These bills could then be sold on the secondary bill market in the City. As Clapham puts it, 'a smooth channel had been cut, down which the aggregated northern surpluses flowed south'. In this way 'all free British capital was sucked' into the international money market from the provinces and Britain's domestic economy opened up and exposed to the full vagaries of the international economy.[2] This process was intensified in the 1870s, with the development of the telegraph and telegraphic transfer. In doing so, it prefigured the impact that technological advances in communication had on the Euromarkets in the 1970s. For it had the effect of bringing the financial centres of the world closer together. Where formerly the slow speed of communication resulted in often wide differences in interest rates set in London, other West European centres and New York, which was three weeks away, the ability to move funds around quickly changed everything. Capital flows became extremely sensitive to interest rate differentials. They also became sensitive to what the market perceived were the relative strengths and weaknesses of the competing financial centres.

With the City firmly established as the largest and most efficient international financial centre and sterling regarded by the world as 'good as gold', London became an entrepôt centre for mobile short-term capital attracted from all over the world. These funds, in turn, began to be utilised by the discount market to finance acceptance credits. The nature of this business had also changed, as the 'bill' had evolved from being a means to finance a particular contract/shipment on behalf of British merchants, to being an open line of credit which customers could draw upon. Bills were being used, not only to finance international trade, but increasingly as negotiable instruments in themselves, backed, not by goods-in-transit, but by other bills. In this way, City banks began, not only to finance trade that had no direct involvement with the British economy, but also speculative activities that actually worked against the effective functioning of sterling itself. In addition, with the connection between goods and money severed, the monetary base became open to credit abuse and, hence, the monetary system more susceptible to a crisis in confidence. Then, with the Bank of England guaranteeing to re-discount all bills presented to them by the bill dealers, this eliminated the element of risk, further encouraging over-trading and intensifying any tendency to systemic crisis in the international monetary system. While the crisis of 1857 had prompted the Bank to announce a halt to its re-discounting services, 'in practice', as Scammell (1968: 181, 188) points out, 'the lender-of-last-resort principle was never repudiated by the Bank', given that it continued to offer financial support to bill brokers in difficulty, despite the Bank's ambivalent attitude towards the discount houses which, as will be explained in more detail below, it regarded as commercial rivals. In 1890 the Bank, in an effort to take control of interest rates, formally rescinded the 1858 rule and recommenced its re-discounting services for its regular customers.

The City had turned the political victory of free trade into an economic reality, as British and foreign capital became increasingly available to support sterling as a vehicle for financing international trade in the last quarter of the nineteenth century and as it expanded, through until 1914. The evolution of sterling into a world currency financing 60 per cent of world trade, had also coincided with the international gold standard becoming universal in Europe and the US by 1880. Yet, this was no coincidence. This development of the City into a centre for financing international trade had had the result of increasing the importance of the standard, because this was an automatic mechanism by which individual countries adjusted their prices to each other. A fact which, in turn, required that the Bank of England take 'virtual control' of this institution, developing, as Scammell (1968: 163) describes in his history of the London Discount Market, 'techniques and methods for influencing gold movements, exchange rates and relative price and cost levels, which, assembled together, were to give us later an elaborate mechanism of gold standard procedures'. The development of this mechanism made it imperative that the Bank perfect a means of bank rate control directly responsive to the operation of the discount market. In this way, just as with the Eurodollar market nearly a century later, as Andrew Glyn (1986: 37) put it: 'world' interest rates were 'bound by a golden chain'… to the UK rate of interest.

Public v. private: institutional schizophrenia at the Bank of England

As late as the 1920s, the Bank of England believed that its absolute independence as a central bank could only be guaranteed by its private status and the generation of profits sufficient enough to avoid it having to ask government for financial support. This level of profit could only be made through the Bank's commercial activities, where it competed with the joint-stock banks. However, this meant that the Bank's obligations as a central bank, to control the money market and Britain's gold reserves, to carry out monetary policy for the benefit of Britain's domestic economy and to raise finance necessary for the state to operate effectively, were liable to come into conflict with the obligations it had to its shareholders – the very merchant bankers of the City who were becoming prosperous on the Bill on London – to make profit and pay a dividend. A conflict of interest out of which a destructive 'institutional schizophrenia' would evolve. A conflict of interest that, on a number of occasions resulted in the Bank putting its own and the City's pecuniary gain above its public responsibility, with often debilitating and sometimes catastrophic results for the British economy (Collins, 1988: 191–3). For while the bill business, and the gold standard on which it was grounded, brought great prosperity and prestige to the joint-stocks banks, the discount houses, the merchant banks and the Bank of England itself, to the merchant princes and the Treasury Knights, and in the process established the City of London as the world's premier international financial centre, by opening up and subordinating Britain's domestic economy to the designs and demands of both the bankers and the international economy, Britain was led into two Great Depressions, with devastating results for her industrial base and all those people who depended on it for their livelihood; the first and more modest downturn lasting from 1873 to 1896, and the more spectacular second, beginning in the mid-1920s and continuing into the mid- 1930s, if not later.

The Bank's 'schizophrenia' greatly intensified in the last quarter of the nineteenth century. Something that would end in almost systematic collapse during the financial crisis of 1914. So intense had become the competition between the Inner City and the cash-rich joint-stock banks that as late as 1899 the Inspector of Branches 'wondered whether the Bank's dual position could be maintained'. Yet if a choice did have to be made between a ' "duty to the public" and care of gold, or duty to the proprietors ... and the dividend', he believed the latter should prevail (cited in Mints, 1946: 692). In this view he was at one with Bank tradition itself. As for example, in 1836–37 it kept hold of its government stocks when economic prudence required they be sold off to reduce the nation's money supply. All because the market price of the stocks was too low, and it did not want to take a loss. Then, prior to the crisis of 1847 it kept Bank rate at a competitively low level for too long, so as to increase its own discount business. Then, in the 1870s, not wanting to 'forego revenue by amassing gold', it kept gold reserves at a dangerously low level 'to meet Britain's international liabilities in a crisis', making the British domestic economy unnecessarily sensitive to international gold flows.[3]

Of particular concern for the Bank of England, both in relation to its private interests and its public responsibility, was the fact that the joint-stock banks were not legally bound to keep a cash reserve and could use the full extent of their customers' deposits to maximise their profit. In fact, because this money was lent to the discount market at call or at very short notice, it was regarded by the banks as their liquidity reserves. Taken together, this meant that a 'huge credit pyramid' was erected on the Bank's inadequate gold reserves. This abundance of credit had the effect of pushing down the discount rate, which in turn induced a switch out of sterling into gold – as sterling became less attractive an investment – depleting the Bank's gold reserves even further. This, in turn, had the effect of aggravating what was already a problem for the

Bank, as the price of gold was appreciating, consequent to more industrialised countries having adopted, or reassumed, the gold standard in the 1870s, thereby increasing the world demand for the metal.

To stem gold exports the Bank now had the choice of, either coming to an understanding with the joint-stock banks – which would have had to include some form of an arrangement whereby the Bank would agree not to compete with them for commercial business in future – or to set interest rates in line with the demands of the international rather than the domestic market, in order to attract 'hot money' into London. The Bank chose the latter and raised the discount rate, which it could only then maintain by entering the market and buying sterling at what was now an artificially high rate. An expensive exercise to the Bank. More significantly, it was also detrimental to British trade and industry, which was already suffering from the deflationary effects of falling prices, induced by the shortage of gold, and the loss of those overseas markets situated in the silver standard area (Green, 1988: 590). Now it had to 'shoulder the burden' of a higher bank rate. The joint-stock banks meanwhile, 'made ever higher profits' (De Cecco, 1974: 137). Commercial competition between the Bank of England – and indirectly therefore, the merchant bankers and the Inner City – and the joint-stock banks, with the former carrying responsibility for the monetary system and the latter enjoying 'power without responsibility', was driving Britain's financial system to a state of anarchy and crisis. One proposed solution was to try and attract the joint-stock banks into the banking establishment. This, however, proved difficult, amounting to nothing more than the joint-stock banks agreeing at the behest of Lord Goshen, the Chancellor of the Exchequer, to raise the level of their deposits at the Bank, which, acting under its guise as a commercial bank, the Bank then promptly used to compete with the joint-stock banks for a share of the discount market. This activity, as De Cecco (1974: 99) writes, 'was pursued with the enthusiastic approval of the then manager of the Bank's branches, Ernest Edye, who wrote a memorandum reiterating the need for a radical transformation of the Bank's business clients from a clique of public institutions which tended to generate only unprofitable business towards a purely private trading clientele'. Having returned so vigorously to the role of commercial bankers under Governor Lidderdale, the Bank continued to develop their commercial banking operations throughout the 1890s, not only in the discount market, but also by lending money to the Stock Market.

The Bank was successful, increasing its securities and advances from £33 million to £89 million between 1889 and 1899, and its dividend from 7 to 10 per cent in 1897, where it remained until 1904 (Clapham, 1944: 370; De Cecco, 1974: 99), yet not as successful as the joint-stock banks, whose deposit base during the same period, had grown from £500 million to £850 million (and would rise to £1226 million by 1914). Taking that together with the fact that the 1890s had seen many of these commercial banks amalgamate into five large banking groups, meant that their power had increased immensely, in relation to that of the Bank of England. So that the Bank's control over the money market was further reduced during this period. In addition, to the chagrin of the Inner City, the joint-stock banks began to undermine the merchant banks' monopoly of the accepting business by competing directly for bills. This challenge reached its apogee in 1914 when the banks used the opportunity of the financial crisis to try and destroy the Inner City and take over the international finance business (De Cecco, 1974: 132; Peters, 1993: 134; Kynaston, 1994: 310).

With war in Europe imminent, the international financial market began to collapse, with stock exchanges closing and gold deliveries ceasing. The joint-stock banks reaction was to call in their loans, draining money from the system. With funds no longer available to finance international trade, new bill business at a standstill, and payment on the great volume of outstanding bills threatened by the inability of foreign drawees to make effective payment in wartime, the merchant banks and the discount houses were pushed to the verge of bankruptcy. At the same time, Stock Exchange dealers, who financed their business through bank loans secured on the collateral value of their share portfolios, were forced to dump their stocks on the market to recover the funds needed to repay the banks. This had the effect of pushing down prices and reducing the value of their collateral so that the banks then required them to reduce their debts still further. Then, the commercial banks, anticipating a convertibility crisis, consequent to the nation's limited gold reserves, removed their own gold reserves from the Bank, while at the same time refusing to pay out their own customers in specie, offering five pound notes instead of sovereigns and then telling their customers to exchange the notes for gold at the Bank of England. These actions, naturally, provoked the very crisis the commercial banks had feared would take place (De Cecco, 1974: 145).

Having once chosen to engage the joint-stock banks in competition it was impossible now for the Bank to apply 'moral suasion' and co-opt them into taking responsibility for monetary policy. Instead they fought out their struggle for commercial dominance of the discount market right up to 1914 in an increasingly anarchic financial market, with the

Inner City and the joint-stock banks locked in battle, and the government and the British state caught in the middle. Whilst the Treasury tended naturally to side with the Inner City in viewing the culprits in this situation as being the irresponsible joint-stock banks, Lloyd George and his Cabinet were generally sympathetic to their position without, at least initially, fully understanding the nature of the conflict for dominance of the market. Yet, in the end, the merchant banks and the discount houses were only saved from bankruptcy by Government intervention, first, on 3 August, when a moratorium was placed on bills of exchange for a month, and then later when Bank of England loans of fiduciary paper were made available to guarantee their past and future transactions in the discount market. This had the effect of strengthening the Bank's hand by giving it 'enormous influence over the discount market', which the accepting houses could do little about, given their very weak position at that time (De Cecco, 1974: 133, 168).

The merchant banks in their capacity as 'accepting houses', were asked to form a syndicate – the Accepting Houses Committee – with joint-liability, which could obtain loans from the Bank at 2 per cent over Bank rate. Lloyd George called a conference to decide how the 'spoils' of the discount market were to be divided up between the Bank and the joint-stock banks, with general opinion believing that the latter would end up inheriting the bulk of the acceptance business. Yet to the annoyance of the banks, Lloyd George 'succeeded in confining their gains, by defending the City from their attack' (De Cecco, 1974: 168–9). It was the Bank that came best out of the 1914 crisis. A crisis which, as De Cecco (1974: 155) put it, 'brought out the leitmotifs of recent British financial history: the rivalry between the bankers and the BoE, and the traditional alliance in an emergency between the Inner City and the Government against the bankers'. However, the tension that existed between the Bank and the Government in relation to the carrying out of monetary policy did not subside. Giuseppi (1966: 140) writes of the Bank of that time, that having become 'so great in the nation's counsels it would soon have to make up its mind ... whether it wished to remain master in its own rich but private house or, accepting even greater burdens of responsibility, relinquish some of its independence'. But nothing much changed, as the struggle to return sterling to the gold standard in the 1920s makes clear.

The return to gold

The advent of war and the end of *Pax Britannica* brought the virtual collapse of the open international economic system, with the *de facto* suspension of the gold standard, so too the doctrine of *laissez-faire* and the free market. The international liberal economy was at a standstill. Tariff barriers were erected and exchange controls introduced. Governments were forced to intervene in the operation of their respective central banks. Production was brought under political control to secure its subordination to the war effort, while the necessity of ensuring the support of the working class meant the government needed to give more priority to its needs. Four years later, the end of war brought the additional problems of pent-up inflation, government debt, war debts and reparations, all adding to a tendency towards political and economic chaos. Taken together, the economic situation that existed in the immediate post-war period had the effect of heavily 'politicising' financial and monetary affairs. The response of the world's private and public bankers to this dangerous situation, was to launch, as Helleiner (1991: 62) writes, 'a remarkable political offensive ... to restore the pre-war liberal monetary and financial order'. An offensive led by a coterie of merchant bankers from London and New York, through the Financial Commission of the League of Nations, and at the international monetary conferences in Brussels and Genoa, in 1920 and 1922, convened with the idea of coming to an agreement for reconstructing an international monetary system. Yet significantly, the monetary proposals adopted at Genoa were based largely on proposals put forward by the British delegation, dominated as it was by members of the Bank of England.

Prior to 1914, City oligarchies had feared establishing the Bank of England as an independent power base. It remained, in fact, as Moran (1991: 63) puts it, a 'rather amateurish institution' run by a part-time Court drawn from the aristocracy of merchant banking, which elected, on a rota basis, a part-time Governor and Deputy Governor, for periods of normally not more than two years.[4] This allowed successive incumbents to combine quasi-state business at the Bank with private business in the City. But this suited the City, which wanted to avoid the danger that a permanent governor might utilise the enormous potential power that resided in the office, to establish an independent power base and become a 'little "monarch" in the City' (Bagehot, 1906: 226). For, above all else, the bankers feared such a personage would precipitate a call for the state to take control of the Bank and carve out a role for itself in regulating and managing the City.

This situation was turned on its head by the Great War. Before 1914, the Bank could still confidently proclaim that 'the Government has no voice in the management of the Bank' (cited in Chapman, 1968: 72).

But when the politicising of monetary affairs, before, during and after the war, went as far as to call for the government to intervene in the City, the very fear that had kept the City from releasing the latent authority of the Bank, now determined for it a more powerful role. In the face of a potentially democratic state, the City needed the Bank to act as its 'praetorian guard'. This change led directly to Montagu Norman becoming the first full-time Governor of the Bank in 1922, and remaining in this position for 22 years. His job was to ensure a 'return to normalcy', in other words, the re-establishment of the pre-1914 international monetary system based on gold. In truth, even before the war had come to an end, Britain's dominant class had set about reconstructing the international liberal economy. Returning to gold 'without delay', had been defined by the 1918 Cunliffe Committee (the Committee on Currency and Foreign Exchanges), as the major object of Britain's post-war monetary policy. As their Report stressed: 'nothing can contribute more to a speedy recovery from the effects of war, and to the rehabilitation of the foreign exchanges, than the re-establishment of the currency upon a sound basis'. The following year Parliament decreed, effectively, that sterling would return to the gold standard in 1925.[5] But behind the guise of this economic rationale stood two others. The first was concerned with prestige and profit. Gold was the fountainhead of the City's 'pre-eminence'. It was the precious metal on which its merchant banks and discount houses had built their reputations and had turned merchant bankers into 'merchant princes' (Byng, 1901, cited in Newton and Porter, 1988: 11). More prosaically, if a self-regulating market for global capital could be recreated, by definition, this would have the fortuitous effect of reconvening the profit stream blocked since 1914 and getting the City back into business. This was especially pertinent, given that the growing economic power of a US made even stronger by war, had convinced the City bankers that New York was seeking to take over control of international finance and needed to be repelled (Cain and Hopkins (1993b: 6). The second was political. Because if the war, and its aftermath, had unleashed dangerous democratic forces to challenge the *status quo*, a return to gold would provide a value-free rationale, one based on unquestionable economic logic, with which to block such expectations, keep the City free of any future government interference and ensure a return to the pre-war social and political order.

If the horrors of war had been met resolutely head-on by the British working man, after 1918, the British Establishment were similarly ready to face the horrors of peace: pent-up inflation and democratic expectations. Clearly, a return to balanced budgeting, to bring government spending and the involvement of the state in the economy back to 'minimalist' pre-war levels, was essential. Public borrowing necessary to prosecute the war, had been of such a high level that it had resulted in a glut of Treasury Bills on the market. So many, in fact, that they were determining short-term interest and not 'bank rate'. In other words, without the automatic discipline of the gold standard on the state's money supply and budgetary practice, just as the Treasury had lost control over public expenditure, so the Bank of England had enjoyed a similar experience in relation to the money market. That a return to gold first required a drastic reduction in the money supply, meant fortuitously, that short of raising taxes, government spending would have to be cut and with it the supply of Treasury bills.

The beauty of the gold standard lay in the fact that it was, ostensibly, an 'automatic', self-regulating monetary mechanism. Supposedly operating outside of politics, it offered an unchallengeable, technically based rationale for 'the cessation of government borrowing', and, by extension, government spending. Being free from political manipulation it became a constitutional barrier to the policies of any parliament elected to pursue the interests of the working class. As the *Bankers' Magazine* explained, 'a return to gold would prevent future "unsound" experiments by Socialist Governments which might divert the English people from the only real solution of their problems – economy and hard work'. Or, in the words of Cunliffe Committee member, Lord Bradbury, 'the gold standard was knave proof'.[6]

Lower public borrowing would, in turn, put pressure on the Government to cut unemployment benefit, while higher rates of interest that could be expected to accompany a return to gold at the old par would also increase unemployment. Yet, both these consequences, as Montagu Norman later admitted, were welcomed and had been deliberately calculated to follow the return to gold (Pollard, 1992: 109). Hence, re-establishing the gold standard would ensure (1) the restoration of the system on which the City's merchant banks had built their fortunes, (2) the return of monetary and budgetary control, that would allow both the Bank and the Treasury to recover their pre-eminent positions in the policy-making process, lost during the war and (3) the dampening of any dangerous socialist aspirations on behalf of the workers. In effect then, restoring the gold standard could be accurately translated as re-establishing the power of the *ancien regime*; the ruling elite of Britain and the Empire – the City–Bank–Treasury nexus. With the Chancellor of the Exchequer 'prophesying ruin for the country if expenditure were not cut drastically', and the *Daily Mail* determined to do its bit to rid the country of the evil of 'squandermania' in public spending, once again, the British Establishment had no reason to doubt that both its political and pecuniary interests were also those of the British nation and its people.[7] Clearly then, the gold standard was regarded as 'non-political' only in the sense that it removed the struggle for control of economic policy from the political arena. It was, of course, highly political, especially as its operation would result in the wholesale destruction of large sections of British industry and, with it, the pauperisation of millions of British people. That these calamitous events took place while the City's merchant banking community became ever more prosperous, could be explained away by reference to the unavoidable consequences of the self-regulating mechanism of the gold standard. Just as with the forces of nature, no one could be held responsible for the vagaries of economic forces.

The plan to return sterling to the gold standard after the war, and most importantly, to do so at the pre-war parity of $4.86, was regarded, with only limited opposition from some industrialists, as the only basis for bringing about both the revival of Britain's greatness, and the re-imposition of world monetary order. That this policy was also an essential pre-requisite for the re-establishment of sterling as the major international trading currency of the world and the reconvening of City fortunes, did not go wholly unnoticed. At least not by the Governor of the Bank of France, Emile Moreau, who said of Montagu Norman and his attempts to create a central bankers' alliance to run the world's monetary system, independent of government: 'All his monetary alliances are calculated to make sterling the universal instrument of exchange' (cited in Boyce, 1987: 199). Yet, much as Norman might have wished, the mechanism could not be rebuilt. Sterling's role as global currency in the nineteenth century was backed up with Britain's wealth and economic dominance. This was no longer the case after the Great War, with Britain reduced to relying mostly on 'symbolic capital' instead. While the City never really considered this reality, it did accept that before gold could return to claim its thorny crown, the British economy would have to be subjected to drastic deflationary measures. For otherwise, it would be impossible to push up the price of sterling from $3.75, where it stood in 1921, to its old pre-war parity of $4.86 This deflationary policy was rationalised as a necessary measure to curtail the inflationary tendencies that had built up during the war. Immediately upon the Armistice, in November 1918, the Bank had tried to increase Bank rate, but the government having complained of excessive rates during the last year of the war and sensitive to the cost of financing war debt, resisted. But by 1919 the Government was prepared to cut expenditure by

36 per cent. The Bank was regaining control and Bank rate and Treasury bill rate increased sharply; to 6 per cent in November and 7 per cent in April 1920. Yet this policy continued even after the 1919 inflationary boom had turned into depression from the second half of 1920 onwards. Hence in 1920, Government expenditure was reduced by a further 30 per cent and Bank rate increased again to 7 per cent where it stayed for 12 months (Boyce, 1987: 33; Howson, 1993: 3; Cottrell, 1995: 82). Not surprisingly, between 1920 and 1922 GDP fell by 6 per cent, standing in 1921 at its lowest level since the nineteenth century, in real terms. By 1922 consumers' expenditure stood below the level of 1910, with unemployment at 12.6 per cent; having peaked, in the strike-affected June of 1921, at 20.6 per cent. Sterling, on the other hand, which in February 1920 stood at a low of \$3.40, had by the end of 1922 risen to \$4.635. Yet, the Bank and the Treasury still regarded the Cunliffe Report as their 'marching orders' (Moggridge, 1969: 16).

The Treasury had been well aware of where these deflationary measures were leading. As their only economist, Director of Financial Enquiries, Ralph Hawtrey predicted, there would be an 'acute and serious unemployment crisis'. Yet he did not regard this as a good enough reason for abandoning the return to gold. More important was to maintain the City as the world's financial capital. Because as he told the Treasury's new Controller of Finance, Sir Otto Niemeyer, the 'greatest factor in the material prosperity of this country is not manufacturing ... but commerce. The diversion of commerce to other centres is the severest loss to which we could be exposed'.[8] Two months later, Norman giving evidence to the Chamberlain/Bradbury Committee, used the same argument; seeing a 'shrinking form sterling' in Europe as a threat to the City's position as the world's foremost financial centre. Something that could only be overcome by a return to the gold standard.[9] He even instilled a fear in the Committee that without a return to gold, sterling might soon be replaced by the German mark as the international medium. Sir Charles Addis, Head of the Hong Kong & Shanghai Bank and a director of the Bank, had already made his view of the gold standard clear, observing in his 1922 Presidential Address to the Institute of Bankers:

> To suppose that a people so conservative by instinct, so tenacious of custom, so careful of tradition, could be induced to trample on their monetary past and to relinquish the dearly purchased gold standard, which rightly or wrongly they believe to be bound up with the prestige of their national credit and their supremacy in international finance, is to live in a world of illusion. (cited in Dayer, 1988)

To the Chamberlain/Bradbury Committee, however, Addis offered a somewhat more mundane argument. That it was not Britain's trade that would be endangered if the gold standard was restored, but London's financial interests if it were not. He warned the committee that sterling was being replaced by 'gold dollar credits' as a means of financing far-eastern trade with the US, and that once traders got used to using dollars instead of sterling it would be very difficult to get them to switch back. Banks, he said, would be forced to transfer their accepting and discounting business to New York. In any case, he continued, falling prices were far better for the economy and 'social harmony' than inflation. So much so that the sacrifices associated with deflation were 'not too high a price to pay for the substantial benefit to the trade of this country and its working classes, and also, although [he] put it last, for the recovery of the City of London of its former position as the world's financial engine'.[10]

The clear and over-riding concern of the Bank of England and the British Government alike, in the immediate post-war period, was to re-establish the City's nineteenth-century institutional structure for the private provision of international credit and liquidity. Of course, if a self-regulating market for global capital could be recreated, this would also have the fortuitous effect for the City of reconvening the profit stream that had been blocked in 1914, and keeping it free from future state interference. Nevertheless by 1923, such was the difficulty in achieving the necessary pre-requisite for this happening – a return to gold at the old par – that even the Bank was inclined to recommend that the return to gold be postponed until 1930. However, when the following year, the Dawes Plan and loan provided the basis for a solution to the problem of German reparations, restoring confidence in the German currency which itself now joined the gold standard, and signalling that finally the way was open to begin rebuilding Germany and Europe, the Bank became frantic that the City would loose out to the US and New York, as the accompanying boom in international commerce inevitably came to be financed through dollars and even marks, rather than sterling. As Addis complained, 'Europe is the "promised land" to America: to be possessed without even competition' (Boyce, 1987: 59).

This meant only one thing. Sterling would have to be returned to the bosom of gold as soon as possible. Only then could, as Addis put it, 'the pound look the dollar in the face'. So as 1924 drew to a close, a return to gold came to be increasingly regarded as inevitable, and speculators began buying sterling in anticipation of the event itself. This had the desired effect of pushing up its price *vis-à-vis* the dollar, and the nearer the pound got to the old par the easier it became to contemplate taking 'the final plunge'. Yet, the further sterling rose against other currencies the more difficult it became for British manufacturers to compete in both international and domestic markets. By 1925, when the decision to return to gold was finally taken, there had already been four years of deflation and stagnation, and money wages and other costs had been pushed down by about 40 per cent, as British industry struggled unsuccessfully to keep their prices competitive internationally, especially with those in the US. Together this had the inevitable effect, in the medium-to-long-term, of weakening confidence in the ability of Britain to maintain sterling at such an uncompetitive and damaging rate, to the point that it would threaten to collapse, thereby provoking an outflow of gold – a situation which could only be countered by the continued pursuance of even harsher deflationary policies (Pollard, 1970: 3).

With the economy stagnant and Britain's manufacturing industries in a desperate position, especially those involved in exports, in a situation of chronic unemployment, on 28 April 1925 Britain returned to the gold standard at the old pre-war par of $4.86. The consequence of these policies was that while the remainder of the industrialised world experienced mild expansion until 1924, quickening to an economic boom in 1929, Britain stagnated, with low investment, high unemployment, and little chance of bringing about any effective programme of industrial rationalisation designed to make British industry more competitive. Yet this cut little ice in the City. But then by 1927, with the economy in deep depression and millions of people unemployed, Bank of England shares rose to £265 (from £150 in 1920) and bank dividends to over 16 per cent (Pollard, 1970: 3; Boyce, 1987: 152).

After the 1929 crash and the consequent world depression, Britain's position became ever more depressed. Yet even then, the Bank persisted with deflationary policies, effectively putting on 'the brake ... while going uphill' (Pollard, 1970: 3). In 1931, with the struggle to return to gold having greatly weakened sterling, Britain now came increasingly under the power of international speculative capital, as she relied more and more on short-term, footloose capital to maintain parity on the gold standard. The controllers of this so-called 'hot money' demanded higher interest rates and the even stricter application of 'sound money' policies, as an inducement to hold sterling, which had the effect of tightening, still further, the deflationary noose around Britain's domestic economy, a process that was to be repeated, with similar results after the Second World War.

Yet, all was to no avail, as massive disequilibrating short-term capital movements intensified. With the collapse of Kreditanstalt and the freezing of foreign assets in Germany, the international financial crisis of 1931 began to unfold, and the pound's stability came increasingly into question. London's addiction to short-term capital now worked against it, hastening the evaporation of confidence, and £200 million of hot money flowed out of London in the summer of 1931. By the second half of July gold was leaving the country at a rate of £12–15 million a week, and by the end of the month gold reserves dropped to £133 million (Stewart, 1967: 71). By August, Britain was forced to apply to the US and France for a loan of £80 million, which they agreed to, on condition that Britain implemented the recommendations of the May Committee and made substantial cuts in public expenditure, especially unemployment pay.[11] This was, as van der Pijl (1984) describes, a 'last ditch' effort by 'comprador liberals', determined to maintain the 'automatism of subordinating national economic policy to the interests of money capital'. It was ultimately unsuccessful, as nothing could stop the flight from sterling, and on 21 September 1931 Britain suspended gold payments, ending Britain's disastrous experiment with the gold standard and allowed sterling to find its own level again.

In the end it was as simple as that. Sterling immediately fell to $3.80 and by November bottomed out at $3.145, a 35 per cent drop on the old par. Nothing much else happened. No bangs only whimpers. In the puzzled - aftermath of anti-climax, Sidney Webb, Colonial Secretary in Macdonald's Government, expressed the feeling of many when he famously remarked: 'Nobody told us we could do this.' Britain's ten year struggle to revive the gold standard was over. All the sacrifices made by British industry and the British people had amounted to nothing. Yet, as Pollard (1970: 3) observed, 'instead of the catastrophe forecast by the City, there was instant relief and the headlong plunge to the depth of depression was halted' (Pollard, 1970: 3).

In terms of Britain's own national interests, while in the nineteenth century the gold–sterling exchange standard had invariably reacted to domestic economic fluctuations by placing the burden of adjustment overseas, the new gold standard had done the opposite, placing it firmly and squarely on Britain's domestic economy, with disastrous consequences for British industry (Pollard, 1970: 24). But providing an explanation for returning to gold at the old par becomes ever more pertinent, when one considers the health of the international monetary system. Prior to 1914 the gold standard was, in reality, a gold–sterling exchange standard, with sterling providing the international liquidity necessary for the international economy to function effectively. Cutting back the global circulation of sterling after 1918, in order to facilitate the return to gold, was then nonsensical, for it was removing international liquidity from the system – the very material basis without which a successful resumption of the pre-war international trading system would prove impossible. If Britain had only 'symbolic capital' to keep the gold standard system going, the adjustment process integral to its operation was almost certainly doomed to end in a severe deflationary crisis for the world economy. Especially given that those countries that were running trade surpluses, the US and France, were unwilling to reflate in line with their increased gold reserves, as the classical specie flow mechanism of the gold standard required them to do. Yet, policies which appear misguided and foolish when looked at in terms of the national interest, may sometimes appear quite rational from the point of view of a special interest group. As Ingham (1984: 186) explains, the return to gold demonstrated the historical disjuncture between commercial and productive capital. Viewed from this perspective, these events were perfectly explicable, 'financially; institutionally; in the form and extent of political representation; and by the social and cultural divisions which were to be found within the ruling class'.

Vested interest was to be found in the City rather than with manufacturing. Nevertheless, as Pollard (1970: 16, 23) points out, to remain profitable, much of the business carried out in the City relied more on a prosperous industry than a return to gold, including overseas trade, genuine (as opposed to speculative) capital exports, and a large part of the banking sector, insurance and shipping. In fact only the merchant and overseas bankers really stood to gain. What Pollard describes as 'that tiny section of the community ... with annual earnings of not more than £60–65 million, and for whose sake all the sacrifices were made'. Representatives of this section, through their control of the Bank Court and sections of the Treasury, dominated the monetary authorities and were able 'to present policies favourable to itself as policies favourable to the national interest'. To them, the restoration in confidence in sterling, by fixing its value against gold, was considered an essential pre-requisite to reviving London's bill business, which had been lost in 1914 and had not returned during the deflationary years that followed the Great War. Adams Brown Jr (1970: 65), writing in 1929 agreed, seeing 'commercial interest' as opposed to 'financial interest' or 'banking', as the predominant force behind the re-imposition of the gold standard. It was certainly the only beneficiary. For while Britain's manufacturing base had become characterised by declining industries, bankruptcies, mass unemployment and poverty, the City had been transformed into a centre for massive short-term funds, as speculative and very lucrative hot money flows intensified. It was a case of sacrifices from the people, but profits for the City.

After gold

As late as 16 May 1930 Sir Richard Hopkins of the Treasury was able to tell the Macmillan Committee of Enquiry into Finance and Industry, set up by the Macdonald Government in response to the economic crisis, that 'the control of the currency is exclusively a matter for the Bank of England. It is not a matter in which the Government intervenes'. With the suspension of the gold standard in September 1931 this changed and control of monetary policy returned to the political arena, bringing automatic operational demotion for the Bank of England and the eclipse of the power of the merchant bankers (Kunz, 1987: 6, 189). This new reality was confirmed the following April, when the Exchange Equalisation Account (EEA) was created to manage exchange operations, and official responsibility for sterling passed to the Treasury.[12] The British Government's economic policy was now re-prioritised in favour of Britain's domestic economy and away from the City. Not surprisingly then, Britain's domestic industry began to recover.[13] A second merger boom developed. Support grew for the 'industrial modernisation movement' that had first emerged in the 1890s, and the ideology of 'monopoly capital'. A programme of industrial restructuring was advocated. By 1937 Britain had reached the highest level of output in her history, unemployment was at its lowest for six years and average real incomes were over 10 per cent higher than they had been in the brief but catastrophic 'second golden age'.[14]

However, while Treasury and even City opinion accepted that in the aftermath of the events of 1931 there was no immediate alternative to managed money, it was still hoped that eventually there could be another return to gold. There was little awareness that the previous 'return to gold' had been a disaster, nor that pegging national currencies to gold at an overvalued rate might not have been the best policy. Montagu Norman was unable to accept that the bankers' masterly plan for a better world was over (Kunz, 1987: 71; Kynaston, 1999: 363). He longed for the time when the City would recover its dominance in international finance. Hence, reversing the City's fortunes defined much of Bank thinking and policy. To this end, the Bank of England and the Treasury 'gold clique' continued to 'hanker' for a *second* return to gold, even after Britain's economic position had improved. By January 1933 Sir Charles Addis was becoming optimistic, expecting that 'fundamental economic forces, led by an invisible hand', were working towards the imminent 'restoration of London to its former predominance over the international market'. While this was not to be, Addis continued to argue that 'a return to gold should be the immediate objective of British monetary policy' (cited in Dayer, 1988: 244–50). It is not therefore surprising that despite Britain's industrial revival and a world economic recovery by 1937, a report to Cabinet written in that same year by the Committee on Economic Information continued to present the case for a return to gold, thus:

> Yet the prosperity of the country is bound up with the revival of international trade, and if it were true that a restoration of some sort of international gold standard is a condition of any large relaxation of trade barriers, and would in fact secure such relaxation, we, of all countries, should be prepared to examine the question. ... Finally, the return to fixed parities would facilitate the resumption of inter-national lending for the financing of trade on an important scale.[15]

Because although the end of gold had brought welcome relief to Britain's industrial sector, the City, detached as it was from much of its international customer base, was declining to its lowest point for 200 years, especially those institutions relying on the profit generated from the issuing of foreign loans and the financing of international trade – the merchant banks and the discount houses.[16] Montagu Norman, who took the opportunity of the Lord Mayor's Banquet, both in 1936 and 1937, to lament the 'sorry plight' of his 'friends' in the dis-count market, was determined they should survive (cited in Kynaston, 1999: 389). To secure for them at least a degree of profitability, Norman organised three gentlemen's agreements between the discount houses and the clearing banks, whereby the latter agreed not to compete for Treasury Bills, allowing the former to create a cosy cartel; bidding for the bills as a syndicate before sharing them out on a quota basis. He also engineered a similar relationship with regard to the accepting houses, offering the Bank of England's finest discounting terms only to those merchant bankers who were members of the Accepting Houses Committee. He even went as far as to make available the Bank's own funds when the situation demanded it; lending, at very favourable rates, £1 million to Lazards, £340,000 to Higginson & Co. and 'almost certainly' £100,000 to Hambros in 1932 (Kynaston, 1999: 355–9).

The City, meanwhile, realising that the international financial system was at a standstill and not about to be re-launched in the immediate future, had very quickly latched onto the only practical alternative international forum through which international banking could survive: the British Empire, which was, as Kynaston (1999: 363) puts it, 'a halfway house between economic internationalism and economic nationalism'. While certainly an 'imperial currency area' had existed since the nineteenth century, this was a fundamentally new development.[17] Hence, as early as February 1932 *Lloyd's Bank Monthly Review* was able to write that a 'sterling bloc' had begun to emerge, which, it believed, 'would confirm the Bill on London in its traditional position of the medium of world commerce, and would be an insurance against any loss of financial prestige and business due to the depreciation of the pound against gold' (cited in Kynaston, 1999: 363). Once again we see the twin concerns of 'City prestige' and 'merchant profit' to the fore.

The Treasury joined the City in welcoming the development of a Sterling Bloc, although Norman and the Bank, still dreaming about a return to gold, were slow to recognise that this was a means of restoring the City's international position (Kynaston, 1999: 364). In March the Committee on Financial Questions recommended the consolidation of the sterling group and also the possible adoption of a common monetary policy for the British Empire (Dayer, 1988: 239). Then in August, with the British Government erecting a tariff wall around Britain and the Empire, and a system of Imperial Preference being agreed at the Imperial Conference in Ottawa, the Sterling Bloc quickly became a more concrete notion. It was further consolidated and institutionalised as the 1930s progressed, especially as a result of the introduction of Exchange Controls in 1939.[18] This resulted in external transactions being tightly controlled while internal ones remained free. In addition, major holdings of sterling were pooled, via the relevant central banks of the Sterling Bloc countries, with the Bank of England at the centre, forming a nexus that allowed what could be described as 'imperial liquidity' to be made available when and where necessary. With the outbreak of the Second World War this informal grouping was transformed into a formal organisation, the Sterling Area. Member states belonging to this organisation received sterling for both exports to Britain and in exchange for any gold and foreign exchange earned from international trade.

While the events of 1931 had destroyed much of the Bank of England's power and prestige, the Treasury had been more fortunate. It had actually increased its power over monetary policy – at the expense of the Bank – and been able to retain control of Britain's economic management, perpetuating the so called Treasury View of balanced budgets and sound money, despite the end of gold and the popularising of Keynesian economic theory (Howson, 1993: 5). It was only with the advent of war, and especially with the appointment of Churchill as Prime Minister in 1940, that the Treasury experienced *de facto* demotion within government and entered a period of relative obscurity. Thus, again, as in the First World War, when it became imperative that an effective 'national productive effort' be organised, control of the economy was taken away from the Treasury.

With the Treasury losing control of economic management, and the Bank no longer responsible for monetary policy, with a near-bankrupt City unable to rely totally on the international economy and forced to look towards domestic capital accumulation for survival, with Britain then emerging from the Second World War with reserves of $2–3 billion with which to finance sterling liabilities of around $12 billion, it might have been expected that a *structural* change would have taken place 'in the relationship between the different forms of capitalism in Britain, and between them and the state' (Overbeek, 1993: 112).[19] Yet, it did not. The disastrous return to gold and the ensuing economic depression, mass unemployment, hunger marches and national strikes – these events had made little difference, because nothing essentially changed. So although the City–Bank–Treasury nexus was certainly forced to adapt to the realities of the 1930s and 1940s, its institutional structure was able to emerge intact into the 1950s. In the post-war period, therefore, industrial capital would remain subordinate in the making of economic policy, which had the effect of hastening Britain's decline as a world economic power, while sterling was revived as an international reserve and vehicle currency and the City recovered to become the world's foremost international financial centre. As Ingham (1984: 200) makes clear, 'the dominant class had been shaken by the 1931 crisis and the City's low ebb, but it was able to hold on in its unchanged institutional framework, bide its time, and ultimately prosper in commercial capital's spectacular (if largely unexpected) revival in the mid-1950s'. As the next chapter will demonstrate, it was in setting out to bring about this revival that the City's merchant and overseas bankers discovered and nurtured a nascent foreign market in dollars that had established itself on their doorstep, and harnessed it to their own business in international banking and commerce. It is from within the institutional arrangements and cultural and social milieu attached to these activities that the evolution of the Euromarkets should be understood.

4
Restoring Sterling after 1945

While the advent of the Eurodollar market greatly increased the international use of the dollar and reduced that of sterling, its effect, inevitably, was to reduce New York's importance as an international financial centre. Yet why should New York's loss be London's gain and not say Paris's or Zurich's? The Bank of England (1964: 103) claims that it was 'an entirely natural development' for the City to become the centre for the Eurodollar market. Political economist Eugene Verslusyen (1981: 14) agrees, although his explanation is somewhat more illuminating. He sees the City's position at the centre of the Eurocurrency system as stemming directly from the fact that it became 'solidly anchored' in an 'institutional framework – particularly the merchant banks', which had 'reached maturity nearly one hundred years' earlier. A framework which, against all expectations, 'reassert[ed] itself' after 1951.

For certainly, if the resurrection of the City as the world's foremost international financial centre, and, for that matter, the Bank of England as the 'praetorian guard' for the City's merchant banking community after 1945, depended directly on the restoration of sterling as an international reserve and vehicle currency, then such an event would have been regarded as a most unlikely occurrence. What was surely more certain at the end of the war, was that because of the bankrupt position of Britain's economy and the consequent decline of her international role, as Mayhew (1999) puts it: a 'significant weakening of sterling after 1945 was inevitable'. Set that reality within the political topography of the immediate post-war period – with the City closed, the Treasury still under a political cloud and the 'Treasury View' of 'stable money' and 'balanced budgets' apparently eclipsed by the Keynesian idea of counter-cyclical demand management, a new Labour Government in possession of an overwhelming mandate for change, committed to a

'welfare state', full employment, 'national capitalism' and the nationalisation of the Bank of England – it might have appeared, as Fred Block
(1977: 60) suggests, that 'the forces in Britain that would tend to
favour ... a limited role for sterling were considerably stronger than those
that preferred a restoration of sterling's international role'.

Yet to hold this view is to totally underestimate the institutional
power and position of the City–Bank–Treasury nexus, which, as the last
chapter demonstrated, had gone to extreme lengths in the inter-war
years to return sterling to the gold standard, in the belief that this would
counter rising competition from the US, check unruly democratic
elements and restore the basis for the City's nineteenth-century pre-
eminence. Nothing much had changed. This nexus remained at the
heart of the British Establishment, despite the restrictions imposed by a
war economy and the election of a socialist government. Hence right up
into the late 1960s, poor, industrially inept Britain, tried to do the
impossible – to finance a welfare state while simultaneously attempting
to recreate its role as a world power and run an international currency.
While this latter aim would ultimately end in failure, it would guarantee
the City's post-war revival.   •

Central to understanding the City's recovery, is the role played by the
Bank of England, which re-emerged with its institutional independence
virtually intact after the Second World War, despite, both, nationalisation and the countervailing political and economic forces which were
set against it. It did this by working within the Attlee Government's
uncritical commitment to the Empire. This ensured that the restoration
of sterling's international role became the single most defining political
economic project of the immediate post-war era, even if the Government
remained blissfully unaware of the fact. This, in turn, guaranteed the
survival of the City, which otherwise would almost certainly not have
recovered its former position as the world's premier financial centre in
the 1970s (Ingham, 1984: 204), although, ironically, only after sterling
itself had been jettisoned and effectively replaced by the Eurodollar as a
global money medium. Finally, this led directly to what Blank (1977:
685) describes as the 'dramatic reassertion of the liberal state' in 1979 –
a remarkable turn-around when considered from the perspective of
Labour's 1945 landslide election victory, because at that time the only
institution of any significance that believed in the liberal cause was the
Bank of England. And if domestically it was faced by seemingly
insurmountable problems, internationally its power and independence
were also threatened by the interests of the new hegemonic global
power – America.

America v. Britain: creating an international monetary system

At the end of the Second World War a major problem for the US was how to prevent its economy from falling back into the depression of the 1930s. Now with an extended production capacity as a result of war, they needed foreign markets into which they could sell their 'export surplus'. Here was the rationale for the US to take up the role vacated by Britain and re-create an open world economy. But first, the 'drift' towards 'national capitalism', which began in 1914, and had been gathering an ever faster pace since 1929, would have to be reversed. However, the Bretton Woods agreement had created a problem in allowing member states to retain controls over current transactions for five years. The internationalists regarded this as disastrous for the creation of a multilateral world economy, especially in relation to Britain and the dismantling of the Sterling Area. With the death of Roosevelt in 1945, the influence of US Treasury Secretary Henry Morgenthau and his assistant, Director of Monetary Research Harry Dexter White came to an end. This brought about a dramatic decline in power of the Treasury *vis-à-vis* the US State Department, opening the way for the opponents of the New Deal and the New York banking community to have American foreign policy identify more with their interests, both ideologically and financially (Burnham, 1990: 39–42). They ignored the strictures of Bretton Woods, especially with regard to the setting up of the IMF; fearing that 'extensive national or international intervention would eliminate the role that private international bankers had historically played' (Block, 1977: 53). Their solution, the Key Currency Plan, returned to a self-regulating system for international trade or capital transactions and strove to counter moves to bilateralism and other aspects of national capitalism.

While it was too late for the American bankers to prevent the creation of the IMF and the Bretton Woods system, the State Department was able to have US international monetary policy reconfigured in such a way as to reflect the Key Currency proposals. It did this by having the US apply financial leverage on a bankrupt Europe to achieve their aims. In the case of Britain, the US wished to prise open the British Empire Oyster and put an end to Imperial Preference (Kolko and Kolko, 1972: 65). It manipulated the flow of Lend–Lease aid to keep British currency reserves at a bare minimum, then without warning cut it off so that Britain was forced to accept a US loan instead.[1] This was made conditional, on Britain removing the preferential tariffs established in 1933, opening up the Sterling Area and agreeing to restore sterling's convertibility with the dollar within one year. A second dimension of the US strategy, was its desire to see the pound restored to its international role, so as to plug what came to be known as the 'dollar gap' with additional international liquidity, that Europe and the world could use to purchase her 'export surplus'. While these two strategies proved to be, at least in the short run, inherently contradictory, they were ultimately to be the means of restoring the City, and fortuitously for the New York Financial community, of thereby creating, once more, an institutional structure for international banking, which America's decentralised and, as Peter Burnham puts it, 'institutionally inappropriate' banking system, could not provide.

Yet if members of the New York banking community had expected to simply renew their inter-war alliance with the Bank of England and the City, in the pursuit of a new wave of internationalism, they were to be disappointed. Because, although the Bank of England also opposed the Bretton Woods Agreement, this was not because it believed the plan needed to be more internationalist. In fact, the Inner City was to follow a very pragmatic strategy of its own, cutting a narrow path between the international interests of an overwhelmingly dominant US and a national capitalist commitment to prioritising Britain's domestic economy, as pursued by the Attlee Government. For, although Britain had been committed to work towards multilateralism as early as 1941, when it accepted Article VII of the Lend–Lease agreement with the US, the Bank was, at the very same time, planning for a post-war international economy in which international trade would function through a system of payments agreements between different currency blocs, rather than in one open multilateral system.[2] As Helleiner (1991: 78) puts it, 'the 1920s axis between the bankers of New York and the City of London had been shattered'.

When these views are considered alongside the Bank's pre-war belief in a self-regulating international financial system, it may appear that the Bank's 'essential institutional autonomy' had not survived and that, in fact, as early as 1942 Montagu Norman's Bank had ceased to exist. Yet this would be wrong. The Bank's view flowed naturally from the belief that 'exchange controls' would become the 'almost universal rule' in the post-war world, given Britain's commitment to re-constructing a fixed, rather than a floating exchange rate system. Otherwise a recurrence of the mass capital movements that had been so damaging before 1931 would inevitably take place, with a consequent loss of gold (Howson, 1993: 54). More importantly, however, was the fact that behind the Bank's proposals was its determination to see sterling preserved as an international currency, and by extension, as Sir Wilfred Eady, Joint Second Secretary at the Treasury described in 1944, its 'almost passionate interest in maintaining and restoring London as a monetary centre ...'.[3] This was something the Bank thought was impossible to do in a multilateral system, given Britain's paltry gold reserves, in the face of a dominant US holding the majority of the world's gold stocks (Pressnell, 1986: 97). As US Ambassador to London, John Winant, explained to Washington, the Bank was convinced 'financial control will leave London and sterling exchange will be replaced by dollar exchange'. To the Bank, the solution to all these concerns was not to be found in a multilateral system as, defined at Bretton Woods, but rather from within the Sterling Bloc.[4]

In effect, Bank of England policy was to continue where it had left off in 1939, and it was in the context of the post-war reaffirming of the Sterling Bloc and the legacy of Empire, that the Bank was able to push through the decision to restore sterling as an international currency, withstand attempts to redefine its institutional structure within the state and regain its institutional autonomy in the teeth of the post-war Welfare State.[5] As Per Jacobsson, the Director-General of the IMF said, 'the Crown and the £ sterling are the twin pillars of British greatness' (cited in Davenport, 1974: 99). This belief, which had been inculcated into the City–Bank–Treasury nexus in the nineteenth century, had not been destroyed by the collapse of the gold standard and the international economy in 1931. It re-emerged after 1945 to instil a determination to re-establish the City as the foremost international financial centre in the world.

Securing the Bank's institutional autonomy

When the Bank of England appointed Montagu Norman as their full-time Governor in 1920 they had appointed a person ideally suited to lead the City in what was first an ideological struggle. Norman's 'big idea', according to the Governor of the Bank of France, was that stability in world affairs could only be achieved if the central banks succeeded in taking economic problems 'out of the political realm'. And by being on the gold standard, monetary policy was removed from government control and therefore technically regarded as being 'outside politics' (Williamson, 1984: 105). The belief that monetary policy in the hands of the Bank, as opposed to the politicians, is by definition 'free from political influences', as the 1931 Macmillan Committee described it, is a credo which has regained some prominence in recent years.

Lord Cobbold, who was Governor of the Bank in the 1950s, once described Norman, as having 'no politics'. Of course, it was precisely his actions in regard to returning to the gold standard in 1925 and the consequent effect of subjecting the British economy to the automatic disciplines of international monetary pressures, that brought the Bank of England into disrepute, and were considered highly political by those in the Labour Party that did not side with MacDonald's National Government.

They formed the basis of the Attlee Government which nationalised the Bank in 1946, when as Hugh Dalton, the Labour Chancellor, exclaimed triumphantly, 'power, in British central banking, has now moved from British private financiers and the City "establishment" to the Chancellor of the Exchequer, not an "establishment figure", but a senior Minister, publicly responsible to Parliament' (Dalton, 1962: 47). Yet Dalton never intended such power to include any direct control or influence over the banking industry. Even Ernest Bevin, trade unionist and senior Labour politician and the only member of the Macmillan Committee to call for the abandonment of the gold standard, believed that while the Bank should become a public corporation, 'it should remain free from political influence' (cited in Cairncross, 1988: 62), echoing former Labour Chancellor and National Government turncoat, Philip Snowdon, who said in 1928, 'I have no desire at all to see a central bank under political interference'. It was not, therefore, that prescient of the *Economist* when it predicted in 1945 that 'the nationalized Bank of 1946 will not differ in any fundamental way from the privately owned Bank of 1945'. Ten years later, a Treasury paper concluded, '[i]t would be a mistake to think of the 1946 Act, or any other stages in this process as representing any fundamental change or break with the past'. There was 'no abrupt break with Montagu Norman's legacy', nor with the Bank of England's distinctive view on economic policy. In fact, nationalisation was almost entirely irrelevant. As for Bank personnel, as Ham (1981: 33) explains, the Bank had gone 'out of its way to equip itself with 1930 vintage veterans'. Very few of its senior executives were replaced and it continued to be run by a Chief Executive and a Court of part-time directors who were mostly Old Etonians drawn from the ranks of the merchant banks. People who still regarded themselves as 'princes of the City'. This tradition continued until well into the 1960s. In keeping with this relationship, as late as 1961 the Bank still regarded the London Discount Houses as 'its children'.[6]

Yet during the period leading up to nationalisation, not everyone at the Bank and in the City were that confident public ownership would allow it to retain its independence. Hence it put considerable energy into a damage limitation strategy. It was Norman, just before retirement, in 1944, who 'command[ed] the response of the Bank' to Whitehall, and under whose direction the Bank started to consider constitutional change (Fforde, 1992: 1), convinced that nationalisation would be an inevitable consequence of the return of a Labour Government. Nevertheless, they were determined, as Cobbold confirms, that 'as much of the Bank's independence should be retained as possible ... and our thinking and our homework was directed to this end'.[7] Norman, at the Centenary Luncheon of the *Economist* (1944: 18) in September 1943, put out a marker, when, quoting Walter Bagehot he said 'we can often effect by the indirect compulsion of public opinion what other countries must effect by the direct compulsion of Government', and he added significantly, 'it is an advantage which we should be slow to sacrifice'. What could he have meant?

When Norman retired, according to former Bank director and official historian, John Fforde (1992: 2): 'his creation simply sailed on without him, trained to work as he had taught it'. Yet, much had still to be done to secure his legacy. Perhaps the person more responsible for doing this was Lord Catto, who succeeded Norman on 14 February 1946, becoming the first Governor of a nationalised Bank of England. Catto had been a partner at Morgan Grenville and became a Bank of England director in 1940 and also the Bank's financial advisor at the Treasury, where he is credited with having done 'much to protect the Bank's interests' (Kynaston, 1999: 472). Cobbold certainly believed that it was largely down to Catto that the Bank 'achieved considerable success in maintaining, both *de facto* and to some extent in the legislation, an existence independent of the Treasury'. Hence, during the second reading of the Bank of England Bill in the House of Lords, Catto requested the wording be changed to 'ensure that to all intents and purposes the same relationship will exist in future between the Treasury and the Bank as has existed in the past'.[8] Naturally, by definition, therefore, this also meant the continuation of the Bank's non-political status. For as Catto pointed out,

> The avoidance of politics is a time-honoured tradition of the Bank of England: indeed it is one of the very corner stones of its policy without which its centuries-old relations with Governments would have been impossible.

Five days later, at a farewell dinner for Norman given by the Bank, Catto announced, 'we put up a fight behind the scenes and obtained every point we considered essential to the well-being of this great and ancient institution'. Cobbold was convinced that this would not have been possible without Catto. Had Norman or 'or any of the regular City Leaders' been in charge, he believed Dalton would have 'ridden roughshod over Bank and City and the factual independence of the Bank would have disappeared without trace'. This did not happen and it was Catto's plebeian upbringing, in contrast to Dalton's aristocratic background, that he felt prevented the Chancellor from 'standing up to a public row with Catto'. Dalton, in Cobbold's words 'had met his match'.[9] So, as the *Economist* opined in regard to nationalisation of the Bank, 'nothing could well be more moderate'. After Catto, came the first Governor appointed from within the Bank, who had been long groomed to become Norman's successor, Cameron Cobbold himself. Just as Dalton was overawed by Catto, so were most Conservative Chancellors by Cobbold, a fact that helped Norman's protégé keep his Bank, as Fforde (1992: 2–3) writes, 'substantially unchanged until the late 1950s'. While this may imply that Cobbold strived to maintain the *status quo*, in fact, in the face of a Labour Government taking responsibility for macroeconomic policy in order to manage the domestic economy and maintain full employment, he had to wage what Howson (1993: 8) describes as 'a long-drawn-out campaign ... to restore the Bank's pre-war position in the UK financial system'. He had, in other words, to revive monetary policy and the Bank's central role in its operation. The *Banker* (1960: 778) wrote of Cobbold on his retirement, that 'his Governorship has been amongst the most decisive in the Bank's long history', guiding it, in the 'dismantling of much of the wartime apparatus of control, the reopening of the commodity exchanges', reviving, 'the international functions of the City', and rediscovering 'monetary policy and the return to flexible money rates'.

In 1961 Cobbold was followed by the 3rd Earl of Cromer, a merchant banker and member of the Baring family, who at 42 became the youngest Governor of the Bank of England since the eighteenth century. As the Rothschilds family wrote to the Barings family, the City was 'very thrilled ... to feel that the Merchant Banking Community should be so well represented by the honour'. Cromer also impressed the society magazine, the *Tatler*, especially his 'love of the country' and his 'Tudor House in Westerham, Kent ... complete with a Jersey herd'. Cromer, they remarked with enthusiasm 'has Prince Philip's gift of speaking crisply to the point with an economy of words and a neat sense of humour', all invaluable gifts now made available for the benefit of the Governorship (cited in Kynaston, 2002: 254–7). Not surprisingly then, Cromer was able to re-assert the dominant role of Governor within the

Bank's executive. Until he retired in 1966, after falling out with the Wilson Government, there was then, as Spiegelberg (1973: 154) puts it, 'a dynastic formidableness' about the succession of 'ducal figures in the City' to the Governorship. Even then, he was succeeded by Leslie O'Brien, a Bank official who had been Norman's last private secretary and an 'unstinting admirer'. And in July 1973 when O'Brien himself retired, he was followed by Gordon Richardson, a merchant banker from Schroders, who, according to a colleague, 'had a merchant prince's idea of the role of City grandees' (Kelly, 1976: 60; Widlake, 1986: 51; Fay, 1988: 67).

Thus up until Richardson's succession, if not his retirement ten years later, it can be argued that the Bank of England was still recognisably Montagu Norman's creature, behaving as though hardly anything had changed; and not much had. Most importantly, the Treasury's position *vis-à-vis* the banking sector was, in practical terms, unaltered. For, the Treasury was not empowered by the 1946 Act to issue directives directly to the banking community, but only on the initiative of the Bank. And, although, the Treasury had the statutory power to issue directions to the Bank, it never had, and was unlikely ever to do so. This was the essence of the Bank's victory over Dalton and socialism. As Cobbold admits, they were desperate to prevent the Treasury gaining direct control over the commercial banks. This they achieved by convincing Dalton that such powers should be, as Cobbold puts it, 'limited to the initiative of the Bank'. In addition, the Bank continued to have complete autonomy over its internal affairs. As Cobbold explains with regard to the catch-all phrase 'affairs of the Bank' which was used to define the Bank's area of relative autonomy in the 1946 Act,

> [it] seemed a very appropriate generic wording to give us what we wanted to achieve, which was to have as much freedom as possible for the Governors and the Court to manage the internal administration of the Bank without interference from Whitehall. I do not recollect much detailed discussion of what exactly the phrase would cover. In fact I'm pretty sure that Catto and I would have been keen not to discuss it in detail, which might have given rise to limitation or restriction of the Court's freedom in these matters.[10]

Hence, nationalisation did not empower the government of the day to dismiss the Governor and Deputy Governor. Neither did it require the Bank to publish accounts, nor be subject to the spending limits usually applied to public bodies. The Bank continued to hire its own staff, and was not required to reveal, even to the Treasury, the salaries of its senior officials. It still maintained its traditional secrecy. It still continued to depend for direction and leadership upon the City's small merchant banking community. Whenever anyone questioned the Bank's 'independence', it was peculiarly defensive, acting as though its 'dignity were affronted'. It even complained to the Federal Reserve Board when it was listed in an American magazine 'among those central banks that are not independent of government' (Fay, 1988: 30). In its defence, it might have argued that nationalisation had, if anything, legitimised its independence, or quoted Harold Macmillan, who believed that the Bank had become far more independent since nationalisation. Not only because it was freed from the control of its shareholders, but also because it gave the Bank an *ex officio* claim to be represented in government. Yet, although its power to influence government policy had increased, it retained the right to take public positions at variance with those aspects of policy it disagreed.[11] So, while nationalisation, as Daunton (1993: 199) writes, 'reinforced the status quo', based on providing expertise on monetary policy of a narrow technical nature, which the government of the day was largely unqualified to challenge, at the same time it allowed the Bank 'to avoid direct public responsibilities', by transferring those to the Treasury.

This is confirmed by Cobbold, whose personal view was that 'if the Bank had continued as a privately owned institution ... [its] position would have been weaker and the Bank would always have been open to accusations, however unfounded, that we were dominated by a court of City oligarchs and acting in private rather than national interests. As a nationally owned body, with Governors and Directors appointed by the Crown, these criticisms fell to the ground'. Then, in addition, while the 1946 Act did not provide government with any more effective control of the commercial banking system, it did give 'legal sanction' to the Bank's 'already very strong persuasive powers' over 'banks and other financial organisations' (Hirsch, 1965: 141). Most importantly, it also continued to have full operational control – or as Brittan (1964: 60) terms it, 'the initiative' – over the manipulation of interest rates until 1959, echoing back to before the war, when as Sir Otto Niemeyer put it, 'a change in bank rate was no more regarded as the business of the Treasury than the colour which the Bank painted its front door'.[12]

The Bank of England remained then, effectively, *de facto* self-governing. An autonomous public institution dominated by private bankers managing its affairs independent of Parliament and the Treasury. Hence, whatever limited power nationalisation may have given the Treasury to control the banking system, as Pollard (1979: 180) points out, 'the City had meanwhile also acquired a firm foothold inside government'. It can be argued, therefore, that the consequence of nationalisation was almost in direct contradiction to its purpose. Taken together, it is not surprising that the Bank welcomed the 1946 Act.

Yet, while the Bank's 'institutional structure' had endured, its 'institutional function' had been dramatically altered; not so much by nationalisation, but by the events of 1931. Prior to this, Britain's economic policy had been, in essence, the Bank of England's monetary policy – there was no other effective policy. Fundamental change only began in 1931 and continued into the post-war period when, for the first time, monetary policy was directed towards domestic concerns (Howson, 1993: 5). The Bank became constrained by the aims of 'national capitalism' and caught in a fissure in the institutional structure of the British state; the contradiction at the heart of the British economy, between the needs of its international and domestic sectors – what Ingham (1984) describes as the 'City v. Industry divide' – the consequence of which was to pit the interests of domestic industry against those of international finance. This fissure had split apart in 1931. But it was re-constituted around the same fault line after 1945, by the Keynesian 'compromise', which preserved the market nexus by hiving off microeconomics and leaving it to 'classical market orthodoxy', while Government relied on Keynesian Demand Management to maintain an adequate level of domestic economic growth, via the development of Britain's industrial base.

This 'transformed' the role of the Bank, as Sir David Eccles (Secretary for State in Macmillan's Government), wrote to the PM in 1960, 'as "the stability of the currency and the exchanges" was joined, some would say superseded, as the prime object of economic policy by a commitment to maintain full-employment, etc'.[13] This, in turn, threatened the ability of sterling to function as an international reserve and trading currency and, in the eyes of the City, prevented London from re-establishing its position as the world's leading international financial centre. Hence, a struggle was initiated between Government and the Bank of England which continued for the next thirty years. So, while the former created and financed the welfare state, took responsibility for maintaining full employment and Britain's domestic economy, the *laissez-faire* minded Bank, and, according to Pringle (1973: 113) '... the most powerful repository of a "liberal" economic philosophy in England', was intent on re-establishing and maintaining a full international role for sterling and the City; thereby, in effect, re-creating the *liberal state*. These essentially antagonistic aims created what Fforde (1992: 395) describes in his history of the Bank of England, as an 'institutional stalemate'. It resulted in the application of an incompatible policy mix, especially in regard to the uneasy compromise between the use of 'market forces' and 'administrative guidance' to determine monetary aggregates. This often led, directly, to a confrontation between the Bank and the Treasury, especially at times of a sterling crisis, when, inevitably, the implementation of deflationary measures to shore up its value and protect its position as an international reserve and trading currency came into conflict with the needs of British industry and employment.

The battle for sterling

While the Bank's over-riding concern in 1945 was to see both sterling and the City restored to their former magnificence, as a 1943 report by the Bank's Post-War Exchange Policy Committee makes clear, the paucity of Britain's reserves meant that in the initial post-war period at least, this could only be achieved by consolidating and extending the Sterling Bloc, rather than within the multilateral system envisaged at Bretton Woods. Again, Bank policy shows a concern for both the prestigious and the pragmatic, with, on the one hand, sterling and the City retaining some semblance of their former glory, and, on the other, gold and currency reserves protected, City incomes reconvened and, hopefully, the balance of payments restored. As for the Treasury, as a note from 1948 makes clear, it was of the opinion that 'the world needs the rehabilitation of sterling in order that a Sterling Bloc may be set up effectively to stand against the dollar block'. Yet it was precisely the Sterling Bloc itself that, potentially, represented the single greatest threat to Britain's reserve position. For during the Second World War Britain's balance of payments position deteriorated from a deficit of £250 million in 1939 to over £1600 million in 1945, rising as a percentage of GDP from 4 to 16 per cent. This was financed by a running down of reserves, the sale of overseas assets, US Lend–Lease and Canadian credits and the accumulation of sterling liabilities to other members of the Sterling Area, accrued as a result of their provision of goods and services to prosecute the war. Hence, by 1945 Britain had only reserves of between $2–3 billion with which to finance sterling liabilities of around $12 billion; a ratio of reserves to short-term liabilities which could only but compound sterling's weakness and make it more susceptible to currency crises.[14]

To the US monetary authorities the solution to this problem was relatively simple. Invoking the principle of 'equality of sacrifice', they suggested that debts to the Sterling Bloc countries be treated as a 'matter of international concern', with a part written off as a contribution to the war effort, and the rest funded by the IMF, especially as some of these liabilities, such as the purchase of goods and services from Egypt which had been used entirely to defend Egypt itself, were highly questionable. Yet the Bank of England was concerned that Britain should not renege on these debts and the British Government repeatedly dismissed these suggestions. The decision to pin sterling's future as an international currency on the Sterling Area was crucial. For while it frustrated the US, by implying that full convertibility of sterling with the dollar would be delayed, and hence too, the setting up of the Bretton Woods system, it also left Britain with a potential call on its reserves that fatally weakened sterling as an international currency, ultimately defeating the purpose of the exercise.[15]

Even without this burden, the vulnerability of Britain's external position should have been perfectly clear much earlier than 15 July 1947, when, in accordance with the terms of the 1945 Anglo-American Loan Agreement, and in keeping with the Key Currency/Bretton Woods approach to re-establishing a system of multilateral world commerce, convertibility with the dollar was restored. However, despite the fact that $1890 million of Britain's dollar reserves, over half the value of the US loan, had been lost in the first six months of 1947, the Bank of England was much more optimistic than it had been in 1943 or 1945, believing irrationally that convertibility would not lead to a drain of Britain's dollar reserves. For given the conditions of the time, with a world shortage of dollars and a great demand for US goods, it should have surprised no one that the holders of these accumulated sterling balances began to exchange them for dollars so rapidly that in just over one month Britain's reserves were almost depleted and, on 20 August, convertibility was suspended (Plowden, 1989: 5–13). Sterling's vulnerability, however, did not end with the suspension of convertibility. The Bank's decision to honour the sterling liabilities condemned Britain to spend the next quarter-century setting uncompetitive interest rates and deflating her domestic economy, in order to shore up sterling's inherent weak position so that it could keep sterling holders sweet and continue to operate as an international currency.

Sterling's weakness led to another currency crisis in 1948, then to devaluation in 1949, a further eight crises between 1950 and 1967, with the last one ending in a second devaluation, followed by four more before the end of 1969. Whilst the traditional cause of a currency crisis is a trade-induced balance of payments deficit, that occurs when there is an excess of imports over exports – and Britain's export performance certainly was inadequate – most of sterling's problems were brought on by sterling's role as an international reserve and vehicle currency. For, a small deficit on trading account most often led to a disproportionately higher deficit on capital account and international banking account, as short-term speculative capital and official monetary reserves moved out of sterling in anticipation of devaluation.

The British monetary authorities reacted to this problem by keeping interest rates relatively high to make London more attractive to foreign capital, inducing 'hot money' inflows, while simultaneously deflating the economy and reducing imports to bolster the trading account, in effect, subjecting the British economy to the same monetary policy so damaging in the inter-war period. Not surprisingly then, this strategy, though successful in the short-term, could only have the ultimate effect of making British industry less competitive, thereby further damaging Britain's export performance and leading to more intractable balance of payments problems and the further weakening of sterling. Just as in the inter-war period, the interests of the City took precedence over those of industry and the economy became dependent once more upon large funds of speculative, footloose capital that would, as Pollard (1970: 2) puts it, 'at the first sign of danger turn against sterling, leave London and turn a temporary embarrassment into a rout', hot money, in otherwords.[16]

While all this was happening, the British Government was actually pressing ahead with the removal of controls on the use of sterling. This followed on naturally, and unquestionably, from the conviction that the City's international position had to be restored, which even the Attlee Government supported. Strange (1971: 232) explains this as a consequence of its 'widespread ignorance' of and 'indifference' to Britain's position as 'host to a future international financial centre'. Hence, the policy which gave priority to re-establishing sterling as an international currency was dictated by bankers and civil servants, 'with little reference to Ministers who neither understood nor had much interest in what they were doing'. For, surprisingly, the Labour Party never really questioned 'the "international financial vocation" of the British ruling class' (De Cecco, 1976: 381; Clarke, 1988: 254). The Attlee Government's inability to define a 'clear policy position on the economic significance of the City's external role', meant they could not disentangle this question from their wider commitment to the restoration of Britain as a world power, or as Perry Anderson (1987: 43) claims, the 'historic structures of Britain's imperial economy'. Couple this fact with the 'non-event' of Bank of England nationalisation, and it is not incongruous that the 'first step' in the restoration of the City was taken by a

Labour Government, when it arranged for the London Foreign Exchange market to re-open in December 1951.

The Bank, meanwhile, had started trying to persuade the Government to go further and re-establish the London Bond Market. Thus began a recurring theme in relations between the Bank and the Treasury that was to continue throughout the 1950s and into the 1960s, with the former repeatedly arguing how essential such a capital market was for the re-establishment of both sterling's and the City's international status, and the latter unwilling to countenance such a move for fear it would only aggravate sterling's weak position and provoke another devaluation. The Bank had strongly opposed the 1949 devaluation and while it was regarded by many as a pre-requisite for the success of British exports and, by extension, British industry, a second devaluation, as a Treasury report makes clear, would 'certainly' mean 'the end of the Sterling Area as it now exists', to be replaced by other currencies, 'particularly the Deutschemark'. Yet while devaluation might certainly bring an end to sterling's international role, exchange controls, essential to prevent this from happening, were, as George Bolton, Advisor to the Governors of the Bank of England, accurately observed as early as 1943, also 'likely to be incompatible with the idea of sterling as an international currency', and the attraction of London as financial centre.[17] This posed a dilemma, for the very functioning of sterling as an international currency was undermining its ability to carry out this role, requiring, as its position got weaker, the application of more, not less, exchange control. The City and the Bank's preferred solution was for monetary policy to revert to one based on a self-regulating market mechanism and away from one based on administrative guidance and physical controls, and for public spending to be radically reduced – something that the 1944 commitment to full employment and creation of a Welfare State could not allow. The dilemma ultimately remained unresolved, that is, until it was realised that the future of London as a financial market was not directly dependent on sterling's continued role as an international currency. It is not surprising, therefore, that the history of sterling after 1945 is inexorably entwined with the question of exchange control, the constraints this placed on both the resuscitation of the London Bill and the re-creation of a London Capital Market and the struggle waged by the City and the Bank to have them removed.

European Payments Union

But in the immediate period after the 1947 debacle, exchange control was not an issue. It was not until 1950 that progress towards freer conditions re-started, when a system of bilateral relations between European countries was replaced with a regional multilateral settlement, the European Payments Union (EPU), which the whole Sterling Area could link up to through Britain's membership. The Bank of England, which had, only a short time before, hoped to extend the sterling zone to take in the major countries of Western Europe, was now faced instead with what it felt would be the inevitable downgrading of sterling's reserve position and the consequent undermining of Britain's 'global role'. Events which it believed would naturally follow from the creation of the EPU. In addition, the Bank was concerned that this might lead to the creation of a rival 'European currency unit'.[18] Nevertheless, Britain eventually agreed to become a member of the EPU, but on terms which led Bolton to lament in a note to Cobbold that the 'special position of sterling has virtually disappeared' (cited in Fforde, 1992: 213). The EPU was duly established on 19th September 1950 and became an overwhelming success, contributing to an expansion of world trade. Rather than restrict sterling as an international trading and investment currency, it therefore had the opposite effect.

Not surprisingly, as Fforde (1992: 216) points out, 'the EPU was appreciated by relatively few in the Treasury and the Bank'. The latter believing that sterling's survival as an international currency depended almost exclusively on its relationship with the dollar. So by 1951, the Bank, in an effort to resolve the dilemma of a weak sterling attempting to be convertible with the dollar at a fixed rate of $2.80, in accordance with the Bretton Woods agreement, came up with a masterly plan. Instead of championing the Sterling Area, they now saw a rapid move to full convertibility at any price – a 'dash to freedom' – as the only way of re-establishing both the City's and sterling's international role. A plan that came to be known by the ominous title: Operation Robot. This dramatic reversal of policy followed what Helleiner (1991: 118) describes as a 'turn towards multilateralism of conservative financial groups within the UK', who wished to bring an end to the EPU. Not only because they felt it operated as a barrier to sterling's international future, but also because they believed, as Block (1977: 101) explains, that it 'substituted an intergovernmental credit mechanism for the historic credit-providing role of British bankers'. In their animosity towards the EPU the British were joined by US neo-liberals and its international banking community, who regarded this quasi-socialist institution as the foremost barrier to achieving full multilateral convertibility. There was only one problem for the Bank – the Attlee Government. For while it might not have questioned the 'international financial vocation' of the

British establishment, it remained committed to a 'cheap money' policy, whereby very low interest rates kept down the cost of both government borrowing and industrial investment. Cobbold had been striving since 1945 to persuade the government to re-introduce a traditional monetary policy, but without success. This was the key to re-establishing the Bank's control and power, especially as the Treasury believed it to be an area of expertise its lack of technical knowledge precluded it from entering. It was also a pre-requisite to any 'dash for freedom' and a floating of sterling. Cobbold had to wait until a Conservative Government was elected in late 1951 to get his way.[19]

The return of the Conservatives saw Labour's concept of the Sterling Area as a 'defensive currency area' replaced by a philosophy of 'sterling strong and free', that was in perfect harmony with the campaign to have exchange controls removed and full convertibility of sterling restored. Yet there is no real doubt that the driving force behind this strategy was the Bank of England. In fact, as Britton makes clear, some 'very senior British Cabinet Ministers insisted privately that sterling's international role was a burden which they would only be too pleased to be rid'. Yet this view was never made 'effective' as 'official policy'. This remained unchanged, and in line with the Bank's view that nothing should cast doubt on Britain's commitment to 'the continuation of sterling as a reserve currency' (Brittan, 1964: 278; Hirsch, 1965: 45; Blank, 1977: 686).

Operation Robot

While the countries of Western Europe were working towards the liberalisation of trade as an essential prerequisite to moving to convertibility, the Bank of England's priority was inclined to the reverse. This again reflected the dominance of City interests in Bank policy making, which naturally, as Hinton (1987: 105) points out, required that priority be given to restoring sterling as 'a medium of international trade and finance'. This, in turn, demanded that sterling be convertible. Hence, although Britain was the country most dependent on the EPU, it was the one most eager to dispense with it. So it was, with sterling coming under tremendous speculative pressure in the aftermath of the Korean War boom, that the Bank began advocating their plan to create a currency union between Britain and the US, by setting sterling 'free' and making it fully convertible (to non-residents) with the dollar at a floating rate of exchange.[20] The immediate reaction of Edwin Plowden (1989: 144), the Treasury's Chief Planning Officer, was 'one of great puzzlement', as given sterling's weakness this would inevitably mean devaluation, something which the Bank had always been against. As well as terminating Britain's participation in the EPU it might also bring an end to the Bretton Woods System itself, even before it was up and running. The commercial rationale for Robot, that it would stimulate a rise in dollar earnings consequent to an increase in exports to the US, was unconvincing. Clearly Robot was concerned with resurrecting sterling's international role, which itself could not be detached from matters of 'national prestige'. George Bolton, for one, saw Robot 'almost wholly in such terms'. He wished to see Britain restored to its position as a leading world money power. Something he believed was the 'only international policy which guaranteed the nation's survival in worthwhile form' (Milward, 1992: 354).

Of course, Robot was not merely a plan for resurrecting sterling's international role, it was also a means by which a self-regulating market mechanism for running the British economy could be re-established. So that, as Lord Cherwell explained to Churchill, now Prime Minister again, it would 'be taken out of the hands of politicians and planners and handed over to financiers and bankers who alone understand these things'. Robot would, therefore, once again, not only put the foreign confidence in sterling and Britain's external balance as the first priority in domestic economic policy formulation, but would, at the same time, restore the Bank to its former position of strength in the formulation of such policy. Britain could then expect an immediate return to the deflationary policies of the 1920s, as the Bank struggled to maintain an increasingly overvalued pound, calling for a substantial rise in interest rates, so as to both dampen domestic demand and therefore Britain's import bill, and attract short-term foreign capital into London. Rather than precipitate a large sterling devaluation, a Robot-induced convertibility, would almost certainly have acted, as Andrew Shonfield (1958: 207) explained in 1957, as 'a ruthless and effective disciplinarian of the home economy', just like the gold standard of the inter-war years. Perhaps this was something that did not occur to the puzzled Plowden. Although 'Robot' was supported by Cobbold, the Chancellor of the Exchequer R. A. Butler and, for a time, most of the Cabinet and Churchill, on 29 February 1952, after lengthy discussions, the plan was rejected for fear that it would lead to inflation and unemployment. Churchill had been here before, when as Chancellor he had authorised the return to gold in 1925, much against his own instincts. Nevertheless he was 'looking forward to the day when sterling could be set free' again. So the issue did not go away.[21] It was repeatedly thrown back to Government in different guises until the so-called Collective Approach reached a height of absurdity, depending as it did on the US (or the IMF) being willing to provide $5 billion of reserves to support sterling. Not surprisingly, it was rejected at the Anglo-American talks in March 1953.

While the Bank had been defeated over Robot, the re-introduction of monetary policy in 1951 had, at least, given the City, as Cobbold pointed out, 'a chance of furbishing up the dealing techniques for which it has long been famed' and showing that 'London has not lost its pre-eminence in financial skill and knowledge'. In addition, the 'stalling', as John Fforde (1992: 492) describes this long drawn-out process that followed the end of Robot, provided the Bank with an opportunity to formulate a more low-key approach to re-establishing sterling convertibility. Bolton began to develop plans to 'harden' the EPU and widen the transferability of sterling by dismantling the restrictions hampering trading in a form of transferable sterling known as cheap-sterling, which was, in effect, a black-market currency used in trading outside the Sterling Area at a discounted rate with the dollar, set purely by the market. Cobbold had, meanwhile to content himself with 'easing up a bit here and there, getting commodity markets going' (cited in Fforde, 1992: 406). So by October 1953, he announced in the Governor's annual Mansion House Speech to the City, that the reopening of various commodity markets and the extra business this was bringing London, was 'helping to make sterling a more useful and desirable currency throughout the world'. Moreover, he added, the restoration of arbitrage facilities between London and leading European financial centres allowing both spot and forward rates of exchange to be offered, also meant that the Foreign Exchange Market was once more functioning effectively.[22] One week later Bolton circulated a plan to move towards 'back-door convertibility'. The first stage was to unify all the categories of transferable sterling (non-dollar, non-resident sterling), and remove all barriers restricting dealing in it. The second stage was the removal of the barrier between the Transferable Sterling Account and Dollar Sterling Account Areas, thereby establishing *de facto* convertibility. While the Treasury was in favour of most of Stage 1, including the re-opening of the London Gold Market, it was not prepared to agree to Stage 2. Cobbold was not, however, 'too disheartened', as, according to Fforde, he had begun 'to exploit the tactical flexibility of the Bank's new course'. As the *Economist* put it, 'With head tucked well into a new protective shell the objective is now to crawl like a crustacean to freedom' (Harris, 1972: 231; Fforde, 1992: 505). On 22 March 1954, the London Gold Market was reopened and, at the same time, all restrictions on the movement of non-resident sterling outside of the dollar area were removed. Butler wrote to Churchill, 'I believe [this] will help to strengthen sterling as an international currency and London as an international financial centre.' A note in the Chancellor's Cabinet folder adds, this will 'enhance the prestige of the City ... and ... increase world confidence in sterling'. This was a signal to the Bank that it was time to go all the way. But to its frustration the Government was still unwilling to take a risk on full convertibility and even the Americans were ambivalent to the idea, as were the other members of the EPU, for complex and conflicting economic and political reasons.[23]

The climacteric of 1955

If for one moment the Bank grudgingly accepted that its 'stability without commitment' policy was at an end, and with it any hopes for a Robot-style floating exchange rate, it did little to communicate this reality to the City and the financial press. In fact it did quite the opposite. It ignored the Government's wishes and fed rumours through the BIS in Basle that full convertibility was at hand. With the consequence that Britain entered what Schonfeld (1958: 196) calls 'the Climacteric of 1955' and a three-year long, speculation-driven, sterling crisis. As the market, responding to the easing of exchange controls on currency flows and convinced – despite the Treasury's declared intent to consolidate sterling's position and not put Britain's reserves under any greater risk – that just as in the 1920s 'the Bank had more or less taken over direction of British policy', concluded, both that the pound was to be set free, and, given its weakness, that its price would inevitably float downwards by 5 per cent.

As 1955 began sterling was already under pressure and bank rate was raised by 0.5 per cent, from 3 to 3.5 per cent. But as Shonfield observed, 'the City of London hardly noticed' and in February it had to go up again by 1 per cent. If there was anyone in the City still unconvinced of the Bank's ability to push through convertibility at any price, this surely was the point where all remaining doubts were extinguished. For on the very same day that pressure on sterling demanded bank rate be raised for the second time in weeks, the Bank also announced that in future it would intervene to support the unofficial currency, transferable sterling, which meant that whenever its price threatened to fall, the Bank had to enter this black market and buy up any foreign-held sterling offered for sale, paying for it out of Britain's paltry dollar reserves. From this time on, the rate for transferable sterling was never allowed to fall much below the official rate.

This was a big breakthrough, made possible only after Cobbold had mounted a 'sustained offensive' to win support from the Treasury and the Prime Minister (Fforde, 1992: 526). For it meant, as far as the Bank was concerned, and as it now pointed out to anyone who would listen, that in practice sterling was fully convertible – 'only the British Government refused to take official cognizance of the fact'. But just in case the world remained in any doubt as to where all these manoeu-vrings were leading, as Bolton advised his colleagues, it was 'essential to make plain to all that UK policy remains firmly directed towards ... the maintenance and the growth of the use of sterling as an international currency'.[24] Nevertheless, in fact, the Bank's actions only had the effect of engendering a feeling that currency regulations were not so important and that if official convertibility really was imminent, given the increasing weakness of sterling, it would be convertibility at a devalued rate. Not surprisingly acceptance business revived, as expanding world trade took to using commercial credit in a currency which was expected to fall in value. Such was the speculative crisis against sterling in the summer of 1955, and the deflationary measures the Government felt it necessary to apply in response, a significant 'stop' phase in the evolution of Britain's post-war economy was soon in progress. For no government with inad-equate reserves and a convertible currency to defend could risk stimu-lating a Keynesian type industrial investment boom. While Robot had been thwarted, convertibility and the need to re-establish sterling's international status had finally, but inevitably, become the 'ruthless disciplinarian' of Britain's domestic economy that Schonfield had predicted. Now it was surely possible to conclude, as he did, that behind the Bank of England's monetary manoeuvrings of the 1950s, 'it was possible to discern the same larger objective as that which was ultimately attained by Montagu Norman in the 1920s'.

If 1955 had been 'the year of the great economic disillusion', as Schonfield describes it, when the government's inability to comprehend that its attempt to ensure both economic expansion 'at home' and a strong and convertible sterling abroad, was 'beckoning Britain in opposite direc-tions', then the following years brought no great enlightenment either. In February 1956 a Bank report stressed that 'international regard for sterling is of over-riding importance' and that Her Majesty's Government is pur-suing an inevitable policy of 'restoring freedom of use of sterling'. In May, the Treasury's Sir Leslie Rowan, one of the architects of Robot, claimed that an 'essential characteristic of sterling' was that it was 'the major trading or international currency in the world', and as such it was important 'for the world that [it] should resume its full role as a medium of world trade and exchange'. By August another major sterling crisis was underway. On this occasion Britain's trading account remained in surplus, the run on sterling being brought about by large withdrawals of sterling following the Suez crisis. The Treasury began to consider a devaluation of transferable sterling. The Bank strongly opposed any 'going backwards on convertibility' and made it clear to the Chancellor of the Exchequer, Harold Macmillan, that devaluation would mean an end to the Sterling Area and sterling's international role. Interestingly, the Bank could have done more itself to reduce sterling's weakness, but chose not to. In particular, it was reluctant to put a stop to the draining away of reserves through what was known as the Kuwait and Hong Kong gaps – open markets for sterling – that were putting further strain on Britain's position. Instead, the following month, Cobbold used his Mansion House speech to make a veiled criticism of rising Government spending, which was undermining Britain's balance of payments position and sterling's strength.[25]

Meanwhile, acceptance business was continuing to rise. By March 1957 credits outstanding with the NSA (Non Sterling Area) had risen dramatically higher to £178 million, as again 'acceptance facilities were being used as a method of speculating against sterling', in the expectation of a devaluation. At the end of June, with another crisis imminent, the Bank had to go on a PR offensive, responding to the suggestion that Britain would be better off if sterling's international role was terminated, by pointing out that it 'is the currency most widely used by traders all over the world' and talking up its 'unrivalled advantages ... as an international currency'. Nevertheless, when the crisis began for real in August, it re-ignited a great debate on whether the Sterling Area was holding back Britain's growth, and tensions between the Treasury and the Bank, that had been simmering for some time, began to boil over. By September, as yet another speculation-led sterling crisis erupted, Cobbold felt it necessary to express his conviction that 'our prosperity and standard of living will suffer a mortal blow if the pound goes again'. He demanded more of the old medicine: deflation. The Government, now led by Harold Macmillan, disagreed. So while Cobbold insisted that bank rate be increased from 5 per cent to 7 per cent and public sector capital spending capped, the Prime Minister and his Chancellor, Peter Thorneycroft, demanded that the clearing banks reduce their lending instead. While on previous occasions, the banks had reluctantly complied with the Government's wishes, this time they refused. They dug in and Cobbold, sympathetic to their position, 'refused to give them a direction' (Hall, 1991: 126–7). Macmillan and Thorneycroft were so furious they determined to force the Bank of England to accede to their demands, by law if necessary. When, to their astonishment, they discovered there was nothing in the 1946 Act the Treasury could use to make the Bank comply with its directions, they tried to dismiss Cobbold instead. This also proved impossible. It seemed to Fforde (1992: 680) that, 'the unexploded bomb dropped by the Act was in danger of going off', as the Chancellor began to look for a way of issuing directions to the clearing banks himself, threatening to impose on them 'an advances limit by Act of Parliament', in order that the Treasury could itself gain control over commercial bank lending. When the Bank found out, Deputy Governor Humphrey Mynors, warned the Chancellor that 'to take fresh powers ... would raise the gravest questions of the relations between the government and the banking system'. Cobbold was more direct. He threatened that should new legislation be introduced giving the Treasury direct control of the money supply and the banking sector, this might lead to the Bank refusing, 'or forcing others to refuse, to meet the Government's cheques'. In effect, Cobbold had threatened to make the Government bankrupt. He then gave a speech announcing that only he, the Governor of the Bank of England, had the power to direct the banks. For a time the Chancellor persisted. He established a working party to consider, both, how the Treasury could control bank credit and how the law could be amended to provide the Treasury with the 'power it thought it had already'. But, in the end, undoubtedly, as Robert Hall (1991: 127), Director of the Treasury's 'Economic Section', wrote in his diary, Thorneycroft got 'cold feet'. Nothing more was heard about amending the 1946 Act.[26]

Remarkably, Thorneycroft re-emerged, almost immediately, as a 'hard money fanatic', a prototypical monetarist, often credited as a pioneer of Thatcherism. Such was the extent of his transformation, that Samuel Brittan distinguished his pre- and post-conversion personae in terms of Thorneycroft I and Thorneycroft II. Hence, while on 9 April, Thorneycroft I had talked about the immorality of using 'savage deflationary policies' to depress demand and employment, 'to the point at which employers cannot afford to pay and workers are in no position to ask for higher wages', by 24 September, Thorneycroft II was telling the IMF that 'if inflationary pressures grow ... other aspects of policy may have to be adjusted, but the strain will not be placed on the value of the pound sterling'. He re-iterated this message to the City the following month when he told the Lord Mayor's Banquet: 'If one can regard the economy as an electric current, we are ensuring that if the current overloads it, the fuse will not be the pound sterling. The strain must be taken in other areas of policy.'[27] Thorneycroft, like most of his predecessors and successors at the Treasury, was, in the final instance, prepared to sacrifice all other aspects of the British economy to save sterling. The debate with the Bank of England, and indirectly, with the City, was only over the means to achieve this. Whatever method was chosen, the aim was to reduce the level of imports, so as to improve Britain's balance of payments and strengthen sterling's price in the foreign exchange market.

Macmillan, for his part, was left waiting upon Cobbold's retirement. He wrote revealingly, in August 1960, 'Cobbold is meant to be retiring on January 1, and should at all costs be held to this decision'. Not that his departure would make any difference now. On 19 September, interest rates were increased substantially, from 5 to 7 per cent, a level not experienced since 1920. Sterling was saved without any inconvenience to the City. Nevertheless, while in the end Macmillan had acceded to the Governor's demands, he did make sure that this rise would be accompanied by a ban on re-finance credits and sterling credits to finance non-sterling international trade. Interestingly, both these measures, in different ways, led directly to the development of the Eurodollar market. The latter, by cutting off sterling as a form of global credit used by the City's merchant and overseas banks to conduct their international dealing. The former, by ratcheting up the cost of credit to Britain's domestic economy, especially business and local government. Together they stimulated demand for a cheaper alternative, which was found in the dollar deposits that had been collecting in European and Canadian banks.

In any event, the Bank had won its battle with the Treasury. Control of monetary policy and, through this, control of the banking sector and the City had been wrested from the state and became increasingly the domain of the Bank. It is perhaps not a coincidence that after 1957 rentier incomes, as van der Pijl (1984: 192) points out, emerged as 'the most rapidly growing sector of personal income'. Of course so long as the post-war political consensus endured, with its commitment to full employment, this only led to an intensification of the institutional struggle at the heart of the British economy whenever sterling came under threat. For, as the following decade would demonstrate, the successful use of the Eurodollar as a surrogate currency for sterling, did not in any way temper the City's and the Bank's enthusiasm to see the latter returned to its former position as a fully operational international currency. Consequently, while the 1957 sterling crisis had been the most perilous since 1931, within four months the Bank was demanding that the ban on acceptance credits be relaxed.[28] The Treasury resisted, heroically, although Cobbold, who was himself being pressured by the City banks, continued trying to persuade the Government right through to the end of that year. The move to full convertibility was not to be halted either and the following June, Cobbold told the BBC that he regarded 'the sterling system as one of Britain's major and lasting contributions to the world'. In December 1958 transferable sterling was finally merged with dollar account sterling, making all sterling held by non-residents fully convertible with the dollar and all other currencies. With official convertibility finally achieved, the Bank turned its attention back to the removal of exchange controls. In May 1959 Sir George Bolton, now chairman of the Bank of London & South America, gave a speech in which he said,

> We have passed through several crises since 1945, in many of which I have been personally involved, but I can assure you that at no time, once we had set our course, did we consider failure as even a remote possibility. ... The course we set was simple ... it was to balance the budget, to repay our debts and restore the value and position of sterling. On this simple but sound policy which I assure you has been, and will be followed by every British Government we have been able to rebuild our domestic economy and foreign trade, restore the international use of sterling and the London market and to participate in investment abroad.[29]

By this time the Eurodollar market was expanding rapidly and with it the involvement of London's merchant banks. Nevertheless, the City and the Bank were still pressurising the Treasury to have the restrictions on sterling removed, with Cobbold warning that to continue the ban would damage both British and Commonwealth exports. However, the Treasury was inclined to doubt Cobbold's argument. For while the Board of Trade had been inundated with complaints regarding the ban on re-finance credits from banks and accepting houses, it had not received any from British exporters. On 1 June, a Bank draft paper on sterling remarked that 'the whole world benefits from the strength of sterling'. On 8 July, Cobbold informed the Treasury 'that a decision against removing the ban would be foolish and he would be unable to support it in the City'. By November he was telling the Treasury that the Bank could not defend the ban with the City. The Chancellor would have to explain it, in person, to a deputation from the Accepting Houses Committee.[30] In the same month Bolton, no doubt hoping to push the Treasury into a corner on the issue, gave a rallying speech in which he heralded finally the revival of sterling. He said,

> One great battle in which I have personally participated ... under the inspired leadership of the Governor, has been the fight to revive and

sustain the international position of sterling. At many times this was a fight against great odds because for a long period, we had few supporters. ... However, there is no doubt that the revival is here, sterling is more secure than it has been for two generations.[31]

But, in reality, to the City's merchant bankers, sterling's endemic weakness, which they largely put down to the effect of profligate government spending and socialist wickedness, and the consequent restrictions imposed on its use as global money, meant their reliance on the Eurodollar market as a surrogate for the London Discount Market was becoming ever stronger. Nevertheless, while this market guaranteed to a great extent that their profitable business as intermediaries in the organising of short-term global credit continued, they still believed they were losing out. Not only in terms of the prestige gained from running a successful international vehicle currency, but also because they were omitted from the formerly lucrative business of issuing sterling bonds. Exchange controls prevented the City's Foreign Bond Market from being restored to its pre-1931 glory and, hence, the global market for long-term capital had moved to New York. Even bonds issued on behalf of European institutions could only be done through the US capital market, with the New York banks picking up the commissions that had once been the prerogative of the City's merchant banks. Not surprisingly then, the City continued to push the Treasury to have exchange controls removed. But by the end of 1960, once again, the climate turned sharply against easing restrictions, as 'hot money' – much of which was emanating from the Eurodollar market – began flowing into Britain at such a rate that it prompted a parliamentary question to be asked in the House of Commons and suggestions to be made that, if anything, Britain should follow the German and Swiss examples and restrict such capital flows.[32]

The Bank was incredulous that Parliament could even consider such a move and began to draft and re-draft an effective reply. The first draft argued the cost–benefits of allowing such short-term capital flows, especially that they have 'supported the reserves during a period of some weakness in the overseas trading position'. But this only prompted an internal memo to the effect that the Bank should not even attempt to make such an argument, because '[s]urely the Treasury ought to stand firm in this matter on grounds of principle and on the damage that would be done to the standing of London and of sterling if we attempted to follow the Swiss or German examples'. While the Swiss and German authorities had blocked the flow of Eurodollars into their domestic markets, fearful, both, of the upward pressure this would place on their currencies and the inflationary effect of an expanding money supply, the Bank could only think in terms of the effective functioning of the City. In addition, with arguments eerily prescient of the rhetoric of Thatcherism and the monetarism experiment of the 1980s, it is clear that, even as early as 1960, the Bank viewed 'hot money' flows as almost a mechanism by which the financial markets discipline profligate government. More importantly, the higher interest offered in the City's Eurodollar market – a rate which was itself being pushed up by the higher rates pertaining in Britain – was attracting outflows of short-term capital from the US, to the extent that it was beginning to cause difficulties for the US payments position, a problem that would eventually lead to the collapse of the Dollar–Gold Standard and hence the Bretton Woods System. Yet the Bank of England was unwilling to contemplate any restrictions on such flows. Clearly, if restrictions had been applied in 1960, the City's Eurodollar market, would, most probably, not have developed as rapidly, or for that matter, in quite the same form, as it did.[33]

In March 1961 re-valuation of the Deutsche mark provoked intensive speculation against sterling and Britain entered another currency crisis that lasted until July. Nevertheless, this did not prevent Bolton from again writing to the Prime Minister and telling him that exchange controls were 'a confession of weakness'. Then, in July, the Bank's Executive Director, Maurice Parsons, wrote that 'the UK can only maintain the international status of sterling by abandoning Exchange Controls entirely'. In the same month Lord Cromer, who had succeeded Cobbold as Governor, wrote to the Chancellor and expressed his concern that exchange controls were restraining 'the foreign earning power of the City' and diverting 'much unique expertise in the fields of international finance ... to studying take-over bids'.[34]

Yet to a great degree this was simply rhetoric, for the code of self-regulation on which City dealing operated made evasion of exchange controls relatively simple. As Lord Richie, Chairman of the Stock Exchange admitted in 1961: 'exchange control permission for the passing of money from one country to another in return for securities can normally be arranged without much difficulty by a broker or banker'. This confirms what Schonfield (1958: 210) was himself told as far back as 1955, by someone 'holding high and responsible position in the field', that in fact, 'nobody but small fry ... takes any notice of exchange controls now'. In otherwords, while rigid exchange controls undoubtedly prohibited those small to medium sized manufacturers from transferring money overseas in the course of their international business, City merchant and overseas banks 'could usually get clearance from the Bank of England to channel funds wherever and whenever they wanted' (Hinton, 1987: 4). Nevertheless, by the middle of 1961, with sterling under intensive pressure again, exchange controls had not so much been eased, as tightened. The Bank was furious, pointing out in response, that of 'overriding consideration was the maintenance of the status of sterling as an international currency', a currency 'still … more used than the dollar to finance world trade'. Then, as was almost inevitable in a sterling crisis, the problem of 'hot money' resurfaced, prompting, once again, the Bank to go on the defensive and report that 'However much we dislike hot money, we cannot be international bankers and refuse to accept money. We cannot have an international currency and deny its use internationally. … London is the finest centre for the employment and investment of money. If we take a swipe at that, we shall do lasting damage to sterling.'

It would have come as no surprise to the Treasury when, two weeks later, despite sterling's continued problems, the Bank began pushing once again for a sterling bond market. This time the matter arose out of the issue of the Government providing credit to underwrite Britain's export industry, like its European competitors. Cromer saw this as potentially 'dangerous' and told Macmillan's latest Chancellor, Selwyn Lloyd, that Britain should 'get back to the system of days gone by when overseas borrowers could raise money in London' on the Foreign Bond Market. Nor would it have seemed so incongruous that despite sterling's ills, Cromer continued to express his objections to the continuing ban on refinance credits, for, as he wrote to the Treasury, 'To forbid this is to deny that sterling is an international currency and that London is the money centre of the world'.[35]

At the beginning of 1962, the Bank, on learning that the Treasury was examining what changes might need to be made to exchange controls if Britain were to join the European Common Market, decided to 'pull out all the stops to plead for building up London as the financial centre of Europe'. Cromer called for a 'recasting of stamp duty' which would 'open up the way for the reintroduction of bearer securities … rather than the contrary', which he felt was 'prejudicial to the general standing and business of the London market'. He pointed out that greater liberalism in world trade necessitated a greater mobility of capital. He reminded the Chancellor that as London was the only 'genuinely international centre in Europe', ending the restrictions would allow it to take up its natural role as the financial centre of Europe. More significantly, he suggested that the Government should authorise the establishment of a foreign capital market in the City, something he claimed would take pressure off sterling, *implying for the first time that it was possible to separate the fortunes of sterling and the City*. Interestingly, within four months, important correspondence, meetings and discussions began taking place, between members of the City's leading merchant banks and the Bank of England, especially between Cromer and Bolton, where plans were laid which culminated in the establishment of the Eurobond market. Finally, on 5 February, Cromer proposed that the Treasury should widen the scope of its examination to 'embrace the related question of how London may be allowed to re-establish its position as the main financial intermediary in the world, thus ensuring that the balance of payments be no longer denied earnings that the services of the City can provide'. All these suggestions emanated from the final realisation that sterling's endemic weakness was preventing the City from fully functioning as it should do.[36]

Another idea put into operation at this time, after the Treasury was finally persuaded to agree, was the provision of official support to the forward exchange market for sterling, the hope being that if the Bank intervened to prop up the future price of sterling, this would allay market fears and dampen speculative tendencies (Strange, 1971: 237). However, while this measure was designed to reduce the risk from holding onto sterling, it also reduced the risk from moving into sterling, so that short-term capital, attracted by Britain's relatively high interest rates, began to flow out of both the Eurodollar market and, to the annoyance of the US monetary authorities, the US domestic money market, thereby exacerbating the US balance of payments problem and increasing the potential risk to the further depletion of their declining gold stock. From the point of view of Britain's domestic economy, this foreign capital, by flowing into a parallel money market, where it was being bid for by local authorities and hire-purchase companies, was eroding the Government's policy of credit stringency. As for the Eurodollar market, which will be discussed in greater detail in Chapters 5 and 6, this action was helping to create a smooth *transmission belt*, linking the US and European money markets, making capital flows increasingly sensitive to interest rate differentials. A month later, Herr Von Belling, of the Dresdener Bank, said, in a discussion he had with a Bank of England representative, that if Bank Rate went down to 4 per cent in the U.K. 'the Euro-dollar market would "disappear" '.[37]

The US had also interpreted Britain's actions very negatively. The US Treasury had begun to worry about sterling and the Bank's determination to promote it at all costs, regardless of the problems it posed for the dollar and the damage that may be inflicted on the international monetary system. In March US Treasury Secretary Dillon told President Kennedy as much and made his views clear to the Bank. A few weeks later, a Bank report stressed that 'sterling must remain strong', adding that the 'counterpart to sterling as a reserve currency is the financial and market mechanism of the City of London'. A second report, written in June, re-affirms this view. It states 'Sterling should ... remain as the world's most important trading currency and the London Money Market and Foreign Exchange Markets as the most efficient centres in which to place money and to deal in foreign exchange'.[38] Not surprisingly then, three weeks later Cromer again attempted to persuade the Chancellor to ease exchange controls. Yet all the Bank's admonishments were having little effect. In keeping with true National Capitalism doctrine, Head of the Treasury's Finance Group, Sir Dennis Rickett pointed out, 'we do not want too much capital investment overseas and too little in modernization and expansion at home'. Macmillan's final Chancellor, Reginald Maudling, heartily agreed, to the extent that just a short time later, he went as far as to argue that Britain should be freed from the inhibitions of a reserve currency status. A furious Parsons wrote to Cromer,

> Ever since the end of the war our efforts in the Bank ... have been in the direction of restoring the status of sterling both as a trading and reserve currency. ... If the Government wishes to move in the direction described ... We can discard immediately any idea of getting rid of security sterling and of re-opening the Foreign Bond Market.[39]

Towards the end of 1962, the functioning of the Eurodollar market in creating a freer flow of international capital was already threatening the US and the Dollar–Gold Standard.[40] As Dillon explained to President Kennedy, demand by Italian banks for Eurodollars had pushed up Eurodollar rates, putting pressure on sterling, as short-term capital moved out of Britain to take advantage of higher returns. This forced the Bank of England to reduce the cost of forward cover on sterling, increasing the covered differential between London and New York from 0.25 per cent to 0.75 per cent, so that funds began to move out of the US to Britain. The pressure this placed on the dollar prompted the US Treasury to request the Bank alter its policy. This time it was 'reasonably co-operative', increasing the cost of forward cover again by 0.125 per cent, so that the covered differential narrowed again to just over 0.50 per cent. As 1963 began, Cromer widened his campaign to re-create a London capital market. He even tried, without success, to persuade the Inland Revenue to reduce stamp duty on future bearer bond issues, whether sterling or Eurobond

issues. As he told Chancellor Maudling, he placed 'the greatest importance on the alleviation of this tax, which is a serious impediment to
additional earning of foreign exchange by the City of London'. He wrote
again on 6 and 30 March, each time taking the opportunity to press
once again for 'the further liberalisation of Exchange Control'. Four days
later, on 3 April , the British Government finally lifted the ban on the
issue of bearer securities denominated in foreign currencies and
removed stamp duty. In effect, giving the green light for the establishment of the Eurobond market. Nevertheless, by the end of the month
Cromer was back fighting the sterling cause, writing to Head of the
Treasury, Sir William Armstrong, that 'exchange control is an infringe-
ment of the rights of the citizen ... I therefore regard [it] ethically as
wrong'. He ended his letter by recalling 'the contempt mixed with pity'
that was felt in Britain when 'exchange control was imposed by Hitler'
in 1930s Germany. And as 1963 came to a close, the Bank was again
debating how to convince the Treasury to relax exchange controls, in
the hope 'that as time went by it would be possible for even more countries to borrow here in sterling terms'. But with the balance of payments
position worsening and an election due, the Macmillan Government
refused. If the Bank and the bankers were despondent they should not
have been. As Kynaston (2002: 275) points out, '1963 had been the most
important year since 1914 in the history of London as an international
financial centre'. The Eurobond market had been born.[41]

The great unmentionable

In October 1964 Labour returned to government promising to 'forge' a
New Britain, replacing Tory Keynesian *laissez-faire* policies with French-
style indicative planning. The modernisation movement, which from
the Boer War had called for Britain to become a modern industrial society, similar to the US and Germany, was finally seizing the day. In terms
of Labour ideology, as historian Ben Pimlott (1992: 349) explains, 'ethi-
cal socialism was giving way to socialism that was "scientific" '. The
Treasury and the Bank of England, however, had other ideas. Sterling
was overvalued and sucking in cheap imports to the extent that Britain's
trade deficit had reached a massive and disturbing £800 million. Not
surprisingly, another sterling crisis was already on the way, the first of
eight that were to dog Labour. A Treasury note awaited the new
Government, warning them off devaluation, in no uncertain terms.
They need not have worried. On Labour's first morning in office, the
new Prime Minister, Harold Wilson, his Chancellor, James Callaghan

and George Brown, Deputy PM and head of a spanking new agency – the Department for Economic Affairs (DEA), the first executive agency in peacetime Britain dedicated to productive capital and Britain's industrial development – met alone in the Cabinet room, to open the books and get down to some serious socialist business for the first time in 13 years. As they eased themselves into the trappings of power, they came to the shocking realisation that everything they had accused the Conservatives of during the election campaign was true, only worse. They quickly reached agreement. They ruled against devaluation. It was their first, and certainly their worst decision.

In truth, it had been taken months, perhaps years, if not a century earlier, as they each came to view devaluation both from their own unique perspective and within the wider imperatives of Britain's historical state structure: Brown, in pragmatic terms, as an attack on a working class having to pay more for imported goods, especially foodstuffs; Callaghan, as both an erosion of Britain's global status and a breach of trust to sterling holders worldwide; Wilson, in essentially 'nationalist' terms, as an assault on Britain's greatness. Hence, while openly contemptuous of the City and its 'monied interests', in 1958 he had told Parliament that the 'strength of sterling' would be Labour's 'first and primary consideration.' Now as Prime Minister, he was certain that devaluation, as he put it 'would have the most dangerous consequences'.[42] Yet this decision committed Labour into supporting sterling in the face of an onslaught of speculative selling. On 23 November bank rate was raised by 2 per cent, in an attempt to dampen the domestic economy while attracting 'hot money' into Britain. But it was not enough. It took a £3 billion support package from other central banks to save the pound. But it had to be pushed on Cromer who preferred that Wilson change his economic policies in line with orthodox Bank thinking on public spending, taxation and monetary policy. A champagne celebration was arranged in 10 Downing Street. But this was only the beginning. The following June, sterling came under attack again, and remained so until September. Cromer called once more for an end to exchange controls and re-iterated his belief 'that the future well being of this country and its position and influence in the world depend on a strong pound'.[43]

From the very beginning devaluation had become the Great Unmentionable; never discussed in Cabinet – banned even. So in March 1966 when yet one more internal report appeared calling for a competitive pound, Wilson ordered it be burnt. Less than three months later, another sterling crisis began, continuing on until September and prompting what the *Economist* described as 'perhaps the biggest deflationary package that any advanced industrial nation has imposed on itself since Keynesian economics began', as Wilson attempted to reduce demand by more than £500 million; raising interest rates and taxes, cutting public spending and freezing wages, prices and dividends. As the *Sunday Times* remarked, Wilson's 'determination to avoid devaluation had become an obsession'.[44] Nevertheless, by the following May he could no nothing but look on, as yet one more currency crisis erupted, culminating finally in the decision to devalue sterling by 14.3 per cent to $2.40, on 18 November 1967. The Bank of England's view of this catastrophe is made clear by Assistant to the Governors, Roy Bridge, who turning down an invitation to Downing Street, wrote that he had 'refused for reasons of conscience an invitation to sup at No. 11 with the devil'. He described this occasion as the "Mad Hatter's Tea Party – 1967 Post Devaluation Version." But perhaps Bridge could look for some solace in the Clarke Report published in the same year which pointed to the future, recommending that 'the Bank of England and the leading banking associations examine exchange control regulations with the specific purpose of removing restrictions which are hindering the banks' role as major parts of an international financial market and whose removal would not undermine the pound'.[45]

While sterling continued to come under pressure and threatened to oust the Wilson Government, nevertheless, as Strange (1971: 141) points out, 'from 1968 onwards, there seemed to be a remarkable lowering of the temperature of debate in British financial circles about [its] fate ... and much less anxiety about its long-term role as a vehicle currency'. It even started to be 'occasionally argued' that Britain's high interest rate policy 'could be easily dropped'. Nevertheless, this did not happen until the beginning of 1969, when Eurodollar rates went over 11 per cent, and the practice of keeping the London short-term rate for sterling above that pertaining for the Eurodollar was quietly discontinued. It seemed that sterling's role as an international currency was at an end. The struggle for sterling was over, or was it?

Sterling and City divorce

At a conference organised by the Institute of Bankers in 1961 some very important questions were asked: 'how did sterling and the City of London survive the 20 years 1938 to 1958? ... how ... do we account for the recovery from the abyss?' The explanation provided is fascinating, both as an articulation of the interests of internationalism and as an illumination of the incestuous nature of the relationship between the

Bank and the City. It is also damning evidence of the role played by the Bank, surreptitiously acting to help the City's merchant banking community avoid restrictions placed on the use of sterling by the British state, while, at the same time, placing total reliance upon their 'honour' to 'obey the spirit as well as the letter of exchange control'. But this should come as no great shock, for as the conference report confirms, even 15 years after nationalisation, the Bank was still regarded as an institution working more on behalf of the market than on behalf of the state. Certainly, the Bank of England is not 'the authorities' mentioned in paragraph two. The Institute of Bankers explains the City's post-war recovery as thus:

> The first explanation is no doubt the force of sheer inertia or the momentum behind a highly integrated system. Structures of this kind do not collapse suddenly. The second reason was the British genius for improvisation and for making the best of a bad job. This was admirably illustrated by the way in which the commodity markets were gradually reopened and were allowed to function as genuinely international and free markets in spite of the persistence of exchange control. This was done by commodity market schemes which were devised under the benevolent eye of the Bank of England. Under these, recognized firms ... were given complete freedom to deal in their particular commodities, buying and selling in any part of the world, undeterred by all the paraphernalia of exchange control. ... This was putting the markets on their honour to obey the spirit as well as the letter of exchange control. It paid many times over.
>
> Another reason for this recovery is that, despite exchange control, sterling remained an international currency almost in spite of ourselves. ... The outside world found that it could not do without a trader's currency. It made sterling, or rather the particular type of sterling which it held, convertible against our own wishes, and against our efforts. We frowned on 'transferable sterling' but it flourished in markets such as Zurich, Amsterdam and New York. ... The authorities here endeavoured on many occasions to check the development of this particular market. But in the end they had to adopt an attitude of dignified tolerance towards it. They even allowed British banks, disguised in the form of overseas agents and subsidiaries, to partake in the business. Here was a tremendous compliment to sterling paid by the outside world. Sterling's first major step in the return to convertibility was taken by foreign traders and bankers – in spite of ourselves.[46]

It was the restoration of sterling as an international currency and the City as the world's foremost financial centre, together and as one, that became the single most defining political economic project of the immediate post-war era in Britain. A project pursued and largely achieved in the face of overwhelming countervailing forces – that is, Britain's very limited currency reserves at the end of the Second World War, the nationalisation of the Bank of England, substantial war debts to Sterling Bloc countries, Keynesian minded governments of both persuasions committed to full employment and the development of the national economy, a dominant US hegemon determined to undermine Imperial Preference and the Sterling Bloc, the existence of a vastly more powerful international currency in the form of the US dollar, operating from a vastly richer international financial market based in New York. Each of these factors alone had the potential of undermining and ultimately destroying the ability of sterling to carry out its role as an international currency. Yet, as this chapter has made clear, the project was pursued unhesitatingly and unstintingly, without, it seems, any prior or subsequent debate by the PM, the Treasury, by Cabinet, Government or Parliament. Central to the success of this project was the role played by the Bank of England, which after 1945 set about re-establishing the hegemony of international financial capital, just as it had done after 1918, and with it the liberal state. Yet, unlike the earlier period, the Bank had first to ensure that the hegemony of traditional monetary policy and the private exercise of monetary authority was re-established at the core of Britain's economic policy-making process.

If as Peter Hall (1986b: 68) explains, policies are made by 'policy-makers ... profoundly influenced by the labyrinth of institutionalized relations that are history's legacy to every society', such relations ensured retention of the Bank of England's institutional independence beyond nationalisation in 1946. This, in turn, ensured the 'rediscovery' of monetary policy in November 1951, thereby freeing the Bank's hands again, after 19 years, allowing the Bank to remain the single most powerful repository for liberal thought in Britain and defeat any attempt by government to take some statutory control of the banking sector and credit creation in the 1950s. It also led directly to the City regaining its privileged access to the economic decision-making process, and the eventual resurrection of an institutional state structure reminiscent of that which defined the pre-1931 (if not the pre-1914), City–Bank–Treasury nexus, because 1951 heralded not merely the end of the use of direct controls but the beginning of a return to monetary policy being controlled, not by the Bank, but, given the regulatory system, by the market, which is why the event is so significant. It allowed the Bank to regain a position powerful enough to begin to re-establish a position of independence, for itself and for the interests of *financial capital* in the City; the 'end result' of which, was to 'leave the locus of power within the UK financial system much as it had been in the early 1930s' (Howson, 1988: 564). This first necessitated the re-opening of City markets, an early return to convertibility, the removal of exchange controls and other restrictions, and the re-establishment of sterling as the world's reserve and vehicle currency and, hence, the City as its most important financial centre. This formed the basis of Bank policy throughout these years, which was extended to include the championing of London as an entrepôt *offshore* market, when it eventually became clear that the fortunes of the City and those of sterling had 'drifted apart'. For while it might not be possible to resurrect sterling's international role, at least once substituted with the Eurodollar, its decline could be separated from that of the City. Finally, as McRae and Cairncross (1973: 17) put it: 'London had a currency in which to operate worldwide ... largely insulating it from sterling's difficulties'.

5
The State, the City and the Euromarkets

The purpose of this chapter is three-fold, first, to examine how in the process of the new global money medium becoming anchored in the old institutional framework, it was adjusted and reconfigured to stand outside the regulated international financial system; how the 'historical mechanisms' inherited from the old London bill market that existed in the *free* international financial structure of the nineteenth century were fused with new techniques and utilised to overcome the 'obstructions' created as a result of the highly restrictive international financial system created at Bretton Woods. Second, it is to unpack the institution defined by the all-embracing term 'Euromarket', in order to disentangle what are in reality two distinct financial instruments, the Eurodollar and the Eurobond. Revealing, in the process, the considerable confusion that has hitherto contributed to a misunderstanding of the role of those agencies responsible for these financial innovations. A fact which is directly responsible for the prevalence of much of the state v. market dichotomic analysis which so dominates discussion of the Euromarkets. Finally, it is to then re-appropriate the new evidence so as to establish the extent to which each of the component parts of the City–Bank–Treasury nexus was involved in what would appear to have been a fundamental redrawing of British sovereignty.

Locating the historic mechanisms in the Eurodollar market

When the 1957 restrictions on sterling deprived the City's merchant banks of the means with which to finance their international business, they simply applied the same syndication techniques which they had traditionally used to mobilise large amounts of capital in their accept-ance credit business, to the hitherto latent market for non-resident dollars. The very techniques that had been evolved in the nineteenth century to finance international trade – the routine business of discounting and collecting deposits (Young, 1966: 54; Forsyth, 1987: 148). It was these 'historic mechanisms' which allowed the merchant banks to aggregate the small amounts of surplus dollars that had been acquired by international banks in the City, New York and Western Europe, in the course of their day-to-day business, into large dollar loans, which they were then able to offer at more competitive rates than those available in New York at that time.[1] Of course, in carrying out Eurodollar business, the individuals and firms belonging to the City's merchant banking community, by co-operating in both the informal ongoing practices of collecting and discounting, and in the setting up of rules for carrying out such activities, imposed a set of cultural and social institutional norms on this new international money market, which had been developed in the nineteenth century as the basis of governance by what was, in effect, *a private regime* (Porter, 1993: 33). In this way they defined and, in turn, were defined by the architecture of the international financial system that evolved after 1957.

The Eurodollar market utilised many of the other practices which characterised the Victorian money market centred around the Bill on London; most notably, as Ingham (1982: 217) points out, how the activity of Eurobankers acting as wholesale bankers and middlemen, did, itself, determine the 'tenuous and discontinuous' nature of the relationship between the borrowers and lenders, and how the Eurodollar had a duel function, acting as both, finance for the borrowers and lenders, and as a negotiable instrument for the bankers. While Ingham sees the relationships between the City institutions as *financial*, he sees the Eurodollar market as being characterised by *practices* which are 'fundamentally *commerical*' as opposed to financial, in that discounting and short-term lending 'pre-empt any financial control of the borrowers by the intermediaries'. In addition, as Young (1966: 55) makes clear, the banks and firms in Western Europe and New York which possessed the ex-patriate dollars, 'had been the clients of the accepting houses in the days when the London bill was king'. They continued to rely on the expertise and the reputation of the City's merchant banks regardless of the currency that was being traded. The enduring nature of these relationships and techniques, in turn, allowed a set of social institutions, linked up through the co-operation of those firms involved in the syndicate to perpetuate a 'private regime' of the ninetieth century into the 1960s and beyond (Porter, 1993: 33). Thus, in anchoring the Eurodollar within this framework, a parallel international money market evolved that operated outside the state system of 'national' banking regulation, recreating the, essentially, private global credit network that had developed in the heyday of *the Pax Britannica* (Germain, 1997: 49).

Clearly, the nascent Eurodollar market inherited a large part of its institutional structure and techniques from the City's Victorian system for financing international trade. Techniques and practices which had been developed a century earlier, to accommodate the rise of the City as the world's entrepôt market for capital, proved to be extremely adaptable to the international monetary and trading conditions emerging at the end of the 1950s and calling for a new *entrepôt* centre. However, these were not only the 'historical mechanisms' which the City's banks adapted to the operation of the Eurodollar market. There was also those techniques developed during the highly restrictive post-war period, to facilitate their burgeoning international business as the world recovery got underway. These were the techniques of currency and interest rate swaps and back-to-back loans which were used to get round exchange control, leading to the development of swap-like financial instruments in the late 1970s and a full international swap market in the early 1980s. Financial innovations, or as Forsyth (1987: 148–9) puts it euphemistically, 'remarkable' tools, by which 'institutional imperfections in the international capital markets could be exploited'.[2]

Holmes and Klopstock (1960a: 9) point out also, that, whereas in European financial centres there is a close connection between the foreign exchange market and the money market, reflected in, for example, the fact that in most banks the chief foreign exchange dealer is also responsible for overseeing their money position, this 'linkage ... is virtually unheard of in the United states'. Add to this the fact that because banks domiciled in England operate, largely, under a code of 'self-regulation', English law is regarded as more suitable than continental law on which to base a legal framework for carrying out international financial transactions (Plender and Wallace, 1985: 27). The City's merchant and overseas banks also had a particular advantage that even UK clearing banks did not possess – they were not subject to liquidity requirements and, therefore, were perfectly suited to maximising income from the business of organising credit (BIS, 1964: 139). Finally, in addition to the accident of geography, of London lying between the other major financial centres New York and Tokyo and the fact that English is the lingua franca of modern finance, London retained the services of people technically skilled to operate in the foreign exchange market.[3]

Sir George Bolton: The Bank of England's 'market man'

Of the many writers who single out Sir George Bolton as being a very significant figure in the development of the Eurodollar market and the post-war revival of the City of London financial sector, only Richard Fry (1970: 13–16) attempts to provide an explanation for this. He says, that before London's merchant banks could, 'discover' the Eurodollar, they had first 'to throw aside the paralysing effects of three decades of control and restriction'. He identifies the Conservative Government's return to an active monetary policy in November 1951 as one of the earliest acts which brought about necessary change, followed by a steady loosening of exchange controls, and the opening of old City markets for international business. He claims that 'each new turn led to intensive technical discussions between the bankers and merchants concerned and officials at the Bank and the Treasury'. But he does add, 'it may be going too far to suggest that this amounted to a deliberate, farsighted policy, conceived mainly in the Bank of England and supported by a few of the most senior officials at the Treasury and Board of Trade'. Unfortunately, Fry provides no details of these 'discussions', nor any information about the operation of the policy-making process which could be considered to have nurtured the Eurodollar market. He does, nevertheless, describe how financial innovation was possible within the British banking system, where supervision was 'permissive rather than mandatory'. In such a regulatory situation, he claims, policies are 'made effective by people'. Thus, 'it was up to the bankers and traders to make the best of it', which they did, by 'merely' pursuing the opportunity the City had been given 'to develop profitable business'. As he explains, the City employed

> enterprising men with bold ideas and technical ingenuity ... who refused to accept ... that England no longer had the resources to run an important centre of world finance. One of these was Sir George Bolton ... one of the leading spirits in the creation of the new international money markets which gave London its chance.[4]

For 26 years Bolton was the Bank of England's 'market man', and probably Britain's foremost expert on foreign exchange. He has been variously described as a 'champion of global free-enterprise', a 'merchant adventurer' and as the 'most influential and well-known of all British bankers'. Bolton began his career as a foreign exchange dealer in the City in 1920, with merchant bankers Helbert, Wagg & Co. and after the collapse of the gold standard in 1931 was recruited by Montagu Norman himself to help run the Bank's Foreign Exchange Section that Norman had created to 'manage' sterling. He was made Principal of the Section in 1936, and Advisor to the Governors on exchange and monetary policy in 1941, where he became increasingly influential in matters of sterling and foreign exchange. He is also credited with having persuaded Keynes of the benefits of continuing the Sterling Area into the post-war period (Cottrell, 1995: 111). He represented Britain at the Bretton Woods talks in 1944, and also helped devise the European Payments Union.

Bolton was made an 'Executive Director' of the Bank in 1948, and a Director of the Bank of International Settlements (BIS). He had hoped to become Governor, but that job went to Cameron Cobbold, in 1949. However it was with Cobbold as Governor and Bolton his most 'influential advisor', that his position in the Bank's policy-making process reached its pinnacle. For Cobbold's main concern was to recover 'an independent role for the Bank' (Howson, 1991: 85). He was thus preoccupied with the task of resurrecting monetary policy, a necessary prerequisite in any battle to restoring the Bank's pre-war position in Britain's financial system. Given, in addition, that Cobbold's experience had been in domestic money, the Governor felt inclined to leave foreign exchange matters and relations with other central banks to Bolton. As Fforde (1992: 196), writes, 'by the autumn of 1949 [Bolton] had acquired a personal ascendancy in the Bank on most questions of external financial policy'. While he had been responsible for developing the apparatus of foreign exchange control after 1931, and especially in preparation for the Second World War, he remained a 'dealer at heart', who was instinctively opposed to any bureaucratic interference with the functioning of the market. He therefore used his position at the Bank to promote the liberalisation of financial markets, return sterling to convertibility and remove exchange controls as soon as was possible after 1945. But after the failure of the ROBOT plan for a floating pound in 1952, of which he was one of the chief architects, his influence at the Bank waned. While he spent the next five years supervising the re-opening of City markets and the dismantling of controls which would take Britain nearer to a return to convertibility, he ultimately became frustrated with the slow pace of change and the policy of maintaining restrictions on the use of sterling. Finally, Bolton retired from the Bank in 1957 because, as he explained, 'he thought Government policy was going to lead to the extinction of sterling'.[5]

It was becoming routine for retiring Deputy Governors to be offered the chairmanship of a major bank in the City, and for top Bank officials, directorships. Hence, in 1962 Standard Bank – another overseas bank that helped to get the Eurodollar market started – appointed Executive Director Cyril Hawker as their chairman, with Cyril Hamilton (Deputy Chief Cashier), becoming his deputy. Sir John Stevens, also an Executive Director, became Managing Director of Morgan Grenfell in 1967 and Chairman in 1972. Sir Kenneth Peppiatt, Chief Cashier and then Executive Director, became a Director of Coutts. And much later, in 1973 when Governor O'Brien retired he became an official advisor to Morgan Guaranty and Morgan Grenfell, and President of the British Bankers Association. Bolton, himself, became chairman of the Bank of London & South America [BOLSA]. And when in 1970 Bolton finally retired, he was succeeded by Sir Maurice Parsons formerly, Deputy Governor and Montagu Norman's private secretary.[6] In Bolton's case, he had been recruited by Sir Francis Glyn, his predecessor as Chairman of BOLSA . Glyn had come to the Bank as early as 1948, to ask Cobbold's advice on which retiring Bank official might be suitable to appoint as a new full-time Director. Bank of England papers show that Glyn returned to the Bank in 1949, 1952 and 1955, until, according to a note written by Cobbold in January 1957, 'further consideration culminated in the appointment of Sir George Bolton as Deputy Chairman'. The gamekeeper had turned poacher. Glyn had chosen wisely. Bolton was not only Britain's foremost expert on foreign exchange who was to remain on the Bank Court, he was also very well connected, in both the worlds of international finance and monetary regulation, with the President of the Federal Reserve Bank of New York, Alfred Hayes amongst his close friends. Most importantly for BOLSA, Bolton had, as Jones (1993: 264) describes, a 'strategic view' that few, if any, of his contemporaries in international banking possessed. He arrived at his new job equipped with the prescient belief that BOLSA's future prosperity was not dependent on sterling. In fact, as he told the *Banker*, it was his conviction that sterling's international use 'would virtually cease', that had prompted BOLSA to make 'a deliberate withdrawal from sterling activities' and buy dollar deposits 'at the going rate', as an alternative medium for financing international trade.[7]

Yet having said this, two years after joining BOLSA Bolton was still calling for a restoration of 'the international use of sterling', which he fully expected to see in the near future. However, these contradictory statements should be considered in the light of the fact that, regardless of the profitable Eurodollar business being carried out in London, it was not until the 1967 devaluation that the City finally began to think the unthinkable: that sterling's international role might be coming to an end. This suggests that while, as early as 1957, Bolton – in the interests of BOLSA's profitability – was able to detach sterling's decline from the wider context of the fortunes of London as a financial centre, he still, perhaps, held on, as did the City in general, to a desire to see it restored to its former glory. Nevertheless, Bolton arrived at BOLSA in 1957 and immediately began to utilise the dollar deposits he found at his disposal. In fact he had been made Deputy Chairman of BOLSA in 1956, while still at the Bank of England, and had himself written the memorandum placed before the BOLSA Board of Directors on 28 May 1957, recommending his appointment. It reads like a Declaration of Intent; a manifesto for a new global currency for the City:

> London ... has barely succeeded in maintaining its international banking system following the loss of political influence by the UK, the weakened position of sterling and the incapacity of the London Market to increase its foreign investment net. ... Whatever may be the future of banks engaged exclusively in domestic banking, those whose main business is to maintain and develop a position in the foreign field will have to adapt their structure to meet the needs of the time.

Three months later, on 27 August 1957, Bolton became Chairman of BOLSA. In September, BOLSA's London Branch recorded having $3.69 million in dollar deposits. By the end of 1957 this was $10.57 million, rising to $106.21 million in 1958, $281.91 million by 1960 and $417.91 million by 1964. In 1960/1, BOLSA re-organised and re-named their European Department the 'International Department', the functions of which were 'to control and expand the international business of the bank', and employed a team of young dealers who were sent out to major European and US cities to canvass for dollar deposits. They also bought the merchant bank Balfour Williamson to give them a seat on the influential Accepting Houses Committee, which met regularly with the Governor of the Bank of England; and they merged with the Bank of Montreal and took a share in the Mellon Bank of Pittsburgh to tighten their connection with the US and the dollar. Both as a means of attracting dollar deposits and to increase their capital base. By 1962, half of BOLSA's total deposits were kept in London, out of which only one quarter was denominated in sterling, the rest were in Eurodollars and other Eurocurrencies.[8]

Disassociating the Eurodollar and Eurobond markets

A history of BOLSA confirms that with the election of Bolton as chairman it became one of the 'first to grasp the potentialities' of the

Euro-dollar market'. It adds,

> a new approach was necessary ... fundamentally a recognition that
> the international use of sterling would become progressively more
> restricted, and it was in non-sterling finance, and particularly in dollar
> finance, that the scope for the bank's international operations lay.

However, again, no details of what Bolton actually did were forthcoming.
Even Bolton himself says of the innovation of the Eurodollar market,
that it was 'a conscious effort by a number of us to create a money market
from the bits and pieces that were floating about. But it wasn't the act of
a cabal: it was more a sort of osmosis'. He does not identify the 'us', the
'bits and pieces', or what the 'conscious efforts' amounted to. However,
in a letter he sent to Lord Cromer, at the Bank of England, on 23 January
1963, he does single out Ernest George Selby, BOLSA's Exchange Dealer as
having been particularly instrumental in creating the market, writing,

> from very small beginnings [Selby] ... has been the leading personality
> in the development of the International Money Market – erroneously
> described as the Euro-dollar market. ... He has developed a worldwide
> personal reputation and is trusted implicitly by every leading bank in
> practically every country in the world, including Russia and the satel-
> lites. Largely as a result of his efforts and personal integrity
> London ... can now tap the surplus resources of every financial centre
> in the world.

Selby had come to BOLSA in 1956 from the Midland Bank, where he had
worked in the Overseas Branch for more than 30 years. It seems highly
likely, therefore, that he brought with him knowledge of the 'swap
techniques' developed at the Midland during 1955, which Schenk
(1998: 225) sees as 'the first stage of the financial innovation which
produced the Eurodollar market'. Yet, notwithstanding Fry's claim that
'technical discussions' took place at the Bank of England between
bankers, merchants and officials from the Bank and the Treasury, there
is no evidence to suggest that either he or Bolton were involved in the
dismantling, or relaxing, of controls and restrictions in relation to the
establishment of a Eurocurrency market in 1957. This can be explained
by the fact that there were none. Thus, when Einzig (1964a: 9) suggested
that the 'British authorities' could have prevented the development of
the Eurodollar market in London, as they had prevented the development of the Eurosterling market in London, by recourse to the powers of

exchange control, he could not have been referring to the application of any clause written in the legislation governing this matter.[9]

The Eurodollar market existed *offshore*. That is, outside of the regulatory reach of UK, or any other national banking law. Yet, importantly, it was not that any unregulated legal entity had been created in which this new market could operate, but rather that a regulated legal entity had been created in which the traditional sterling money market could not. It was the legal restraints imposed by the Defence (Finance) Regulation of 1939 that circumscribed a separate *onshore* market, restricting the movement of sterling within Britain and what became the Sterling Bloc. What remained continued on, as unregulated as before. By default, a realm had been created which existed outside of UK banking regulation, yet remained within British legal and territorial sovereignty; a realm that was legally not *onshore* but spatially not *offshore*, what Johns (1983: 15) refers to as an *onshore external market*, with the UK's money market in sterling thereby being defined as an *onshore internal market*. The Exchange Control Act of 1947 only reconfirmed the existing position, concerned, as it was, with the potential danger of a large movement of sterling capital out of the Sterling Area. It provided no power to control currency dealings which took place outside the *onshore internal area* of the UK and the Scheduled Territories. Oddly, Einzig said as much himself, in an article he wrote for the *Banker* in 1960 in which he explained that non-resident deposits 'do not come within the limits imposed by the Bank of England on the banks' holdings of foreign currencies', which they can increase 'to an unlimited extent without having to ask for permission'. While there were ways the Bank of England might have been able to influence the development of Eurocurrency operations, had it so wished – through their power to decide which banks could deal in foreign exchange and were Authorised Banks, or through the application of balance sheet ratios to Eurocurrency business – these did not include the direct application of exchange control.[10]

Nevertheless, belief that the British Government, through the application of exchange controls, could regulate the Eurodollar market, was widely held. For example, in 1965, the ongoing sterling crisis that had begun in October 1964, and was causing such great problems for the new Labour Government, prompted rumours that it might be forced to apply exchange controls to freeze Eurodollar deposits, held by, not only British banks, but also the London branches of US banks. Such was the strength of these rumours in the US that Charles Coombs, the Vice-President of the Federal Reserve Bank of New York, wrote to the Bank of England to warn them.[11] However, while there were no controls and restrictions in relation to the taking and placing of non-resident dollar deposits and credits in London, there were controls and restrictions on the issuing of foreign dollar bonds in London, at least until 1963. This explains the apparent contradiction of the following two statements made by Lord Cromer:

> the establishment of London as an international financial centre, wherein half of the deposits in the banking sector are for account of non-residents of the UK, has been largely due to freedom from detailed banking legislation (cited in Pringle, 1973: p. iv).

And:

> the wider development of the London capital market is limited by policies that discourage or prohibit the attraction of additional foreign business. ... The barriers that remain here now impede the growth of important contributions to a stronger international economic standing for the country. ... The time has now come when the City once again might well provide an international capital market where the foreigner can not only borrow long-term capital but where, equally important, he will once again wish to place his long-term investment capital. This *entrepôt* business in capital ... would fill a vital and vacant role in Europe in mobilising foreign capital for world economic development.[12]

The former statement refers to the development of the Eurodollar market which began in 1957, and the latter, taken from Cromer's 1962 Mansion House speech, heralds the beginning of the Eurobond market in London in 1963. However, while there is an interplay between the Eurodollar (and all Eurocurrency) and Eurobond markets, as a consequence of the relationship between Eurodollar deposit rates and Eurobond yields, and although the latter did grow out of the need to put to profitable use the large funds being made available in the former, they are distinct markets, that evolved at different times, trading different financial products. The Eurodollar market was created within what remained of the *free* financial market that had evolved in the nineteenth century. While this had been constrained by regulation after the 1931 crisis, it was only in relation to sterling and what became the Sterling Area. When dealing in non-resident deposits and credits of non-resident currencies, business remained as unrestricted as ever it had been. This is alluded to in a Bank of England paper, written by the Deputy Governor,

Sir George Blunden, entitled, 'The Supervision of the UK Banking System':

> There are of course a number of Acts affecting banks. ... But [they] refer to specific activities ... there is no definitive legislative recognition of organisations as banks or legislative sanction for such banking supervision as we undertake ... it has [thus never been possible for the Bank to impose supervision on organisations arbitrarily to meet our own wishes. [Blunden, 1975: 188–90][13]

While not that much had changed in regard to the Bank of England's hands-off view of supervision since the 1882 Bills of Exchange Act, which defined bankers simply as people 'who carry on the business of banking', in the early 1960s a debate on the Eurocurrency markets did take place within the Bank that throws much light on its dealings in, and views on the Euromarkets (cited in Davies, 1994: 423) Thus, a memo written to explain the potential dangers of the burgeoning Eurodollar market of that time, confirms that

> Section 1 of the Exchange Control Act [1947] ... does not prohibit Authorised Dealers. [i.e. Authorised Banks] from dealing in foreign currency deposits between non-residents. The absence of restriction in our Notices recognises this. If foreign currency deposits are switched into sterling, we have the possibility of applying Exchange Control ... but this would be undesirable and extremely difficult. The absence of restriction in our Notices recognises this.

In fact, the only written warning ever given to banks was given in the Memorandum to Authorised Dealers in Foreign Exchange, issued in September 1939, which states, 'it has for a long time been [our] practice to allow the opening by London Banks of foreign currency credits on instructions from, and in favour of, non-residents on condition that no exchange is required from the UK control'. Having said this, where Eurodollars were switched into sterling and technically came under exchange control, the Bank of England considered that applying these restrictions would be 'undesirable and extremely difficult', given that exchange control had not been designed to prevent capital from entering Britain and the Sterling Bloc, but rather to stop it leaving.[14]

The Eurodollar market evolved then, within what remained of the *free* foreign currency market that operated in the City before 1939. It is a wholesale money market which only deals in large amounts of 'footloose' deposits of a temporary, and often questionable nature. While the depositors hold short-term claims on the Eurobanks, the banks in turn, are able to transform these funds into longer-term loans to their customers. In addition, most transactions are unsecured, relying solely on the reputation of the borrower. Finally, because this market was unregulated, Eurobanks were not required to insure deposits or maintain a minimum reserve requirement, and because it does not come under the jurisdiction of any one national banking authority there is no clear lender of last resort to which participants can rely on in times of crisis (Clendenning, 1969: 117).[15] Taken together, this makes for a highly volatile global banking system, easily prone to crises of confidence, and hence permanently at risk of collapse. The Eurobond market, on the other hand, is a market in foreign currency bonds and as such is a market for longer-term capital. It involves no inter-mediation between the lender and the borrower, as investors hold the security [in the form of bearer bonds] issued by the final borrower directly, which can be traded on the secondary bond market. The banks only act to underwrite the placement of the bond.[16]

While, as Chapter 2 made clear, it is generally accepted that the Eurobond market proper was established in July 1963, prior to this, governments, companies and institutions wishing to raise long-term capital by issuing bonds, did so in the US. Yet the US was a very inefficient market for the issuing of foreign bonds. Even as late as the 1960s, US banks operating overseas were essentially catering to the needs of US domestic customers. This explains why, throughout the 1950s and early 1960s, it was not that the majority of US banks missed an opportunity in the Euromarkets, rather that they never realised they had one in the first place. In addition to this, the US capital market had neither knowledge of the European borrowers, nor an inclination to market these bonds to US investors. So non-US buyers had to be found in Europe, where up to 90 per cent of the issues were placed. In fact, this was not difficult, for, as Davis (1992: 111) points out, depositors in the Eurocurrency market were already looking for investment opportunities and buying dollar bonds in the New York, or Yankee, foreign bond market. Therefore, the US investment banks earned commissions and fees from issues that were being sold by Europeans to Europeans. But only a US investment bank was authorised to form and lead a syndicate of local underwriters, which took a minimum commission of 1 per cent; the Europeans receiving, at best, a re-allowance of 0.5 per cent; a situation which prompted Julius Strauss of Strauss, Turnbull and Co., one of the pioneers of the Eurobond market to remark: 'The American house got all the cream but did none of the work' (Kerr, 1984: 16).

In addition, to be allowed to make issues in the US market, European banks had first to be registered with the Securities and Exchange Commission (SEC), which could only be done after meeting the listing, rating and disclosure requirements associated with making an issue in New York; a lengthy and costly process, and one which demanded that information which a borrower might rather keep confidential, was made public. Given all these costs, it is not surprising that, as Peter Spira, formerly of S.G. Warburg and one of the architects of the first Eurobond issue recalls, 'Sir Sigmund took the view that, since most foreign US dollar bonds were sold in Europe, why not create London as the center of the capital markets' (cited in Powell, 1988: 119), though once again, not before Paris had vied unsuccessfully with London for this role.[17]

While Siegmund Warburg is regarded as having been the driving force behind the Eurobond, it is generally accepted that the catalyst for such an innovatory idea was a speech given by US Treasury Secretary Douglas Dillon, in Rome, on 18 May 1962, calling for Europe to develop its own capital markets, rather than have recourse to a US constrained by a growing payments deficit. As he informed President Kennedy, 'the answer ... is not, of course, new controls here but rather fewer controls abroad'. For it was precisely these controls, placed on capital issues in Europe during the crisis of the 1930s that had turned the US capital market into the only effective international capital market in the world. Dillon 'hoped that the Europeans would find a way other than bond issues in New York to meet their needs', although, in calling for the creation of a European capital market to what extent did Dillon envisage a long-term capital market financed with Eurodollars? Certainly, as a department minute makes clear, the US Treasury had by then finally realised that 'the Euro-dollar market at least keeps the dollars in use and prevents them from flowing into the holdings of central banks, from whence they would doubtless be presented for conversion into gold'.[18]

Whatever Dillon envisaged, it was his Rome speech, especially his call that '[n]ew institutional structures must be developed', that perhaps spurred Warburg to travel to Washington in the autumn of 1962. Here, he became aware from his friends at the World Bank that of the $3 billion circulating outside the US at that time, $1 billion was languishing in the short-term inter-bank market, and therefore a potential source of investment capital. It is also claimed that Warburg enlisted the help of his friend, Assistant Secretary of State, George Ball, into persuading Kennedy not to stand in the way of the creation of additional financial markets in dollars outside of the US, as a means of providing Europe with an alternative capital market.[19] Although, according to Dillon, while 'Warburg's initiative was helpful in this regard', that is, in creating the Eurobond market, there was no meeting between Warburg, Ball and Kennedy. He states,

> I was never aware of a Warburg visit to the US, or the intervention on his behalf. The Treasury was not opposed to the issues of Eurobonds, and I never heard of President Kennedy's interest in this matter. ... Since this was a Treasury responsibility, Kennedy would have referred Warburg to us. He did not do so through me and, if Warburg had seen Roosa [Under Secretary for International Monetary Affairs], that would ordinarily have been reported to me. Warburg may have made such a trip, but it was unnecessary, and I never heard of it until I received your letter.[20]

Warburg was not the only prominent City banker in America that autumn. George Bolton was in New York, where his Wall Street contacts told him that because of the growing US balance of payments deficit and dollar problem, American banks were being asked not to make loans to foreigners. He concluded from this that should the banks not comply fully with this request, there was a strong possibility that new legislation would be introduced forcing them to. On returning home Bolton sent off a memo calling for 'the restoration and revival of the London Market machinery to enable issues of foreign loans ... as a matter of immediate importance to the Western World', because, as he added, given 'the isolation and inefficiency of the European capital markets ... the only centre that can help New York is London'. Bolton got it perfectly right. On both counts. On 1 July 1963, the Eurobond market was born. Or, as the the *Banker* put it, 'a novel form of longer-term borrowing in the Euro-dollar market – the precursor, perhaps of many others if President Kennedy's proposed "interest equalization tax" takes effect – was formally launched'. The Autostrade issue. On 18 July, Kennedy unveiled that very tax – the Interest Equalization Tax (IET). Designed to improve the US balance of payments, this acted to discourage American citizens from buying foreign securities on the US capital market. It was just what the nascent Eurobond market needed and less than two weeks later, Warburg was touring the main European central banks and exhorting them to follow the example of the Bank of England and relax restrictions on issuing long-term capital designated in dollars. He told each governor very presciently,

> We can't let the whole international capital market die just because New York closes. Companies must be able to borrow without you

having to create money. Anyway these dollars will arise anyway because reduction in the American payments deficit would make that source dry up: but that will not happen because instead of preventing the outflow from the US, the tax will on the contrary worsen it. The best thing is therefore for you to allow the issue of long-term loans in dollars. Besides, I have just done it a month ago in London with the help of some of your banks. Let them join us in transactions of this kind.

But how had Warburg 'done it … in London?' Perhaps the most authoritive account of the obstacles that had to be surmounted, comes from Warburg's Ian Fraser who describes arranging for the coupons attached to the bearer bonds to be cashed in Luxembourg, to avoid the Inland Revenue's demand for 42.5 per cent income tax on those cashed in Britain, making the issue in Schiphol Airport, Holland, to avoid the 4 per cent stamp duty on bearer bonds issued in Britain, persuading the London Stock Exchange to list the bond, without which the banks in the syndicate would have been unwilling to underwrite the issue – something only achieved after 'a lot of hard work' on the part of Fraser and his Warburg colleagues – finally, overcoming the difficulties set by 'the central banks of France, Holland, Sweden, Denmark and of course Britain, about the exchange control consequences of allowing the bonds to be underwritten, purchased, sold, the coupons cashed and ultimately the bonds redeemed all in a foreign currency – US dollars'. As Fraser writes, 'I had to run round the whole of Western Europe to get everybody in line …'.[21]

From Fraser's account, it would appear that the Bank was less than cooperative. This coincides, as Kynaston (2002: 280) points out, with other claims 'that "one particular hostile authority" was Cromer himself'. Yet, this does not entirely fit with the thesis that the Bank encouraged the Euromarkets. Nor with a Governor who had long championed a return to *laissez-faire* and whose 1962 Mansion House speech called for the City to 'provide an international capital market' once again. Kynaston suggests that this contradiction can perhaps be explained as Cromer having 'one eye on the American reaction', where hostility to a foreign dollar market was growing. There is also the fact that he wanted nothing to get in the way of restoring the City's sterling bond market, not even the Eurodollar. Another explanation, referred to in Chapter 2, revolves around the figure of George Bolton once again, for, many very distinguished commentators argue that it was only when Bolton intervened on Warburg's behalf that Cromer was persuaded of the advantages to the City, of creating this foreign bond market. This includes Atalli (1986: 225), who describes Bolton as overcoming 'the final obstacle' of a 'reluctant and even hostile' Bank of England, 'especially in the person of the governor', who 'demanded exorbitant stamp duties which made the deal impossible', which Bolton 'managed to have ... reduced'. Nevertheless, once again, supporting evidence for these claims is thin on the ground. Instead they appear to be contributing to the creation of an 'oral' history of events which has been handed down from one person to another. Even Cromer himself, while confirming that in the '[e]arly 1960s British merchant banks played a crucial role in the creation of ... the Euro-markets', makes no mention of Bolton, nor explains the nature of this 'crucial role' (Baring, 1976: pp. iii–iv).

In trying to establish whether Bolton's involvement in the birth of the Eurobond market could be verified one way or another, I consequently spoke to Henry Grunfeld, co-founder of Warburgs Bank, who would only say that 'Bolton had been very helpful'. Peter Spira, who had worked with Fraser on the Autostrade issue, also confirmed that Bolton had 'encouraged' Siegmund Warburg in this idea, and 'paved the way with the Governor'. But still the evidence was slim. What was already known, is that Cromer gave an official indication that he hoped the City could re-create its role as an international capital market, in a speech he gave to the Manchester & District Bankers' Institute in March 1962. But at that point, he appeared to see this as a capital market for sterling, or as he put it, 'our' capital (Scott-Quinn, 1975: 31). Yet by the time of his Mansion House speech, six months later, while he once again called for the opening up of the City as an international capital market, he saw this as a consequence of 'mobilising foreign capital'. What had happened in the intervening few months to change Cromer's mindset?[22]

Cromer had been Governor for only a short time when these events took place. And while the Bank had been trying to persuade the Treasury and Government to ease exchange control restrictions and re-establish a sterling bond market since the early 1950s, this campaign had been given new vigour with his appointment. However, within a few weeks of his arrival at the Bank, exchange control was tightened, with new restrictions preventing capital investment in the non-Sterling Area. This prompted Bolton to complain to Cromer that because BOLSA could not now use its sterling capital in South America, it was in danger of being taken over. In October 1961 the Bank began pushing again for a sterling bond market. Then early in 1962, as I explained in the last chapter, Cromer urged the removal of stamp duty, to encourage the opening of a bond market in London. He wrote again to the Chancellor on 30 January

1962, to point out that ending the restrictions would allow it to take up its natural role as the financial centre of Europe. More importantly, he suggested that removal would allow a market for foreign capital to be created in the City that would help ease sterling's vulnerable position, implying for the very first time that the City's future did not necessary rely on Britain running a successful international currency. That, in fact, it was possible to separate the fortunes of sterling and the City bankers. Cromer argued that

> If the time-honoured role of the London capital market in attracting funds from abroad for on-lending elsewhere were re-established, it would considerably ease our position, as compared with the artificial post-war situation in which we have assumed the responsibility of the principal provider of market capital for the sterling area out of our own resource.

A foreign capital market in the City was certainly something Cromer believed would appeal to the Treasury, given its sensitivity to outflows of sterling. Yet within six months Cromer was again attempting to persuade the Chancellor to ease exchange control by explaining it as 'the final step in the reconstruction of sterling as an international currency'. Then the following month Cromer informed Bolton that a market for foreign capital might threaten the future creation of a market for sterling. Bolton had met Cromer at the end of May/ beginning of June of 1962, to discuss a 'certain exchange of ideas' that had been taking place between a 'small group' of representatives from Warburgs, Barings, Samual Montegu and BOLSA, about 'the opening of the London market to a wide variety of borrowers for loans denominated in foreign currencies'. Bolton followed up this meeting by sending a note to Cromer on 6 June 1962, setting out the 'arguments in favour of the proposal' and stressing in his accompanying letter that they 'would not wish to proceed more actively without the general blessing of the authorities'. He also informed Cromer that the 'technical procedures and legal modalities mentioned in the note [had] not been fully worked out' and that they could 'obviously be modified to meet official requirements'.[23]

Cromer replied on 14 June 1962, expressing his desire to discuss Bolton's suggestions further. Bolton wrote again on 11 July, informing Cromer that there had been 'one or two developments', specifically: (1) that 'Charles Hambro had been brought into the group and [had] expressed a wish that Hambros Bank should be associated with this kind of transaction, if ... permitted'; something which, Bolton stressed had been 'greatly welcomed'; (2) that a 'number of tentative proposals [were] building up, including the taking over, from Kuhn Loeb, of a deal to underwrite a $25 million Kingdom of Norway 15-year loan; which Hambros and Warburgs had been especially interested in'. However, no private issues had been made by companies outside the Sterling Area and dealt on the London Stock Exchange since 1934. Bolton was obviously aware of this, as he also pointed out that while he believed the tax and stamp duty problems could be overcome by printing and issuing the bonds in Luxembourg, he anticipated that 'lengthy negotiations would be necessary with the Stock Exchange and/or the Exchange Control in order to obtain a London quotation'; something which he regarded 'as a reflection upon London's ability to revive her former role', although, he added, 'perhaps something is better than nothing'. Cromer replied on 23 July, writing that the Bank was 'sympathetic to this proposal and will give it what practical support [they] can'. He also informed him, that while the 'problems associated with stamp and bearer duty' meant that 'immediate progress cannot be expected', he did not believe that 'any undue difficulty should arise with regard to exchange control as it does not seem that you contemplate the lending of UK funds to non-residents'. Finally, Cromer underlined to Bolton that the Bank did not want to do anything 'inimical to the future opening of the London market in sterling', although he added that he did not believe that Bolton's proposals raise[d] such issues' as far as he could see. Within three months Cromer made his famous speech calling for London to be set up as a centre for 'entrepôt business in capital'.[24]

Bolton, of course, sympathised with Cromer's desire to see a sterling bond market re-opened in London, something which he himself had been calling for since the early 1950s when he worked at the Bank. He continued to argue for this after he moved to BOLSA, especially in 1959, when it became clear to him, even at that early stage, that New York was no longer capable of playing the role of provider of long-term capital. He explained presciently, in a speech he gave to the Dollar Exports Council, that 'the monetary position in North America is such that it is doubtful whether any further progress can be made or, in fact, whether it would be prudent for the US to take on further substantial liabilities'.[25] By 1962, however, Bolton knew that the incapacity of New York to provide sufficient capital for non-residents was equally matched by the impossibility of restoring the sterling bond market in London, given sterling's inherent weakness. This realisation had led Bolton to the gradual exploration of the concept of internationalising the provision of long-term capital, in the first place. Bolton saw the establishment of a foreign bond market in London as the only way of providing, or to be more precise, recycling private international liquidity in the form of dollar credits, without which, he believed, the capitalist world would begin to stagnate.

How then can Bolton's role in developing the concept of using foreign-owned dollars to finance a bond market centred in London be evaluated? For this was not a new idea, and given the evidence of Cromer's note to the Chancellor of January 1962, one with which the Bank was familiar. Even the 1959 Radcliffe Report into the British monetary system remarked that it did not so much matter whether international trade was financed in sterling so long as much of it continued to be financed through London.[26] What is more likely, given that Cromer's views changed between March and October of 1962, is that his meeting and consequent correspondence with Bolton had made him fully aware the City was calling for the establishment in London of a new international capital market, based on issuing foreign bonds financed in Eurodollars rather than sterling. That it would bring great benefits to the City without endangering Britain's external position, meant it did not have to wait for sterling's position to strengthen, and as he wrote to Bolton, this would not necessarily harm the chances of re-establishing a sterling bond market in the future, however slim, in reality, those chances were, because, while the advent of the Eurodollar market proper in 1957 and the Eurobond market in 1963, may have allowed the City to develop its international business despite the weakness of sterling, the Bank, as Brittan (1964: 285) puts it, 'always itches to go beyond these strictly entrepôt activities'. Hence, in November 1963, Cromer told Kleinworts that he 'hoped that as time went by it would be possible for even more countries to borrow here in sterling terms'.

The latter part of 1962 and the early part of 1963 saw Cromer and the Bank working hard to persuade the various authorities to make the legal changes, necessary, if London was to once again boast an international bond market. He talked to the Inland Revenue. He wrote to the Chancellor. By the end of January, as Bank economist Dudley Allen put it, 'approval of the authorities' for a Eurobond issue was secured. Now the Bank started to smoothen the way for the new institution, while, of course, keeping the future of sterling also firmly in mind. Letters went out to other central banks assuring them that the Bank did not anticipate 'a loan of this kind to affect the sterling balance of payments position in any way'. Cromer made speeches on 'The Potentialities of an International Capital market in London'. Even his social life was given up to the cause, through a series of working dinners for City bankers and Whitehall officials, ostensibly to improve the links between the City and government. Cromer's original list of suggestions for discussion topics were 'London Capital Markets' and UK Exchange Control. His diary entry reveals just how little the Bank's cultural frame of reference had changed since the City's nineteenth century apogee, in that he describes the first dinner of 1 May 1963, as having been arranged 'to discuss topic No. 1 – potentialities of developing merchant-adventuring business'. It would seem then that the development of the City's Euromarket was certainly regarded within this tradition. Siegmund Warburg was invited but could not attend. Sir George Bolton did, how ever, and was told by Cromer to 'treat this occasion as confidential as I think it would be prejudicial to the purpose I have in mind if any publicity were to be attracted'.[27]

Within weeks the new market was a reality. Yet even then the Bank remained ambivalent about its existence. In June the Bank of England Quarterly Bulletin (1963: 117) talked longingly about the 'heyday of the foreign bond market.' And by that they meant the old bond market – in sterling. Nevertheless, it went on, 'there is no reason why the UK should not play a useful part by acting as a financial entrepôt, in which funds mobilised from a variety of sources are channelled into foreign loans issued on the London market'. Clearly the Bank still held a torch for sterling. So when Lord Harcourt of Morgan Grenfell called on Deputy Governor Mynors for guidance on whether to join with an Amsterdam bank in a dollar issue made for the City of Oslo, they seemed somewhat hesitant to recommend in favour of such a move. Harcourt was himself confused, wondering why 'a Norwegian City should borrow dollars through a Dutch bank with a market in London', as Mynors reported. Parsons duly wrote to Cromer that they did not want 'to put any obstacle in the way of such issues on the basis that London is thereby conducting a brokerage business, which we are inclined to favour'. But he finished on a rather forlorn note, echoing, no doubt what the Governor was already thinking. That 'we in the Bank would much prefer to see this kind of business done in sterling' (cited in Kynaston, 2001: 282).

Discovering the onshore external market

Bolton played a pivotal role in the creation of *both* the Eurodollar market and the Eurobond market. A fact which is responsible for much of the confusion with regard to this history. Add to this the fact that the Petrofina bond issue took place in 1957 and that the Eurobond market is also sometimes referred to as the 'Eurodollar bond market' – and consequently regarded by many as the Eurodollar market – it is not surprising that the separate histories of these two distinct markets are often erroneously interwoven, as in this quotation from Welsh (1986: 43), where the Russians, Siegmund Warburg and George Bolton are given joint credit for having invented the Eurodollar market:

> Siegmund Warburg may not perhaps be given all the credit for developing the Eurodollar market: oddly enough the historical primacy can probably be given to the Russians who, rather than hold dollars in the US, deposited them with Banque Commerciale pour L'Europe du Nord in Paris ... and other City figures such as Sir George Bolton of Bolsa took up the idea with great enthusiasm.

Welsh is either misinformed, or simply discussing the whole Euromarket phenomenon and not concerned to distinguish between the types of market. Yet by lumping the two together it is easy to conclude that the Eurodollar market – in terms of the origins of offshore finance and its inherent volatility as a potential destabilising factor in the global financial system, a far more important institution – began operating in 1957 as a result of legal changes made by the British state. However, while the state, in the guise of the Bank of England, definitely played a part in the creation of the Eurobond market, a 'state' role in the establishment of the Eurodollar market is more difficult to identify. In fact, given that it appears no relevant banking legislation was either placed upon, or removed from the statute book, which could be considered to have been responsible for its creation, can it really be claimed that the British state played a role in this development? While the exponents of the 'state' view say it can, they are unable to prove it. Their argument is based on largely unsustainable accounts of the Bank's 'fostering', 'encouraging' and 'welcoming' of the market, and on its 'light regulatory touch'. Plender and Wallace (1985: 32–3) can only quote former Chase Manhattan chairman Otto Schoeppler, who said that the Bank made the City 'a very warm place for doing business'. Other than that, the 'many bankers' that have often been mentioned are not named, no dates are given and no meetings are identified. Helleiner cites Kelly (1976: 59), to support his argument, who, in turn, writes that 'Lord Cromer ... called for more international business ... favourable tax treatment of foreigners, and development of the Eurocurrency Markets'. As evidence Kelly cites Cromer's speeches from 1965 onwards. But these only return us again to the Eurobond market, rather than to the development of the earlier Eurodollar market. On the other hand, the exponents of the 'market' view, while rightly pointing out that this innovation was driven by the City's overseas and merchant bankers, ignore the interdependence of the public and private institutions that defined and controlled the 'regulatory space' within which these bankers operated. In fact, both theses, using what Hancher and Moran (1989: 276) describe as the 'dichotomous language of public authority versus private interest', tend to present the 'state' and the 'market' as little more than discrete ahistorical universalities. They are detached from the historical specificity of the British state, and therefore cannot adequately explain the creation and development of the Eurodollar market and offshore finance.

In relation to the role played by the British state in the development of the Euromarkets, all the above references, bar one, describe the help given to it as having come from the Bank of England. An important distinction to make, given the unique position that the Bank, a private bank until 1946, holds in the institutional structure of the British state. The one exception implying that other state institutions, defined within the term 'British financial authorities', also had a part to play; in particular the Treasury. Yet little evidence can be found to sustain this suggestion. Just as successive British governments had unquestionably supported the re-establishment of the City as an international financial centre and come to rely on the inflow of foreign currency to support the reserves, so the Macmillan Government, it seems, instinctively understood the Eurodollar market as an institution beneficial both to the City and the British economy, without really knowing much about it, which was why, in November 1960, when asked if Britain would follow the example of Germany and Switzerland and wish to restrict the inflow of Eurodollar deposits, the government spokesman made it clear that such a move would only damage the City's international reputation, as well as deprive Britain of much needed currency reserves (Kynaston, 2001: 269). The Bank of England must have been pleased with this answer. They wrote it. Taking no chances with the Government's 'instinctive' understanding, it relied on the Treasury knowing almost nothing about how the Eurodollar market operated, and its regulatory implications for Britain's banking system, as a Treasury request for the Bank's help, of 16 June 1961, in gaining 'further understanding' of the 'phenomenon' demonstrates:

> Every now and again one gets rather difficult questions to answer about [the Euro-dollar] ... I myself felt the need of some education ... and was glad to find that a paper had been prepared elsewhere in the Treasury ... to put together such enlightenment as some of my colleagues could lay hands upon. Your knowledge of this subject must be much

more extensive, and I would be grateful if you could look it over and comment on it. ... It would be handy to have a more or less authoritative source of information on the subject. ... I would be much obliged if you could help our further understanding of this topic.

The informal Treasury paper mentioned above, while referring to Holmes and Klopstock's (1960b) seminal report, shows a significant misunderstanding of how the Eurodollar market functioned, believing it to be regulated either by the US or the UK authorities. It states, 'There must be limits to the amounts [of Euro-dollars] which the London banks are permitted by H.M.G. [Her Majesty's Government] to hold ... and limits beyond which they would not wish to hold dollar deposits irrespective of the exchange control regulations'. Interestingly the words 'Bank of England' which were on the original typed document had been crossed out by the Bank and the letters H.M.G. written above in ink. Kynaston (2001: 269) believes that the 'Bank's role was crucial' at this point, in quietening any Government fears about the dangers of 'hot money' flows, attached to the growth of the Eurodollar market. By December 1962 the Treasury had at least been made aware of a plan for a 'foreign currency loan', the object of which, they noted, was 'to make the facilities of the London capital market more widely available and to mop up some of the very volatile Euro-dollars at present in London', in otherwords, the about-to-be-launched Eurobond market. Two years later, newly elected Labour Prime Minister, Harold Wilson, caught in the maelstrom of a sterling crisis that would engulf his Government, asked his advisor Dr Balogh to find out what was going on in the esoteric and unpredictable world of international capital flows. Balogh, in turn, wrote to the Bank of England and asked them a number of pertinent questions which included the following:

1. What conditions govern the amount of foreign exchange that may be held by authorised dealers? Can they shift?
2. What obligation in sterling is implied by the development of the Eurodollar and Eurosterling markets?
3. Was the establishment of legal reserve ratios ever considered in respect of ... Eurodollar and other lending operations involving foreign exchange obligations.[28]

Although, it is impossible to ascertain, conclusively, whether some Treasury officials, members of the Cabinet, or ministers, might have worked towards developing the Eurodollar market, all available evidence suggests otherwise. The Treasury's lack of involvement in Euromarket operations is clear, and their ignorance of these offshore markets is understandable, given their acknowledged lack of expertise in matters of monetary policy. Brittan (1964: 165) confirms this view, writing, with regard to the Conservative Governments' years in office in the 1950s and early 1960s, that they regarded financial affairs as 'an incomprehensible technical exercise divorced from that mainstream of policy'.[29] In any case, Treasury officials would not have involved themselves in what they considered to be the Bank's area of expertise, for, as Sampson (1965: 418) puts it, they regarded the Bank as a 'foreign tribe who must not be interfered with'. Nor could they have relied on the Bank for their knowledge, that is, if Robert Hall (1991: 135) is a reliable witness. He wrote in his diary on 18 December 1957: 'the Bank hardly collaborates with the Treasury at all in internal policy matters – the Chancellor talks to the Governor in private and the Bank neither give us their assessment of the situation, nor of the part they expect monetary policy to play in it'. In this, the Bank's view of the Treasury appears to be not that far removed from what it was in Montagu Norman's day. Norman, who resented Treasury interference, would, most certainly, have had little criticism of those who came after him, if the following extract from a 1959 Bank memo is typical of the Bank's working relationship with the Treasury:[30]

> the Bank have on a number of occasions in the past strongly resisted the Treasury's attempts to obtain fuller information. Thus in March 1955 and again in March 1957 the Deputy Governor refused to allow details of the Authorised bank's positions [in foreign currencies] to be divulged to HM Treasury.

In fact, in July 1962, an internal Bank memo that asked whether the Bank 'had ever sought the Treasury's permission for the acceptance on deposit from, and on-lending to, non-residents, of Eurodollars by UK banks', elicited the reply that 'since [Euro-dollar] transactions ... do not require permission under the Exchange Control Act, 1947, one would not have expected the Treasury's permission to have been sought – nor has it, so far as I can trace'. A suggestion that the Treasury should be informed of the potential dangers of the Eurodollar market on sterling reserves, generated the response, 'I am not anxious for any ... papers to be sent to them yet'. It should not therefore be surprising that as late as 5 June 1963 Sir William Armstrong still needed to ask Cromer whether 'a brief could be prepared explaining how the [Eurodollar] market worked and what its implications were for monetary and exchange management'. Then, on 23 July 1963, Alec Cairncross, Government Economic Advisor at the Treasury, said of the Eurodollar market, 'we are ourselves trying to take stock of all that is involved in the rise of this form of international banking'.[31]

The Bank of England view of the Eurodollar

Clearly then, the 'British state', in relation to the early development of the Eurodollar market, is, in fact, the Bank of England, because only the Bank knew, as Sir George Bolton put it, what was 'going on' (Bolton, 1967a: 7). And to the Bank, this market was not entirely a new phenomenon, as the Bank of England Quarterly Bulletin made clear in June 1964. A highly developed market existed both before and after the First World War, and an active market in both dollars and sterling deposits existed in Berlin and Vienna in the 1920s. But the collapse of the international financial system in 1931 ended the 'international mobilisation of capital through private channels' (Richardson, 1966: 3), although the Bank of England still gave encouragement to City banks at that time to get involved, and stay involved, in such business. George Preston, Principal of the Bank's Dealing & Accounts Office confirms, this in a note from 1962:

> I was involved in Euro dollar deposits in a junior capacity over 30 years ago. London was then borrowing heavily from abroad, especially France, and lending freely to Europe, particularly Germany. When the warning signs became very evident many London banks, with I understand official encouragement, did not pull out the linchpin but Americans and others did. The results will long be remembered. ... The present scale of Euro-dollar operations probably far exceeds anything known in the period to which I refer. ... It is entirely unsecured, many names are 'weak', margins are cut to absurd levels and in consequence there is ... little room to maintain a proper element of liquidity.[32]

Preston goes on to say that he thinks the present situation is 'serious enough to call for some action', but that most of his preoccupations would be removed if they could see a 'return to sound practices'. He suggests that a 'more healthy Euro-dollar market could be achieved if it were found to be possible to insist on appropriate liquidity ratios being kept by all banks for their assets in foreign currency'. However, Preston

ends on a pessimistic note, pointing out that from the limited information at the Bank's disposal, 'it appears the banks are not taking the
necessary care in their currency deposit dealings'. This note was written
as part of the internal debate on the Eurodollar, which continued at the
Bank throughout 1962. It began as an investigation into the workings of
the market, prompted, it appears, by their implications for the British
economy. It involved a number of officials sifting through Bank files,
going back to at least 1939, and reporting their findings and opinions to
their superiors. Although the earliest reference I could find to the use of
the term 'Eurodollar' is on a memo written on 11 August 1960, the more
self-explanatory description 'Foreign Currency Deposits' was used
before that, with, for example, Deputy Governor Mynors requesting an
explanation as to how the taking of foreign currency deposits affects
both Britain's external and internal position on 29 September 1959.[33]
Yet in regard to the actual practice of accepting foreign dollar deposits,
Schenk (1998: 225) claims the Bank of England knew that City banks
were engaged in this activity from as early as June 1955, when they
began swapping them into sterling.

Not surprisingly then, as the archival evidence confirms, Bank
officials were well versed in the technicalities of the Eurodollar market
and certainly aware and concerned of its potential dangers, as, for that
matter, were some of the bankers themselves. Hence, in October 1960, a
Bank official attended a meeting of the Bankers' Sub-Committee and
'enquired whether the Committee were entirely happy with the volume
of business now developing in dollar deposits'. He wrote in his report,
'while the members ... were not unhappy I did get the impression some
of them were rather keeping their fingers crossed'. Then, at a further
meeting two months later, the same official noted that 'some of the
clearers are a little uneasy at the size to which the Euro dollar position
has grown'. Their principal concern however was not related to how the
market – through the process of swapping non-resident dollars into sterling – could be used to overcome Government economic policy in relation to the control of credit and the money supply, but rather to
determine the extent that its existence created a potential call on
Britain's currency and gold reserves. Legally, the operation of the
Eurodollar market did not create such a contingent liability and, according to the Bank of England, the banks were 'well aware' of this. They
knew 'that in theory such lending can only be done on the condition
that no call will be made on the reserves'; although the 'only written
warning to this effect ... was given ... in 1939'. However, in practice,
where 'a bank called upon to repay a deposit it had lent-on, could not

recover the counterpart or obtain it elsewhere, it would *expect* to be able to buy the currency it need[ed] against sterling, thus having a direct impact on the reserves[34] (my emphasis).

This dangerous degree of *uncertainty* arose out of the distinction the Bank of England made between the 'Authorised' and the non-Authorised banks, although how a bank was deemed to be 'authorised' was again, a question of custom rather than law. So, for example, when in 1973, Commerzbank wanted to open a branch in the City, they sent Gottfried Bruder to the Bank to enquire what permissions and regulations needed to be adhered to. None, explained James Keogh, Principal of the Discount Office. So they then asked about the procedure for qualifying as an 'authorised' bank. As Bruder recalls: 'Keogh looked at us and he said "in London a bank is a bank if I consider it to be one" '. That was it, apart from the need to attend what Kynaston (2001: 442) describes as the 'occasional, indispensable afternoon ceremony'. Something which the Bank of Belgium's Philippe Muûls remembers as being obliged 'to go round and have a cup of tea at the Bank of England, from time to time and explain what you were doing'.[35]

Nevertheless, being 'authorised' was important for a bank wanting to operate in the Eurodollar market. For these were banks in 'whose probity the Bank could be confident' and therefore deemed worthy to deal in Eurodollars unrestricted, unlike the 'non-Authorised' banks and finance houses that required permission. But this posed a problem, because, by granting permission, as the Bank put it, to a 'firm of lesser standing', to operate in a foreign currency market, the Bank felt obliged to accept a degree of responsibility over its activities. Should it run into trouble, invest unwisely and require currency from the reserves, the Bank would have no choice but to provide support. Having stood behind the 'firms of lesser standing', the Bank then felt honour bound to support the 'authorised' banks. This uncertainty would explain Preston's concerns and his calling for the imposition of a liquidity ratio on the market. Bizarrely it is also used to explain how the opposite, 'non-regulatory' view prevailed. For although 'reasonable dollar liquidity ratios would be a safeguard ... they would mean admission of responsibility and would remove whatever restraint is achieved by the present uncertainty as to whether the Exchange Equalisation Account would or would not stand behind a bank in default'. Hence, the imposition of a liquidity reserve requirement on the Eurodollar market, consequent to the danger that a contingent liability to the reserves posed for sterling, was an admission of said liability, and, in the Bank's view, therefore inappropriate. In addition, when it was suggested that either the Bank inform the banks that 'we are not behind them', or inform the Treasury that such activities would in future carry a potential call on the reserves, Hamilton concludes that '[b]oth alternatives are fraught with danger of starting something unwelcome'.[36]

Understanding this apparent absurdity is crucial to understanding how the Bank of England regulated the City's banks and their activities. It is not enough to explain, as does a 1965 Bank report on the risks of operating in the Eurodollar market, that '[d]ifficulties could not be guarded against except by a form of banking inspection, which is alien to our system'. It is rather a paradox emanating out of the inherent contradiction in the Bank's institutional position within the UK economy at that time, where it acted as an interface between the state and the market; the 'government's arm in the City, and the City's representative in the government' (McRae and Cairncross, 1973: 193). It explains why the Bank's supervision of the UK banking system was based on two essentially incompatible tenets: to maintain a hands-off approach to the banks themselves, allowing them a high degree of self-regulation, or as the Bank describes it, *flexible freedom*, while simultaneously ensuring that the system itself was secure and not vulnerable to collapse. Which of these concerns – what Moran (1981: 387) calls the two connected problems of *control* and *scandal* – took precedence over the other, in relation to the Eurodollar market, appeared to change according to the perspective from which the *dilemma* was viewed. As one moved up from those Bank officials working at an 'operating' level, to those working at a more senior executive level, so the balance of opinion tended to move in favour of the former concern, and away from the latter. So, for example, with regard to the Midland Bank's use of dollar 'swaps' in June 1955, while Hamilton was prompted to show the Midland a 'warning light', Parsons thought it better 'not to press the Midland any further'. A Sub-Committee Minute of August 1955 shows that the Bank concluded 'that they did not wish to object to banks accepting dollar deposits from non-residents and converting them into sterling through swaps in the London market'. Then in 1959, Preston's senior, Roy Bridge, then Deputy Chief Cashier (Foreign Exchange), reporting on the 'London Market for Foreign Currency Deposits' for Deputy Governor Mynors, concluded, unlike Preston in 1962, that such activities did not pose any threat to Britain's external position and therefore he did not believe 'that this business gives any cause for concern at the present time'. Again, in April 1961, Maurice Parsons, in response to US fears regarding the dangers of the market, pointed out that 'it would not be in the interests of international trade that [the Eurodollar market] should be suppressed', and that in 'ordinary circumstances … the dangers involved appear to be minimal and theoretical, rather than practical'.[37]

The Bank's general attitude to London money market business at that time is illuminated by the evidence of a US Treasury memo, which points out that the 'Bank of England cautions dealers who overtrade and chides those who undertrade. By nature the Bank … thinks the least of an undertrader because they want a home for money'. Nevertheless, it is fair to say, despite the instinctive support the market received from the Bank's senior executive officers, Preston's warning of February 1962 had not gone unheard. It was picked up the following day by Cromer, who counselled H.W.B. Schroder, Chairman of Schroders Bank that trading in the Eurodollar market had 'now reached such proportions as to call for considerable caution in the handling of this type of business'. He goes on to say that it was the doubts attached to the final borrowers' ability to repay the Eurodollar loans that concerned him most. It was in this situation, Cromer concluded, that 'dangers could arise which might prove difficult for all of us'. His central worry with regard to the Eurodollar market, was the potential call on Britain's reserves, something which had prompted the internal Bank debate on the market of 1962 referred to above. However, the Eurodollar market was fast becoming a very important means of attracting short-term hot money flows to shore up Britain's payments position and offer support to sterling. As a Bank note made clear, this was a '[v]ery useful resource for British markets which could not easily dispense with them. If US rates were raised we would probably have to raise our rates to compete'.[38]

By way of finding a solution to their *dilemma*, the Bank began to examine how they could better gain some measure of control over the Eurodollar market, beginning with a greater knowledge of what exactly the banks were up to. As a Bank memo makes clear, they had 'been trying for some time to find out exactly how the banks treat foreign currency deposits', but without too much success, it seems, which is not surprising, since as the memo continues, 'the next step seems to be for us to make more formal enquiries of the active banks – notably BOLSA, the American and the Japanese banks'. That was something which they were 'far from convinced that the Bank would wish to make', although the authorised banks and dealers did provide the Bank with statistics as to their foreign currency holdings and deposits, as they were legally required to do under the Exchange Control Act 1947. Now in July 1962, Hamilton suggested that they define a set of rules for the banks to follow. Certainly, the City's banks could have been expected to comply with any such demands, as they were reluctant to fall out of favour with the Bank. Hence, when Schroders wanted to get into the Eurobusiness in December 1962, they first sent Mr Forsyth and one of their dealers to the Bank to find out 'whether it would be in order for them to give lines of facilities in Eurodollars'. Again, in 1963, when Rothschilds 'were considering the possibilities of floating foreign bond issues in London', Jacob Rothschild phoned the Bank and asked 'whether there was any objection in principal to a dollar issue'.

In addition, while there may not have been legislation prohibiting merchant and overseas banks in the City from operating in the Eurodollar market, as Michael J. Babington-Smith, Director of the Bank and also Deputy Chairman of Glyn Mills Bank, had suggested, it could be controlled via powers granted under Section 34 of the Exchange Control Act enabling the Bank 'to limit the taking of deposits to a stated figure'. However, he added, such measures 'could only be justified if we had very strong grounds for believing that the foundations of the Eurodollar market were showing signs of cracking'. He recommended instead the banks be given 'a gentle warning through the Foreign Exchange Sub-Committee'. Hamilton agreed but thought such a warning should come from a 'higher level with less publicity'. By the time the Bank's top officials met in August 1962, three solutions had been put forward for consideration:

1. Voluntary self-restraint.
2. Liquidity ratios.
3. A hint from the Governor that we are watching the market and request for more detailed and more regular information.

It was felt that (1) 'would be embarrassing to apply' and (2) was 'a non-starter for technical reasons'. This left (3), which was reduced to deciding only to seek more information, 'as a first step', and to do so by way of an informal request by the Governor to the Chairman of the leading half dozen or so banks in the Eurodollar business. A decision was made to approach that gamekeeper turned poacher, Sir George Bolton and BOLSA, and then 'the Accepting Houses with the largest share of the business, i.e. Schroders and Brown, Shipley, the bigger British overseas banks, e.g. Barclays PCO and Chartered and the largest of the Big Five in the currency deposit business ... including the ... Westminster Foreign Bank Ltd'.[39]

No doubt the list must have included Hambros, where, coincidentally, one of the City's most prominent merchant bankers, chairman Sir Charles Hambro, had recently become 'quite alarmed' about the growth of the Eurodollar market, as Deputy Governor Mynors noted. So much so that in

November 1962 he asked the Bank if it could provide some form of 'general guidance to give on the extent to which business in Euro-dollars could be allowed to expand'. In fact, while Hambros Bank had become one of its biggest operators – its non-sterling deposits rising from the equivalent of £9 million to £28 million in the year ending in March 1962 – Sir Charles had become highly critical of how the market was damaging the British economy, by bidding up interest rates and attracting hot money into London, as he had told the *Economist* in May, adding, perhaps in an attempt to allay fears for the future, that it was 'likely to be a temporary phenomenon'. The *FT* explained Hambro's *dilemma* as stemming from his double role as merchant banker and Bank Director – a dilemma which it just so happened, the Bank of England had, to a great extent, finally resolved. As the Commonwealth central bank governors were told the following week, the Eurodollar market was

> a truly international market which performs a useful function in providing relatively easy and cheap access to short-term funds. It has added to international liquidity and stimulated bank competition. ... It has eased the strain on the US balance of payments position in so far as the need for dollar finance might otherwise have been met by US banks direct.

So in January 1963, with Cromer's approval, Mynors sent a letter of reassurance to Hambro, making clear the Bank's view of the Eurodollar 'business'. He wrote,

> It is natural enough that London banks – and merchant banks in particular – with their expertise and international connections, should ... have sought to participate actively in this [Euro-dollar] business. It is par excellence an example of the kind of business which London ought to be able to do both well and profitably. That is why we at the Bank, have never seen any reason to place any obstacles in the way of London taking its full and increasing share. If we were to stop the business here, it would move to other centres with a consequent loss of earnings for London.

Mynors, ignoring the evidence referred to by Preston, assumed the banks will abide by a duty of care developed as a result of past experience. He continued,

> *There are of course risks involved ... we have not however thought that the existence of risks provided any reasons for our seeking to restrict the*

development of this market. We have rather felt that we ought to be able to rely on the judgement of London banks to conduct their operations in accordance with sound banking principles and we have been entitled to assume that, in exercising their banking judgement they would not overlook the experience of 30 years ago. ... The essence of the solution of such problems as there may be probably lies in the observance of the familiar principles:

(a) prudent lending;
(b) suitable geographical distribution of deposits placed (i.e., not too many eggs in one country); and
(c) maintenance of adequate liquidity (in currency) and a reasonable spread of maturity dates; coupled with the realisation that not one bank should take on more business than it can handle within the limits of its present resources.

This is doubtless the policy which you are already following, and I would hope is common to those other merchant banks similarly engaged. To drive the business from London would be wrong as it continues in other places and the reputation of London as a monetary centre would suffer in the process (my emphasis).

It seemed to do the trick with Sir Charles Hambro and by the end of March 1963 his bank's non-sterling deposits had risen to £37 million. Interestingly, a draft of the letter has an extra paragraph which is missing from the final version. In this the Deputy Governor is a little more forthright about what he describes as Hambros and the City's 'sharp increase' in Eurodollar deposits. Something that he believes 'could suggest to a casual observer a measure of overtrading when your deposits are compared to your capital'. He wonders whether Hambros' 'ratio of ... advances to ... deposits could rise to a figure which might seem to be higher than was prudent', leading observers 'to question' the policy they were pursuing, 'namely, the taking of deposits at a seemingly high rate of interest and lending them as to 100 per cent'. However, by 20 June 1963, when Cromer replied to Sir William Armstrong's request for a brief on the Eurodollar market, doubts, for the most part, were under control again. He wrote,

we take it as axiomatic that the canons of good banking will be observed by London banks undertaking operations in the Euro Dollar market. Indeed, our enquiries lead us to believe that the bulk of this business through London is on a bank-to-bank basis; in other words, there is a reputable and responsible intermediary. It would seem that the only serious risk to the UK which might arise would be that of a moratorium on the scale similar to that of the German standstill of 1931. At the present time the reserves of the European countries are considerable and this ... suggests that there would not seem to be any great risk. However the lessons of the past should certainly prevent heavy lending of Euro dollars in the less credit-worthy countries.[40]

In November 1963, discussions with Hermann Abs of Deutsche Bank, first at the British Embassy in Bonn and then with the Board of Trade in London, are also very illuminating as regards the Bank's instinctive support for the Eurodollar market. In Bonn, Abs read out 'a long warning' about the dangers of the Eurodollar market, 'which was under no central bank of control and in which quite small firms were handling enormous sums of money'. He cautioned, 'we should all be very careful indeed about this Market'. He then came to London and spoke to the Secretary of State, where he expressed his 'anxiety about the prospects for the Eurodollar market' and suggested 'that central banks should watch the situation carefully and should have a firm view on it'. Then, before leaving London, Abs followed this up by speaking publicly on the Eurodollar in very similar fashion. Principally, Abs was concerned that German firms, given the absence of exchange control in Germany, were borrowing directly from the Eurodollar market and were accordingly being 'tempted' into using this short-term funding for the wrong purposes, that is, to finance long-term investment, with all the dangers that implied. In otherwords, the old trick of borrowing short and lending long. Abs pointed to the recent collapse of the two Stinnes groups which 'had both been deep in the Eurodollar market'. This prompted the minister to ask his officials for their view on Abs' assessment, which, in turn, led to a written request to the Treasury for help in understanding the market itself and the significance of Abs' comments. This letter was, consequently, passed to the Bank of England where it was received with some consternation.

Cromer advised, 'Let us be cautious without being agitated'. Deputy Governor Mynors wrote to Cromer, 'The subject is so important that I would like to know we are in line with your thinking on it'. George Preston was, as he put it, 'filled with foreboding', much like Abs himself, because, as he continued, 'There are a number of failures on the international horizon which are mixed up with dishonesty, which remind me all too strongly of the events leading up to the 1931 crisis'. But Roy Bridge, who by this time had been made Advisor to the

Governors, thought differently. Believing these events, in themselves, acted as 'an amber light' in warning the market operators to alter their business methods.

Clearly the 1931 crisis still loomed large in Threadneedle Street. Yet there had never been agreement on why it had occurred. Roy Bridge, was convinced 'depression in world trade' rather than 'unsound banking' had been the cause. But then, Bridge had total faith in bankers and banking. So, while he fully understood that the Eurodollar market was a 'natural' unregulated, unsupervised international money market, he was not overly concerned. As he explained to a worried Roy L. Reierson, Chief Economist of the Bankers Trust Company, 'There may indeed be some unsound banking here and there. ... But this is where the experience and the judgement of the international banker should come in'. And even if these masters of the universe did get it wrong now and again, the world could rely on 'the international framework of monetary co-operation' to see it through. Bridge looked at the Eurodollar market and saw its 'underlying reliability'. Reierson, on the other hand, perceived only danger, danger this market posed for the international financial system.[41] The *FT*'s Gordon Tether sided with Bridge. Responding to Abs' public fears he wrote an article entitled, 'How Serious is the Danger of a Euro-dollar Explosion', in which he condemned 'the recent fashion of portraying this phenomenon as a gigantic financial powder-barrel that could be sparked off at any moment should lenders begin to experience difficulty in getting their money back'. Like Bridge, he was confident that there were ways 'in this day and age ... for dealing with such situations' (cited in Kynaston, 2002: 283).

Yet, Roy Bridge aside, perhaps the Bank was more concerned about the Eurodollar market's potential volatility and capacity to run to crisis than it was willing to admit. But the Bank had been pushed on the defensive by Abs and the scandals involving Hugo Stinnes & Co and Ira Haupt. For such was its concern lest the Treasury and Board of Trade begin to believe that the Eurodollar market was a threat to monetary stability, that a detailed four page report was prepared analysing the weakness of the capital structure of the German economy, explaining that the Stinnes group of companies were mismanaged and undercapitalised, that such irresponsible banking practices just would not happen in London and pointing out that other German companies had gone bankrupt that had not been involved in the Eurodollar market. In addition, a draft version of the note includes a reference, missing from the final version, to the importance of London as a Eurodollar market and financial centre. A factor which explains why London banks 'should be free to engage in currency deposit business of the Euro variety'. The report was sent to the Treasury with an accompanying note emphasising that in the Bank's view 'German industry tends to rely to a considerable extent in the absence of an adequate volume of equity and long-term loan capital' on Eurocurrencies. It concluded smugly, 'Thus, the basic weakness is the under-capitalisation of German industry, not the Euro-currency market.'

Prior to Cromer travelling to the BIS in Basle to discuss 'Euro-currencies' during 9–11 November 1963, the Bank of England prepared a graph showing the liabilities of UK banks to non-Sterling Area residents to circulate at the meeting, in order 'to create a good impression and help to dispense any suspicion that we may have anything to hide – a suspicion which can easily arise since the analysis of the London position is so much more complicated than that of the others'. Then, the following month, Bank officials visited the US Treasury where they were asked questions about the UK's 'rules and practices as regards the transactions … [U.K.] banks might undertake in U.S. dollars'. A follow-up letter attempted to clarify the position by explaining that, '[l]ending by Authorised banks against Euro-dollar deposits … is not controlled, as regards amount, nature or tenor. Though cases like Ira Haupt might give us pause, reliance is placed on the commercial prudence of the lenders'. [42] During the course of 1964–44 dollar issues were made in Europe, mainly London, worth a total $681 million. When the Bank made its judgement on the Eurodollar market official in the *Bank of England Quarterly Bulletin* in 1964, traces of its *dilemma* still remained. But generally speaking Roy Bridge's view prevailed. It stated that 'there are risks involved, but the UK authorities have not discouraged London banks from participating in this business, relying on their good judgement in the way they conduct their operations' (BoE, 1964: 107). By February 1965, the Bank had become somewhat dismissive of the dangers inherent in the market, reporting that the banking habit of borrowing short and lending long – the recipe for 'illiquidity' – was 'essentially a straight-forward matter of prudent banking', matters that 'could not be guarded against except by a form of banking operation which is alien to our system.' However, the report continues, while the Bank does not 'attempt to supervise the banks' day-to-day business', it does expect the banks to abide by 'Conventions' when dealing in the Euromarkets, conventions which, should they be 'seriously breached', would prompt serious action. To the point where the Bank 'would not hesitate, if all else failed, to recommend the withdrawal or curtailment of certain permissions granted under the Exchange Control Act'.

However, while the Bank could have used its power over the 'authorised banks', as a 1965 Bank memo to the Treasury explains, to 'issue directions or put down guidelines about balance sheet ratios in relation to Euro-currency business', this was something it would have been very reluctant to do, for 'while liquidity might be assured, profitability could suffer seriously'. The Bank, however, took comfort, and was reassured that such action was unnecessary, simply because the 'banks who do the bulk of the Euro-dollar business are also those who keep very close to the Bank of England for one reason or another'.[43]

6

America and the Euromarkets

In explaining the Euromarkets and the re-emergence of global finance in the late 1950s and early 1960s as being principally driven by actions taken in Britain, by default, this book is also arguing that the US played a far less important role in these innovatory developments than is generally thought. In fact, as this chapter will show, the American banking community had almost no involvement in the Eurodollar market until late 1959 and the US monetary authorities did not really understand how it operated until 1960–62, when forced to recognise its significance in the context of the declining fortunes of the US balance of payments and its impact on US gold stocks and the operation of the Bretton Woods System. Designed to prevent a repeat of the problems experienced under the gold standard of the inter-war years, Bretton Woods was essentially a 'monetary compromise', based not on a pure gold standard, whereby all currencies could be exchanged for gold at a fixed price, but on a Dollar–Gold Standard, which pegged all other currencies to the dollar at, essentially, a fixed rate of exchange, with only the dollar exchangeable for gold on demand, and then only by official foreign holders of dollars – in other words, central banks and other official institutions such as the IMF.

Under Bretton Woods the dollar became the first international reserve currency. Yet this reflected the political reality of the immediate post-1945 period and ignored the potential political and economic problems which could ensue from using a domestic currency as an international reserve currency. It reflected the dominance of the US economy over a Europe and Japan whose productive bases had been virtually wiped out by the Second World War, and a world where the US expected to run balance of payments surpluses and could not envisage international claims on its gold reserves to the extent that the system would collapse. In fact, as the rest of the world exchanged what gold it had for essential products only available in the US in the immediate post-war period, the US accumulated an even larger proportion of the world's gold stocks, and with it, of course, an unhealthy proportion of international liquidity.

This was reflected in the problem of 'dollar shortage', or 'dollar gap', and was eventually overcome by the expansion of the 'paper' element of the Dollar–Gold Standard, which provided the liquidity necessary to drive the recovery of Western Europe and Japan in the 1950s.[1] However, in doing so, from 1956 onwards, the problem of 'dollar shortage' was superseded by the problem of 'dollar surplus', or 'dollar glut'. Thus, the eventual return to convertibility in 1958, a year in which the gold outflow from the US amounted to $2.3 billion, not only reflected a more equal, and necessary re-balancing of the international economy, it also exposed the essential flaw in the monetary compromise that was the Dollar–Gold Standard. The 'paper' element, that is, the dollar, was becoming increasingly debased as currency, to the extent of its expansion relative to the size of the gold stock on which it was based and by virtue of the fact that rising inflation in the US was accentuating its overvaluation (Aglietta, 1985: 172). By the end of 1958 total foreign dollar claims had risen to $15.6 billion and US gold stocks fallen to $20.6 billion. This trend continued until a critical point was reached midway through 1959 when the total amount of foreign dollar claims exceeded the US gold stock. By August 1961 foreign dollar claims stood at $19.7 billion and US gold stock at $17.5 billion. Given the difficulty of revaluing gold in terms of the dollar, this posed a fundamental problem with regard to the US and the Bretton Woods system.[2]

Yet an increase in foreign dollars claims did not necessarily have to result in a corresponding fall in US gold stocks. This depended on the extent of the willingness of (1) private foreigners and (2) central banks, to hold liquid dollar assets. If this were low, the dollar funds of the former would ultimately flow to the latter, making it more likely that, in turn, they would be presented to the Federal Reserve to be exchanged into gold, as central banks acted according to their 'gold traditions' and re-established their gold-to-dollar reserve ratios.[3] But calculating the extent of the willingness to hold dollars was extremely difficult, as it depended on a complex series of political/economic factors. These raised four essential questions which became increasingly pertinent to both the US monetary authorities and those of the other major nation/states, as the relationship between the dollar and US gold deteriorated: (1) at what point and under what conditions would official foreign dollar holders wish to exchange their holdings for gold; (2) what, in the short-term, could be done to prevent this situation from arising; (3) how, in the long-term, could the dollar–gold relationship be reversed; (4) what would then replace the dollar as a means of providing international liquidity. Finding answers to these questions, however, only exposed a set of intractable problems emanating out of the contradiction between the demands of the US domestic economy and US global ambitions, between the role of the dollar as a national currency, and its role as an international reserve currency, which became increasingly problematic as the 1960s progressed.

The depletion of US gold from 1958 onwards, and the conviction that this worrying development was a direct consequence of interest rate differentials in favour of the major European currencies acting as a disincentive to hold dollars, fuelled an increasingly strident public debate in the US on what was the best policy to overcome these problems. This, in turn, was informed by the views of different vested interest groups that tended to reduce the argument to a stark choice between (1) increasing US interest rates as an incentive to keep capital in, and attract capital back to the US, and (2) applying exchange controls as a means of blocking the flow of capital out of the US. Naturally, the interests of international banking, benefiting from the free flow of capital and the financial gains of applying a market price for credit, generally opposed the latter, while industry, requiring a US domestic capital market offering long-term, low-rate investment loans to the domestic economy, tended to oppose the former. The US monetary authorities, especially the Treasury, opposed both solutions and attempted to maintain the 'monetary compromise' by establishing a system of international co-operation designed to prevent further depletion of US gold stocks in the short term, in the belief that the US would be able to improve its economic performance and trade its way out if its deficit problem in the medium-to-long-term. These were the political economic conditions which defined and informed the beginning of the Eurodollar market in 1957, which were inter-woven with its early development through the 1960s, and which were themselves then reconstituted, as the US domestic capital market was increasingly undermined by the inexorable integration of the international monetary system that the creation and operation of the Eurodollar market accelerated. It is in the context of this economic history that the role of the US in the development of the Euromarkets needs to be understood.

US banks operating in the London Eurodollar market

In October 1962, the Bank of England was told by BOLSA's Mr Low, 'that the New York banks were more conscious of openings for business in the Euro-dollar market than they had been'. That would not have been difficult. During the 1950s, while one US bank in Paris was soliciting dollar deposits from French banks and lending them on to Italian banks, this appears to have been the exception rather than the rule. US banks, for the most part, did not participate in the nascent Eurodollar market created by the Communist banks and only began to do so, as Stigum (1978: 137) writes, 'very hesitantly several years later', and then only 'very defensively', after their US customers asked them to do so. For example, in August 1963, one New York bank, Manufacturers Hanover Trust, was extremely critical of the way the market was being operated, especially the practice of creating dollar credit by pyramiding deposits. Their Vice-President, Andrew L. Gomory, wrote to the Bundesbank that it 'is not desirous to lay off deposits and take part in this process of pyramiding. ... In order to return to healthy commercial banking practices, we feel that Euro-dollar deposits should be utilised for loans covering commercial transactions, where the lending bank knows who the *end-user* is'. That they were 'reluctant participants in the market', as Holmes and Klopstock (1960a: 15) put it, is confirmed by a FRBNY report written in at the end of 1961. Also by economist Alexander Sachs, who told Robert Roosa, that 'from personal experience I can attest that some merchant-banking houses in London *and banques d'affaires* in Paris know more and utilise more resourcefully the funds involved in [the Eurodollar market] ... than the American banks' branches'.[4]

According to Oscar L. Altman (1960–61: 322), one of the first economists to study the phenomenon, New York banks did not begin to operate in the market until the summer of 1959, almost two years after it began. This was when, as Holmes and Klopstock (1960a: 7) explain, they 'decided to toss aside their hesitations and use it as a means to recapture, through their branches, some part of the $1 billion worth of time deposits that had escaped them, as money rates reached levels far in excess of Regulation Q'. Al Hayes, President of the Federal Reserve Bank of New York (FRBNY), on asking his staff, in March 1960, why, given the large yield incentive, do US banks not move more of their funds to London, was told by Mr. T. J. Roche that according to the 'conversations' he had had 'with the banks' foreign exchange people ... top management does not approve of such transactions'.

Nevertheless, ultimately, the expansion of the Eurodollar activity encouraged the belated arrival in London of American banks eager to conduct Eurobusiness, although some had previously used their branches in London to provide investment services for their domestic customers, something they were prohibited from doing in the US, under the restrictions of the 1934 Glass–Steagall Act (Coakley, 1988: 73). Either way, in the 1960s the Americans became increasingly appreciative of the Bank of England's 'hands-off' style of regulation, for this meant, as Sampson (1981: 113) writes, 'they could obtain permission for new activities in a few minutes which could take months of negotiating with armies of lawyers in Washington'. Treasury records show that a 'good percentage of the flow of US funds to London [had] been handled by the London offices of the First National City Bank of New York, Morgan Guaranty, Chase, and Brown, Shipley & Co'.[5] By April 1965 they had begun to take over in the City; setting up international consortia banking and developing more innovative financial instruments. To such an extent that very quickly the English merchant banks' domination of the Eurodollar market come to an end.

But was the US banks' belated arrival in London part of an invasion of Europe or an escape from America? As Mayer (1976: 454) describes it, they came to London 'en masse' to avoid the Federal Reserve rules holding down their domestic deposits'. This trend was given even greater stimulus on 18 July 1963, when the growing US balance of payments deficit prompted President Kennedy to introduce the Interest Equalization Tax (IET) as a disincentive to foreign borrowers wanting to tap the US domestic capital market for funds, by attaching a penalty to interest received by US residents on foreign securities, including bank loans, from non-resident entities. This was followed in 1965 by the Voluntary Foreign Credit Restraint Programe (VFCR), which placed voluntary ceilings on loans to non-residents, and in 1968 by the Foreign Direct Investment Program (FDIP), designed to reduce direct overseas investments by US corporations.

Then, in addition, with the Vietnam War driving increased Government spending, the Federal Reserve began to worry that the US economy was overheating. They tightened monetary policy in 1966, (and then again in 1968 and 1969), by reducing the interest rate payable on Certificates of Deposit (CDs) and thereby pushing up the interest premium offered on Treasury Bills, in the hope of attracting investors and thereby reducing the money supply. Their strategy backfired as CDs were cashed and the funds flowed to the Eurodollar market instead, attracted by its higher interest rates. These funds were then returned to the US, as New York banks looking to replenish their reserves, started borrowing, via the interbank market, from their own foreign branches in Europe and other Eurodollar areas. This, in turn, resulted in an increase in the lending of New York banks, precisely the opposite outcome of that envisaged by the Federal Reserve.

While all these measures were meant to strengthen the US's capital account, they had the opposite effect. Not only were foreign dollar holders now discouraged from depositing their dollars in the US money market, but, at the same time, US corporations became unwilling to repatriate capital earned abroad. In fact, they began to cut themselves off from their domestic financial money markets, both depositing their foreign earnings, and raising necessary short- and long-term funding for their foreign subsidiaries, in the Euromarkets. The wider implication of these changes was, as Dosso (1992: 17–18) describes, 'to forge a powerful link between the US, Eurodollar and the European financial markets, and further expose European markets to changes in US domestic and monetary policy'. This led Charles Gordon to conclude that it was 'almost as if [the US authorities] wanted to create a financial centre outside their own shore' (cited in Ramsay, 1998: 22). A different twist to the story of US complicity in the development of the Euromarkets comes from J. Orlin Grabbe (1995), who claims the existence of the Eurodollar market was deliberately kept hidden from the President, implying that powerful interests within the US authorities were covertly re-constructing the international monetary system to further their own interests. He tells the story of Hendrik Houthakker, a junior staff member of the Council of Economic Advisors, who on first discovering the Eurodollar market tried to bring it to the attention of the President, but was told, 'No, we don't want to draw attention to it'. Once again, this is a claim that comes without any verifiable evidence, so we do not even know when Houthakker made his discovery. Grabbe goes on to explain that this experience had such a profound effect on Houthakker, that when he became more powerful, he made sure President Nixon was told what was happening. Of course by the time Nixon came to office in 1969 the Eurodollar market was hardly news.

The Federal Reserve and the continental dollar market

If most American banks avoided the Eurodollar market until late 1959, archival evidence indicates that the Federal Reserve did not even understand what it was until 1960. It also shows that when they did find out, they began to worry, both about the danger this posed for the US payments deficit, and the international financial system itself. For example, on 28 November 1958, with the Eurodollar market proper already one year old, Hayes, at the FRBNY, was sent a report on US foreign gold and dollar holdings, which pointed out that 'in many countries the dollar reserves of commercial banks are closely supervised, if not fully controlled, by the monetary authorities, and are therefore in the last analysis only extensions of the official reserves'. Of course this was not true of Britain, the centre of the Eurodollar market.[6] By March 1960 the FRBNY acknowledged that 'with the development of convertibility, international capital movements had become very complex'. And, while the Federal Reserve had certainly become more knowledgeable about the Eurodollar, archival evidence at this point is somewhat ambivalent. For, although it makes clear the FRBNY had become aware that the BIS believed there was 'approximately $1 billion' in the so-called "European dollars"... managed by commercial banks' which were 'very sensitive to interest rate changes' – and they were certainly becoming increasingly concerned about the extent of vulnerability of US gold stocks to short-term interest rate movements – at the same time, they were puzzled by the nature of certain dealings in the New York money market resulting from the operation of what came to be known as the 'Cano-dollar' market, a Canadian variant of the Eurodollar market.[7] This prompted Hayes to ask what was going on. Why, specifically, the New York Agencies of certain Canadian banks reported a very high level of time deposits held by foreign banks, others showed a very low level of such deposits? From the memo Hayes received in reply, it is clear that the Balance of Payments Division had to ask the Canadian banks themselves what they were doing. It states,

> The Bank of Montreal, the Bank of Nova Scotia, and the Royal Bank of Canada each gave similar explanations for not reporting any time deposits for foreign banks. They said that the interest-earning deposits accounts of foreign banks are held with their head offices and not with the New York agencies. ... On the other hand, representatives of the Canadian banks, explained that all of the deposits held for their head offices are time deposits and that the head office receive the earnings thereon.

The memo concludes, 'It would appear, therefore, that the figures obtained in the time deposit survey are prey to divergent internal accounting procedures. ... Those reporting almost all deposits for their head office as time accounts, take the position that the earnings on the deposits are allocable to the head office, the others take the opposite view that any interest paid on deposits of customers is paid by the head office and not by the agency.' What, in fact, the Banks of Montreal, Nova Scotia and Canada had done, was to hold title to their dollar deposits in Canada, rather than in New York, in a Foreign Dollar Market.

It is clear then, that the FRBNY, as Vice-President Charles Coombs admitted, needed 'to know more about the continental dollar market'.

Accordingly, in June 1960, Holmes and Klopstock, from the bank's Research Department, were sent to Europe to do just that, but only after Hayes contacted the heads of a number of European Central Banks requesting their assistance, including Cobbold at the Bank of England. He wrote,

> For some time we have been increasingly interested in the movements of substantial amounts of foreign-owned dollar balances through the Euro-dollar market and we feel that we should know more about its growth, scope and pattern. ... We would greatly appreciate the assistance of your bank in arranging for Messrs Holmes and Klopstock to meet with merchant banks active in the Euro-dollar market.

In August, Holmes and Klopstock (1960a) duly reported back that the Eurodollar market was an 'interbank market' for dollar deposits. While they recognised this new institution had 'added to the importance of the dollar as an international currency', they also realised that paradoxically, it had 'reduced the importance of New York as a financial centre'. They also concluded that, 'to a considerable extent', the Eurodollar market had 'been promoted by European monetary authorities'; that it was making 'the pursuit of an independent monetary policy in any one country ... far more difficult'; and that its 'pyramiding of dollar assets and liabilities [was] a matter of potential concern to foreign monetary authorities because of the financial risks involved'. They also refer to the fact that the 'phenomenal growth of the operations of Canadian banks in the loan market in New York has also largely been based on balances obtained in the Continental dollar market'. The following month Coombs sent the Holmes and Klopstock Report both to the other Federal Reserve banks and the major US commercial banks, asking for their comments. Their replies give an indication of the varied thinking, both uninformed and astute, amongst US international bankers and central bankers with regard to the Eurodollar market in September/October 1960. For example, Franklin L. Parsons, Director of Research at the Federal Reserve Bank of Minneapolis wrote,

> I had not been aware of the development of the continental dollar market and its impact on domestic monetary policy considerations.

Walter B. Wriston, of the First National City Bank of New York wrote,

> It makes me a little sad to think of a market of this size in our own currency developing outside of our country because it is prevented from finding its natural home in New York.

Arthur G. Boardman Jr, Senior Vice President of the Irving Trust Company wrote,

> I do not favour the lending, borrowing and re-lending of dollars by institutions in non-dollar countries. Under normal conditions the risks may be negligible but in the event of any financial or political crisis, the risks could be large indeed and could have serious repercussions in the foreign exchange markets. ... Once a development of this kind has occurred, it is difficult to check it; it does seem to me that if the American banks had more leeway as to rates under Regulation Q, the problems resulting from the development of the Continental dollar market would be minimised.

Clinton C. Johnson, Executive Vice President of the Chemical Bank New York Trust Company wrote,

> I should like to have you send me three additional copies; one of which I know our Chairman would enjoy reading, another for our London office ...

Robert L. Edwards, Vice President of the Bank of New York wrote,

> Their study is very timely for, as you can well imagine, we have been conscious of the growth of this market in our International Department for some time. I would like some of our senior executive officers to read this study ...

Andrew L. Gomory of the International Banking Department of the Manufacturers Hanover Trust Company wrote,

> The report fully confirms the conviction ... that as long as Regulation Q removes foreign time deposit interest rates from the competition of the free markets of the world and as long as a somewhat provincial attitude toward foreign deposits both by the US Treasury and the judicial authorities prevail, there is little hope for any change in the situation. The loss of foreign trade financing by the New York market is also one of the consequences ...[8]

In the light of the report, both FRBNY and US Treasury officials, separately and independently, spent the next year discussing what could be done to prevent capital outflows resulting from American corporations based in New York City transferring their deposits to Canadian banks, via the banks' New York agencies. These banks were re-circulating US domiciled dollars, in the process transferring ownership abroad and tapping them directly into the 'Eurodollar transmission belt'. Yet even at that late stage, the US monetary authorities were struggling to understand what was going on, although they were becoming more concerned. So that by April 1961, while visiting the BIS in Basle, Coombs made it clear to the Bank of England's representative, Maurice Parsons, that they were 'now inclined to think that this market constitutes a danger to stability'. As Parsons put it, 'American thinking had swung round from an attitude of indifference to one of some hostility'.[9]

The Kennedy administration and the US payments deficit

If the Federal Reserve knew little about the Eurodollar until the end of 1960, it appears the people working in the US Treasury knew even less. While they had used the phrase, 'the so-called "European dollars" ' in March 1960, they did not use the term Eurodollar market until 1961. Nor, it seems, did they brief President Kennedy on its implications for the US dollar position until February 1962.[10] This is surprising for two reasons. First, Robert Roosa who had recently moved from the FRNBY to become Under-Secretary for Monetary affairs at the Treasury, must have been privy to the Holmes and Klopstock report. Although, perhaps, as in Britain, communication between the central bankers and the state officials in the Treasury was fraught with difficulty, as Robert Roosa said 'as soon as I got to the Treasury, I knew enough of the central banks to know that I wasn't welcome. I'd lost my spots' (Roosa, 1972: 94). Second, 1960 had witnessed short-term capital outflows, as Douglas Dillon put it, 'on a scale not seen since the twenties', and this trend continued into the early part of 1961.[11] In fact, throughout Kennedy's Presidency much energy and thought was given over to understanding, explaining and ultimately finding a solution to the persistent US payments deficits and the inter-connected problems of dollar 'over-hang', short-term capital movements and the threat to US gold stocks.

The US Treasury was concerned primarily with how to overcome the short-term capital outflow, and the US banking community had their own idea of how this could be achieved – by the effective abolition of Regulation Q and the raising of interest rates. There was a 'consensus among the bankers that some way should be found, either by statute or by regulation, to remove the limitation on rates of interest paid by member banks on all time deposits other than savings deposits'.[12] This had been argued since 1958, when the worryingly high level of foreign gold purchases of that year was thought by many to be a direct consequence of the low level of US interest rates. It continued to be made over the next few years as the US deficit problem deepened. Higher interest rates, and the reintroduction of more active monetary policy were, of course, exactly what the Kennedy Administration, and Keynesianists in general, wanted to avoid, as this would have a deflationary effect on the domestic economy. Any evidence which ran counter to this theory was therefore welcome. Thus, for example, in June 1960 Treasury thinking on this subject seemed to want to convince critics that an outflow of private dollar holdings, while resulting in a corresponding rise in official dollar holdings, 'may not give rise to large conversions of official balances into [US] gold', as this decision rests with the central banks of those countries whose dollar balances are rising, and not with the market. And central banks may not have wished to convert their dollars into gold and even if they had they may have chosen to acquire it through the London gold market rather than from the US. The attitude of the major European governments and their corresponding central banks was therefore crucial in this regard. Yet, there seems little awareness that where differential interest rates gave rise to an outflow of 'foreign liquid private capital', this would not necessarily result in a corresponding shift into official dollar liabilities'. In addition, once again, where rate differentials resulted in an outflow of US, as opposed to foreign capital, this is seen purely as having the effect of increasing both US gross foreign dollar liabilities and short-term assets abroad.

No mention was made of the alternative, a shift into Eurodollars, which would result in neither a rise in official dollar holdings nor an increase in short-term assets abroad.[13] In fact, successive policy announcements from the US monetary authorities demonstrate an unwillingness to recognise the significance of the Eurodollar market on global monetary affairs. Rather, all thinking seemed to be directed to the development of central bank co-operation, as a means of preventing the loss of US gold stocks that would almost certainly follow the continuing movement out of the dollar that was taking place at an increasing rate, not so much because of interest rate differentials, but out of rising fear of a dollar devaluation. This would have triggered a loss of US gold, had these central banks tried to re-establish their traditional 'gold to dollar ratios' by exchanging some of their newly acquired dollars for US gold. Instead, central bank co-operation, consequent to a meeting in Basle, on 13 March 1961, of the governors of eight leading European central banks, resulted in the Swiss and German central banks, rather than cashing in 'a very substantial part of the dollars they ha[d] indirectly gained from ... the Euro-dollar market' for US gold, lending them instead to the Bank of England, to replenish its reserves.

Hayes believed this to be 'a major development in inter-central bank relations – possibly of historic significance – [that] has actually taken place'.[14] Calleo (1982: 20) refers to the 'the temporizing policy known as ad-hocery', which is generally credited as the work of Roosa, and amounts to the setting up credit lines with other central banks, providing reassurances to foreigners about convertibility and discouraging US corporations from making foreign investments. To these measures can be added the monetary operations, Operation Stretch and Operation Nudge, where the Federal Reserve intervened, to keep the forward cost of dollar swaps down and to maintain short-term interest rates up at their Regulation Q ceiling. Yet, what does this policy say about US Treasury thinking on the Eurodollar market? For, an *offshore* dollar market standing outside of the official international monetary system, creating and trading private international liquidity in the form of a large fund of footloose dollars, is not necessarily affected by 'swap' arrangements nor the costs of forward exchange cover. As the *Banker* put it in 1963, 'No tampering with the forward rate, however, could affect the incentive to switch dollars from New York to the Eurodollar market. ... Here the prime consideration is the differential between money rates in New York and in the Euro-dollar market.'[15] It seems then that while Roosa and Dillon certainly knew about the existence of the Eurodollar market, until as late as the beginning of 1962 they either did not fully appreciate how it operated, or they underestimated its importance. This is perhaps surprising, given that it was the Eurodollar market, by acting, both as a *transmission belt*, linking the US and European money markets, and as a *staging area* for large quantities of footloose, largely foreign-owned dollar capital, that was intensifying the US dollar problem. For the operation of the Eurodollar market was having the effect of making short-term capital movements acutely sensitive and almost instantaneously responsive to interest rate differentials, which were themselves narrowing accordingly, while at the same time allowing for a gathering, or pooling, of liquid dollar capital which was large enough to mount 'market-led' speculative attacks on currencies regarded as 'weak'.[16] Most dangerously for the US position, the Eurodollar market was evolving into not only the primary source of credit for those speculators wishing to bet against the dollar, but also as Einzig (1971: 145) wrote, 'speculation in gold was financed almost entirely with the aid of Euro-dollars'. Rather presciently, Einzig continued, 'should a major dollar scare occur ... billions of Euro-dollars would be borrowed for the purpose of going short in dollars by selling the proceeds of the deposits'.

However, while there may not have been a complete understanding of the problems the Eurodollar market was creating for the US monetary system, there was an increasing awareness of the contrary: that the existence of this market was helping to keep the Dollar–Gold Standard on the road. For, by encouraging private recipients of dollars to hold onto them, the market was keeping dollars out of official reserves and thereby helping to prevent a further reduction in US gold reserves, notwithstanding central bank cooperation. Thus, while in 1960 almost all of the US deficit of $3.9 billion was financed by gold sales plus increased foreign *official* dollar holdings, in 1961 only half of the $2.5 billion deficit was financed this way, the rest being held in *private* dollar holdings.[17] Although, having said that, Dillon appeared to see this as more the consequence of international cooperation and 'ad-hocery'.[18]

The US and the Eurobond

Early in 1962 a new theme of US Treasury policy began to be aired, which was fundamental to the evolution of the Euromarkets, especially the establishment of the Eurobond market. This was to advocate the creation of a European capital market. It evolved out of the Treasury's attempts, not only, to find a solution to the persistent US payments deficit – specifically how to prevent the outflow of US capital – but also, to influence the increasingly vocal public debate on the subject, which was in danger of moving policy in directions that were unacceptable to the Kennedy Administration. For the popular view amongst the bankers and the international financial community was that the US was being lax in applying monetary policy and that, hence, interest rates needed to be raised 'as a deterrent to … foreign borrowing'. A leading advocate of this solution was John Exter of City Bank. Referred to within the US Treasury as the 'British method' it was opposed by them because of over-capacity in the US domestic economy and the connected problem of 'high unemployment'.[19]

An alternative solution to the payments problem, and one that it was rumoured Kennedy favoured, was the imposition of exchange controls. Naturally, this was vociferously opposed by the New York banking community, as Mr Rockefeller of Chase Manhattan made clear in February 1962, when, at a meeting with representatives of the New York City banks, Dillon suggested that the US makes 'more aggressive attempts to attract foreign investment here … and to reduce the incentive of investing abroad'. But Dillon was not implying the Treasury wanted to impose exchange controls. As Chapter 5 made clear, he was genuinely looking to Europe to finance its own development, encouraging European countries to become less reliant on US capital by creating their own capital markets. The answer, as he explained to Kennedy, was 'not ... new controls here but rather fewer controls abroad'.[20] To that end, he further explained that 'the Treasury and other officials are using their influence in every appropriate manner to secure the removal of governmental restrictions, and to encourage the development of local financing institutions ... within other large industrial countries'. Yet, as Dillon also correctly pointed out, 'up to 80 per cent of subscriptions to foreign issues placed in New York comes from foreigners', while the secondary market 'consists almost entirely of foreign buyers'. In other words, most of the capital being raised in the US on behalf of European customers was actually being provided by Europeans. Nevertheless, the following month, Dillon made his famous speech in Rome, pronouncing European capital markets as 'inadequate and out-moded' and making a veiled threat that unless something was changed, 'no solid assurance' could be given that the US capital market would continue to be available to raise foreign investment. Driven by the Treasury's need to see a reversal of the flow of capital between the US and Europe, he exhorted Europe 'to cast off those restrictions that still impede the free flow of capital'. Dillon and Roosa repeated their admonitions to the Europeans throughout the course of 1962 and continued both to check the forces calling for an increase in interest rates, and deny the rumours that the US intended to introduce capital controls. Dillon also chose to scotch an idea that had come to Kennedy's attention, that of asking US banks to voluntarily restrict their export of capital, something which, he explained, was unfeasible and would anyway only benefit foreign banks engaged in 'dollar lending activity'.[21]

Interestingly, the American bankers were not the only ones calling on the Kennedy Administration to tighten US monetary policy. The Europeans also wanted a rise in US interest rates, as a way that 'would at least dry up the Euro-dollar market'. However, the Treasury – which believed the problem was not so much that US rates were too low, but rather that European rates were too high – was becoming increasingly appreciative of the advantages of this market, in keeping foreign-owned dollars out of official reserves, 'from whence they would doubtless be presented for conversion into gold'. It was, therefore, 'by no means clear' that allowing the Eurodollar market to wither and die 'would be a desirable development'.[22] Yet, the debate between the internationalists and the national capitalists, between the nascent monetarists and the Keynesianists, regarding how best to deal with the balance of payments deficit was also taking place within what the *Wall Street Journal* called 'Washington's top financial authorities'. This was brought into the open in February 1963 when George Mitchell a Governor of the Federal Reserve Board, took the opportunity, while giving testimony to Congress, to urge the Kennedy Administration to introduce a special tax on movements of US capital to Europe to discourage European capital borrowing in the US. Mitchell's invitation to give evidence to the House-Senate Economic Committee was itself political. He had been deliberately invited by some Democrats on the committee because he disagreed with the Federal Reserve's Chairman, William Martin, over domestic monetary policy. Martin believed, as did Hayes at the FRBNY, that US interest rates should be raised, while Mitchell agreed with the Democrats that they were already too high.[23] It is in the context of this dispute, that the 'alternative' idea of introducing a tax to discourage foreign borrowing in the US capital market – what became the Interest Equalization Tax – should be viewed.

The *Wall Street Journal*, thought it 'doubtful' such a tax would be introduced, given the Treasury believed it would only result in 'a stampede of US funds to havens abroad'. But Dillon now felt it necessary to inform Kennedy that 'without program changes' the deficit problem would not go away, which, in turn, prompted Kennedy to ask the Cabinet Committee on Balance of Payments to 'survey the alternative courses of action' by the end of March – 'in the light of our new and more sombre expectations'. Within a week Dillon returned to his theme of creating a European Capital market. Nevertheless, the call went out to the advocates of various controversial policy proposals on how to deter the sale of foreign securities in the US capital market, to be ready to discuss the 'magnitude of benefits' that could be expected from their implementation. Dillon now advised Kennedy to refrain from any course of action 'that would frighten the financial community' and that it would be 'inadvisable to take drastic action now of a nature that would be inimical to our long run interests'. He recommended 'a firm decision against any action', adding that the Treasury was trying to persuade European countries of the 'inappropriateness of their using the New York market as a source of capital'. Consequently, no decision was made to introduce capital controls at the meeting of 18 April. The following weeks saw further attempts to head Kennedy off, with news, as Dillon told the New York Clearing House Bank Directors in May, that the 'past year' had seen 'an encouraging acceleration' in the efforts of European countries to liberalise their capital markets.[24]

Yet, notwithstanding an increasing awareness by the US Treasury of the benefits of the Eurodollar market, there is no available archival evidence to indicate that when Dillon first called for a European capital market he envisaged a long-term capital market financed with Eurodollars. For Eurodollars were regarded as essentially US capital and what they wished to see was the creation of a market utilising European capital, so as to reduce dollar outflows from the US. It even appears that only after Eurodollars began to be utilised to provide finance for long-term investment in Europe in early 1963, did it become clear to the US Treasury that this was a way dollar capital could be provided to Europe without aggravating the US deficit. Thus, it was as late as May 1963, that Dillon first introduced Kennedy to the wonders of the Eurobond market, explaining that because 'these dollars have already left the US, there will [be] no immediate effect on our balance of payments nor will there necessarily be in the future. Dollar borrowings abroad should therefore relieve some of the direct pressure on our balance of payments which has been created by foreign borrowings here,' [25] although, this would not apply if the Eurobond market started to be funded with Eurodollars that had been specifically attracted out of the US, a fact not mentioned to Kennedy.

Revealingly, eight months earlier, on 4 September 1962, Sachs wrote to Roosa and Martin and proposed a similar scheme. That is 'the establishment of intermediate-term interest-bearing credit instruments for stated maturities', financed in Eurodollars, as a way of providing 'a functional and flexible means for promoting international liquidity'. What Sachs envisaged, therefore, was 'the transcendence of the prior limitation of Eurodollars to short-term loan transactions'. He suggested the US should 'develop Eurodollars as an instrument for intermediate- and long-term capital issues'. He added by way of explanation, that 'through the extension of the timescape of the interchange in Eurodollars we can be performing the function of a supplier of long-term capital to Europe without aggravating our international payments imbalance'. Sachs wrote four more letters to Roosa and Martin, in July 1963.[26] He was particularly concerned about the proposed IET and suggested that it 'be abandoned and the function be carried out by the establishment of a Foreign Capital Issues Committee of private bankers and Federal Reserve Representatives [to] work on suitable measures for reducing the impact of capital outflows on our balance of payments'. Having already pointed out the dangers of the Eurodollar 'contributing to such reflorescence of both credit and capital extensions across national boundaries' so as to 'constitute a new international banking order', he expanded his idea that a way of preventing European institutions from continuing to pyramid dollar credit, with the ensuing danger of precipitating a further drain of US gold, was the 'supply-manipulation of Eurodollars' to feed a 'capital-hunger' in Europe.

Sachs, who had 'first hand knowledge of the transformations that have been accruing over the past year', believed the US Treasury and the Federal Reserve were unable to grasp both the significance of these developments in the use of Eurodollars and how they connected with the 'deeper issues in US balance of payments management'. He too made mention of the fact that from his 'personal experience' he 'can attest' that London and Paris investment banks 'know more and utilize more resourcefully' Eurodollars than their American counterparts. Later, just one day after it had been signed, Sachs emphasised to Roosa and Martin the implications of the role of the dollar in the Warburg 'Autostrade' issue.[27] Sachs ends one of his letters to Roosa with the observation that 'much more needs to be re-thought and reset in the international account. Here as elsewhere', he exclaims, 'the Pauline imperative applies: "Be ye transformed by the renewing of your mind ..."[28] However, to be fair to Roosa and Dillon and the US Treasury, this process of 'renewal' had started more than a year before, when, in early 1962, like the FRBNY before, they had begun to discover the unique characteristics of the *offshore* market in Eurodollars.

The US Treasury discovers the *offshore* market in foreign dollars

With short-term capital outflows continuing to exacerbate the US balance of payments deficit, especially in the last quarter of 1961, concern had grown in the Treasury to better understand these movements. A memo to Dillon, in August, had already wondered, with regard to an outflow of foreign-owned dollars, 'why so large a proportion of the total ... has taken the form of private dollar holdings rather than official holdings'. It concluded that in part 'this may represent an increase in private holdings from other parts of the world in the Euro-dollar market in London'. Another memo in December then refers to 'the "Eurofund" pool of money, estimated at about $1.2 billion' which was 'alert to rate differentials'. Nevertheless, archival evidence points to the fact that the US Treasury's knowledge of how the Eurodollar market worked and its significance for the US, was even then, very limited. In fact, it shows that it was really only during 1962 that the

Treasury's understanding grew, just as it had done for the FRBNY two years earlier. This explains why reference to the 'Eurodollar market', both in Treasury documents, such as memos to Kennedy and reports on the balance of payments problem, and in speeches by Dillon and Roosa, became increasingly common as the year progressed. For example, when, at the beginning of 1962, large quantities of dollars began to be transferred to Canadian banks, while simultaneously remaining invested in the New York money market, Roosa recognised capital movements which 'seem[ed] to be different in nature'. Just like the FRBNY before it in 1960, the Treasury was puzzled, as a memo from Dillon to Kennedy on 18 January 1962 makes clear, 'we are working ... to analyse this problem further'.[29]

These dollar movements prompted Dillon to inform the Joint Economic Committee of Congress that there 'are serious questions whether our conventional classifications of short-term capital flows accurately reflect their true significance for the balance of payments. This difficult subject is presently a matter of intensive study'. He goes on, 'shifts recorded as an outflow were apparently promptly reinvested in the New York market by agencies of foreign banks'.[30] The use of the word 'apparently' in this context implies that Dillon did not quite understand the nature of these deposits in the Cano-dollar market, which, given that the FRBNY had been aware of what the Canadian banks had been doing since June 1960, is slightly puzzling. It is possible, therefore, that in the absence of any qualification as to what he meant by the 'New York market', or recognition that these 'reinvestments' were of any fundamental significance, that Dillon was talking about the US domestic money market. Yet, at that time, the only rationale for moving American-owned dollar deposits to Canadian banks was precisely the interest premium to be gained from lodging ownership *outside* of the domestic US money market. For, although the Regulation Q ceilings had been raised in 1957, interest could not be paid on time deposits of less than a 30-day maturity, or to corporations on savings deposits, and in New York City no interest could be paid on commercial time deposits at all (McKenzie, 1976: 95). These rules applied equally to all foreign dollar deposits held in the US, and continued to do so until October 1962.[31] They did not, however, apply to dollar 'advances'; that is dollars deposited with foreign banks then advanced back to their agencies in New York. This was, therefore, the only way foreign banks could place funds on the New York market at call. In this way, the agencies of Canadian banks in New York became dominant players in the market for so-called 'street' loans.

The FRBNY's analysis of these particular dollar movements, while somewhat ambivalent and confusing, mentions the all important fact that reserve requirements were not applicable to such dollar deposits. For, while US rules governing reserve requirements were applicable to 'branches' of foreign banks resident in New York, they did not apply to 'agencies' of foreign banks operating in New York, as they were deemed to come under the national banking legislation governing the operations of their Head Office; in this case Canadian banking regulation. However, that reserve requirements were not applicable in any form would suggest that in the case of these deposits, Canadian domestic banking regulation did not apply either, and, as with the treatment of Eurodollars in London, that they were deemed by the Bank of Canada to, exist, effectively, *offshore*.

For, what appears to have taken place was not that the dollars themselves had been transferred to banks domiciled in Canada, as dollars cannot officially leave the US domain, but rather that their title of ownership had left the US. Title was now lodged in a 'Foreign Market for Dollars' operating in Canada. In the case of the Canadian banks, they had increased their deposits denominated in foreign currencies by 165 per cent between 1956 and 1962. While those dollar deposits that concerned Dillon and Roosa were advanced by their Canadian bank owners back to their agencies in New York, to take advantage of a prime lending rate of 4.5+ per cent which had prevailed there since early 1959, a substantial percentage of these increased dollar deposits were re-invested in the Eurodollar market in London and Paris. In this way, Canadian banks played a very important role as suppliers of Eurodollars. The US Treasury appears not to have fully understood the nature and significance of these dollar movements because it was unable to comprehend the essential unique character of a 'foreign dollar market'. Had they consulted the Holmes and Klopstock (1960a: 24) report they would have realised the US banks in question had tapped into the 'Eurodollar transmission belt'.[32] They would not only have been made aware that this market 'greatly facilitates interest arbitrage operations', thereby increasing the sensitivity to interest rate differentials and forward exchange rates, but they would also have been forewarned that should American investors become alert to the possibilities this offered and 'become more sophisticated in the use of exchange markets and money markets abroad ... effects on the United States balance of payments could be considerable'. Nevertheless, the US Treasury was learning more about the Eurodollar market and this knowledge was beginning to filter upwards.

Three weeks after Dillon's 'puzzled' memo to Kennedy, Roosa explained the phenomenon of the Cano-dollar market to the American Bankers Association.[33] Beginning with the fact that short-term capital outflows 'will have accounted for roughly three-quarters of the total deficit in the United States balance of payments' in 1961, he concluded that this did not reflect 'a flight from the dollar', as confidence in the currency was high and foreign private holdings of dollars had risen and gold losses had fallen. Nor, he added, could these movements be explained as a consequence of interest rate differentials, as rates between the world's financial centres had narrowed. So, he asked them: 'What does this mean?' Roosa was perhaps unfamiliar with recent developments in the Eurodollar market, otherwise he would have known, for example, that although interest rate differentials between the US and Europe had narrowed, the differentials required to attract deposits into the Eurodollar market remained (Altman, 1960–61: 325, 1962: 301). Four days later, a Treasury report was produced which explained the Eurodollar and Cano-dollar markets in considerable detail, seemingly for the first time.[34] Referring to them variously as having formed a 'secondary dollar financing system', and 'a competitive banking system in dollars in Europe', through which international trade was being financed, the report stated that 'it is believed that most Euro-dollar deposits are held by foreign bankers and traders, though some US residents make such deposits, particularly in branches of US banks abroad'. Seeing the Cano-dollar market as 'a similar competitive system' to the Eurodollar market, the report then wondered whether the former was going to be 'a steady factor' in the US balance of payments position 'with a trend of its own', and 'if so, why?' The report concluded by pointing out that 'in both 1960 and 1961, a very large part of the growth in recorded outflow of short-term private capital from the US remained denominated in US dollars. That is to say the US holder of these claims was not moving out of the US dollar into a foreign currency'. In fact, according to the report, approximately 75 per cent of the outflow of short-term capital in 1960/61 was not exchanged into foreign currencies. This is very important as it is the earliest reference to the fact the US Treasury was becoming aware that a substantial amount of the dollars flowing out of the US was not, by definition, automatically flowing into other currencies, that, in fact, there existed a 'foreign market for dollars'.[35]

Two days later, on 14 February 1962, Roosa informed Kennedy that the 'balance of payments is worsening', and explained to him some of the intricacies of the Eurodollar market, apparently for the first time.

Yet, three weeks later, another Treasury report referred, rather incredulously once again, to 'significant amounts of dollar claims [are] believed to be held in the form of dollar-denominated deposits in banks abroad, particularly Canada', some of which 'are believed to be employed in the US money market'. Even Henry Alexander, Chairman of Morgan Guaranty, at a meeting between Dillon and the New York banks, 'mentioned the large deposits of US dollars that had been made in Canadian banks with no conversions of the US dollars into Canadian dollars and wondered whether this constituted a real capital outflow'.[36]

Following the panics in the foreign exchange markets that commenced on 28 May 1962, which, it was felt, were a direct consequence of the popular belief that the 'dollar was in trouble', Dillon spoke to the New York Financial Writers Association. Turning to the problem of the US payments deficit, he expressed some bewilderment that the short-term capital outflow of 1961 was almost as great as in 1960, given that in 1961 the 'much improved atmosphere of international cooperation' had brought about a narrowing of interest rate differentials and 'an absence of the speculation against the dollar which had been such a disruptive influence in 1960'. Interestingly, a third of the 1961 outflow came under the category of 'unrecorded transactions'. While the Treasury was 'making efforts to learn more about this mysterious category' Dillon wondered 'what significance, if any, this category carries for our international position I defy anyone to determine with accuracy'.[37]

Of course, if these puzzling transactions concerned dollars flowing into the Eurodollar market, they were not something that could be understood with reference to the traditional international financial system, where all international capital flows are between national financial centres only, where every dollar credit flowing out of the US must, by definition, be flowing into the monetary systems of other countries, becoming, in the process, a dollar liability. Yet, while Eurodollars are ready and willing to flow into whatever country offers their owners the best deal, they can just as well remain *offshore* in a parallel international money market, where the absence of reserve requirements allows banks to operate on narrower margins and hence offer more competitive rates to both borrowers and lenders. Then again, it should not be forgotten that in the early 1960s central banks were themselves probably the largest operators in the Eurodollar market, as those countries running balance of payments surpluses used it to mop up their excess dollars so as to maintain their currency parities within the Bretton Woods System and to control domestic money supply.

While the Kennedy Administration had implemented more than 30 different measures to improve the dollar position, as 1962 progressed it became clear that the deficit problem was intensifying and becoming more intractable. The US Treasury became increasingly concerned that if their policy of 'ad-hocery' was seen not to be working, they would be forced to agree to the use of more drastic measures; principally, either/or both, the raising of interest rates or/and the application of capital controls, neither of which the Kennedy Administration wished to see imposed. It is in the context of this intractable balance of payments problem that we see the US Treasury taking an ever intensifying interest in the operation of the Eurodollar market. For example, meetings in Washington in April, between senior representatives of the US and UK monetary authorities bring up the subject for the first time, and demonstrate US doubts and concerns. Then, in July, a report on short-term capital outflow from the US wondered where exactly the outflow had gone. Then, in September the correspondence between Sachs and Roosa, shows that Sachs, – anticipating the Eurobond market by a matter of some months – had made a proposal 'for supplementing the currency swap transactions by developing Eurodollars into "intermediate-term interest-bearing credit instruments" for stated maturities'. This, he added, had been 'recommended for development "as a functional and flexible means for promoting international liquidity" '. Finally, on 3 October 1962, O. L. Altman drafted an outline for a discussion of Eurodollars at a Treasury meeting on the balance of payments. Questions to be asked included, would global currency holdings be increased through pyramiding? and what would happen if foreign banks operated on a fractional reserve system with regard to dollars, thus creating dollars? The third subject tabled for discussion was 'Need for Information'.[38]

The Treasury's need for information was confirmed two weeks later when John E. Smith, Deputy Manager of the New York branch of the French bank *Societe Generale*, expressed his amazement at the ignorance of the US monetary authorities regarding the Eurodollar market, noting that they had had to send representatives to Europe to 'find out what it is all about'.[39] Now he explained that his bank had 'strongly recommended to the Federal Reserve [that] Regulation Q ... should be rescinded in its entirety'. For the effect of this restriction was that 'the deposits of American corporations are now being successfully solicited by foreign bank agencies and branches in New York and then poured into the Eurodollar market'. He added,

Yesterday I discussed the matter with a representative of the Bank of France, who ... appeared to miss the significance of the ... foreign siphoning off into the Eurodollar market of American corporate deposits. He (like so many others) was only hazily aware that in London, Montreal and in other countries, trading in dollar deposits has assumed greater importance than dealings in foreign exchange. The New York branches and agencies of foreign banks scour the country for American corporate funds, offer terms with which the American banks are forbidden to complete, then transmit them to their offices abroad, which, for consideration of a small brokerage introduce them into the Eurodollar pool.

Smith's concern was that the Eurodollar market, by attracting an outflow of US dollars, was not only exacerbating the payments deficit and eroding confidence in the dollar, but was also allowing dollars to pass into 'foreign control'. By rescinding Regulation Q, Smith believed an end could be brought to the Eurodollar market. But the Treasury dismissed Smith's criticism as over-reaction.[40] They admitted Eurodollar market operations could add to the US deficit, but saw this simply as an alternative way of providing credit to foreign users which otherwise 'might well have been extended by American banks at higher rates of interest' in the conventional way. They concluded therefore, that 'there is no net effect on the US balance of payments unless the amount of deposits which the Euro-dollar market attracts from the US domestic firms is larger than the potential foreign loans by New York banks which will be displaced by dollar financing provided by the Euro-dollar market'. They also rightly disputed the belief that rescinding Regulation Q and raising US rates would eliminate the market, as it was its ability to operate within narrower margins than the New York banks and outside the scope of the regulatory authorities that had driven its expansion, not just the level of interest itself. Most importantly they believed that it might be operating to reduce the drain on US gold reserves due to the fact that its higher interest rate structure might be having the effect of attracting 'more foreign dollar finds into commercial-bank assets and out of official reserves'.

October 1962 also saw release of the Kenen Report on Short-Term Capital Movements and the US Balance of Payments, which concluded that the sensitivity of short-term capital movements to interest rate differentials was 'not decisive', and therefore, by extension, as one Treasury official put it, 'sceptical' of a policy of raising time deposits rates in the US as a way 'to reduce the scope of the Eurodollar market'. If Kenen was to be believed, here was very powerful ammunition with which to counter the bankers' argument for a tightening of monetary policy and the rescission of Regulation Q. It also moved the debate in favour of those advocating the application of capital controls as the only effective method of halting the outflow of capital from the US – a debate that had become increasingly pertinent thorough 1962 and into 1963, as it became clear that no solution had been found to the US payments problem. Added to the findings of the Kenen Report were those of the Bell Report, which had come to the same conclusion. Yet, if the argument seemed to be moving increasingly against the bankers view, the US Treasury was not convinced, and in January 1963 received a report from the FRBNY prepared by Benjamin Cohen which, unlike the previous studies, found that 'private foreign dollar holders ... have demonstrated an important degree of sensitivity to interest rates'; and that short-term capital 'movements to Canada and ... Europe were strongly related to the Euro-dollar differentials'.[41]

It seemed to impress the US Treasury. For now, for the first time, it was more concerned about the effect of rising interest rates in the Eurodollar market than in national markets. So much so that by April a Treasury meeting shows Roosa becoming increasingly frustrated with the attitude of the Europeans in their promotion of the Eurodollar and their habit of using it as a means of 'financing trade ... with other parts of the world'. He singles out the British for particular mention, because they 'seemed to feel' it necessary to push up the interest rate on sterling to keep it ahead of the Eurodollar rate, which had the effect of forcing up the Eurodollar rate. Previously, rising rates for sterling would have only been considered in relation to inducing a movement out of dollars and into sterling. Even so, Sachs, for one, remained sceptical of the Treasury's knowledge of the subject believing that, for example, the committee appointed to examine the US payments problem would find issues such as the Cano-dollar market and 'the convoluted interacting between the extra-liquidity for the Continent by Eurodollars and the expatriated short-term funds of American corporations, beyond it'. He concluded, 'there are huge offsets to our short-term liabilities. But these basic offsets move into and out of what might be called financial clouds. So there are dynamic aspects surpassing and fluctuatingly transforming the rubrics of accounting'. Dillon disagreed and told Kennedy that Bach was 'simply wrong'. That, in fact, the 'short-term rate problem can be measured by the differential between our rates and foreign rates, particularly in the Euro-dollar market, which amounts to about 0.75 per cent of 1 per cent'. Dillon suggested that the President might 'enjoy a talk with the leading man in this particular field, Edward Bernstein'.[42]

Rising awareness of the danger of the Eurodollar market is further evidenced by the fact that, on 22 April 1963, Hayes explained to the

Economic Club of New York that the damaging volume of short-term capital flowing out of the US was 'partly … due to the tendency of corporations, and sometimes banks, to take advantage of the higher rates obtainable abroad, often in the Euro-dollar market'. Then, in June, a FRBNY memo which, while acknowledging the 'usual point that the Euro-dollar market might serve to restrain the flow of dollars to foreign central banks' – making US gold stocks less vulnerable – 'noted a number of disadvantages, such as the risk of credit pyramiding, the balance of payments effects of placements of American corporate funds in the Euro-dollar market, the undercutting of New York as a financial center, etc.'. The memo goes on to ask what can be done to 'limit the growth of the Euro-dollar market or possibly even to curtail its scope'. It concludes that the differential between interest rates offered in New York and the Eurodollar market 'had been and remains the main stimulus to the Euro-dollar market'.[43]

In July, Dillon admitted to Congress that the FRBNY now believed short-term capital flows were sensitive to interest rate differentials after all. That their recent report, in fact, stressed that movements of trade credit to Europe and those funds moving to and from Eurodollar accounts were especially sensitive to such differences. For, while rate differentials were of little importance to foreign official dollar holders – unless, of course, they were encouraged to move their holdings into the Eurodollar market – 'private foreign dollar holders – at least those on the continent of Europe – do seem to be concerned with relative short-term yields here and abroad'. The report estimated that a rise in US rates would be likely to 'reduce private switching out of dollar assets by as much as $600 to $700 million in a year'. This, it continued, would have the effect of 'decreasing the outflow of dollar liabilities to foreign official institutions by the same amount' and consequently, 'while this would not reduce our deficit … it would protect our gold stock'. The report also makes the point, seemingly lost on US Treasury officials up to then, that when US investors 'choose between US money-market assets and Euro-dollar deposits, they naturally pay no attention to the forward exchange market'. Three days later Dillon told the Joint Economic Committee much the same. He also admitted that the sensitivity of short-term capital flows to interest rate differentials was 'an area that has until recently received comparatively little study', though, as he added, he thought this 'perfectly understandable since the free and large scale movement of short-term capital dates only from the end of 1958'. He also announced that he had ordered the banking sector to provide the Treasury with more detailed information on capital movements, and had appointed a committee of business and academic economists, chaired by Edward M. Bernstein, to study the results.[44]

On 14 July, the ABA published a statement calling for higher short-term interest rates, 'strongly commended' the current and previous administration for rejecting direct controls, and re-iterated its opposition to selective controls, as ways of improving the balance of payments position. Two days later the Federal Reserve increased discount rates from 3 to 3.5 per cent and the maximum rate on time deposits and certificates with maturities from 90 days to 1 year, to 4 per cent. According to the *Banker* this action 'was intended primarily to halt the flow of dollars into [the Eurodollar market]'. However, any satisfaction the bankers may have felt was very short-lived, as on 18 July, President Kennedy proposed the Interest Equalization Tax (IET). Two days later *The Times* commented presciently that London had been provided with 'an opportunity for a great expansion of its entrepôt capital issue business, particular in dollar loans'. The *Banker* agreed, recognising the wide scope for evasion of the IET 'through the highly-organised Euro-dollar market, whose operators are unlikely to be slow in seizing any opportunities created by the higher cost of finance to overseas borrowers in New York'. The *Wall Street Journal*, however, seemed somewhat oblivious to the damage the IET was about to wreak on New York as an international financial centre, as were the New York bond markets. Not Morgan Guaranty's Henry Alexander. Legend has it, that he gathered his senior executives together and announced, 'This is a day you will remember forever. It will change the face of American banking and force all the business off to London.'[45]

While these events should have stimulated the US Treasury to gain a better understanding of the evolving international monetary system and the evolution of private international liquidity, archival evidence is somewhat ambivalent in this regard. Thus, when in October 1963 Roosa eventually replied to Sachs' earlier letters he simply informed him that 'we will now be undertaking a very thorough review of the international monetary system in cooperation with other members of the Group of Ten'. He added, casually, 'incidentally, we will hope in the course of these studies to get a better picture of the operations of the Euro-dollar market'. Then, the following day, at a meeting to discuss the progress of the Bernstein Committee, Roosa stated that the US 'needed a new balance-of-payments concept, fundamentally a "change in reserves approach" '. Minutes of the meeting show that 'Mr Roosa noted that we must be aware of the US commercial bank involvement in the Euro-currency market'. If Roosa's reactions seemed to betray a certain degree of complacency, a letter sent to Roosa a few days later, did not. It expressed the rapidly emerging view that the Eurodollar market was dangerous. It stated that it was 'the transnational reservoir of previously transferred expatriated liquid capital ... currently augmenting US corporate liquidity abroad that [was] far more potent than the conventionally designated Euro-dollars derived from the excess of dollars held by European central banks, directly, or indirectly'. The letter called for an 'independent inquiry aimed at uncovering the nature and significance of the volumetrics of the disruptive forces that have come in the wake of ... over-prolonged chronic state of dollar uncertainty, to wit, the corporate "hot money" Euro-dollars'.[46]

The following day, a draft of a report on the 'economic functions performed by the Euro-dollar market' was produced which provided the Treasury with a very comprehensive description of the market, how it operated and who dealt in it. Here, for the first time, a differentiation was made between the two types of institutions seeking deposits in the market – 'credit mobilizers' and 'end users', principally in terms of their 'motive for transaction'. The former, the report explained succinctly, comprised 'from 60 to 100 well-known international banking institutions dispersed in an unregulated world wide market outside the control of any monetary authority ... [trading] freely in dollar deposits with each other', and the latter, institutions seeking funds which were needed, principally, to finance international trade. The report explained that for 'credit mobilizers' transactions in the Eurodollar market were, therefore, essentially an 'interest rate phenomenon' and, as such, they performed a market arbitrage function, while, by contrast, for 'end users' they were made 'largely on the basis of three principal considerations: cost, availability and exchange rate'. It was the former type of operator whose activities had resulted in the pyramiding of 'an international chain of credit transactions', one of four ways in which, the report concluded, the Eurodollar market had aggravated a 'world payments disequilibrium'.[47]

In the same month a report prepared by the FRBNY, again emphasised that 'forward exchange rates do not apply to the Euro-dollar market insofar as the US investor is concerned, since investment in the Euro-dollar ... requires no purchase of foreign exchange'. Hence, it was the higher interest rates available *offshore* that attracted the US short-term investors. However, not everyone was convinced. The following month, when Roosa came to explain the official Treasury view on the nascent Eurobond market, he said the US was 'standing back to observe the evolution of the market for longer-term securities denominated in Eurodollars in Europe and that [they] had not yet taken a position'. He continued that they felt that 'the market was new and tender and that [they] wanted to know more about the way in which it might evolve before forming any judgement, either in principle or with respect to possible action'.[48] A few days later Weir Brown, Deputy to the US Permanent Representative to the OECD, informed the US Treasury that Switzerland opposed the issuing of bonds in London denominated in Swiss francs for fear that the rates offered would attract subscriptions from Swiss residents. For this would have the effect of depleting the Swiss market of franc savings, which, in turn, would push up interest rates in Switzerland, thereby undermining the Swiss policy of keeping them relatively low. Brown wondered whether there were 'implications ... for the US'. Was there 'an analogy between the Swiss position and that of the US with regard to loans floated abroad but denominated in Dollars?' The Swiss believed there was and used it to justify their opposition to the bond issues, claiming 'that Roosa expressed a similar opposition to dollar loans floated on foreign markets'. Roosa denied it. Yet the previous May he had complained to the Bank of England that they should reconsider their *laissez-faire* attitude to the Eurodollar market.

Discussing the Euromarkets with Britain

During 1962, with the deficit problem intensifying and becoming more intractable, the US Treasury's understanding of the Eurodollar market had become, both, more sophisticated and more critical, reflected in the increasing frustration felt by the US at the British attitude to their dollar problems. Beginning on 12 March 1962, Dillon informed Kennedy that the British had made it clear to him they regarded 'sterling as a reserve currency fully equal to the dollar' and that he believed 'they considered the strengthening of sterling as the great need in the present situation, without regard for any affect their actions may have on the dollar'. Dillon added that, 'as we see it, they are, in fact, putting sterling first and the international monetary system second – a totally different attitude from that of the Central Bankers on the continent'. He concluded, 'We cannot continue being tenderly protective of sterling as we carry out our program for full balance of payments equilibrium to defend the dollar'.[49]

US criticism of the Eurodollar market itself became overt during a series of discussions between senior representatives of the US and UK monetary authorities, that also demonstrated the growing gulf of opinion opening up between the two. In April 1961, the Fed's growing 'hostility' towards the market, expressed in conversation with Maurice

Parsons in Basle, had led to some discussion within the Bank. Where the view was that the US, in its determination to maintain 'the restrictive effect of Regulation Q' was itself largely responsible for the growth of the Eurodollar market. Consequently, as Kynaston (2001: 269) points out, the Bank 'refused to be moved from its policy of benign neglect'. With Parsons noting some days later that the market served 'a useful purpose' and concluding, as has already been mentioned in Chapter 5, that 'it would not be in the interests of international trade that it should be suppressed'.[50]

In 1962 the subject came up again. Beginning on 8 March, a very important, high-level meeting took place in Washington, attended by, amongst others, Roosa, Martin of the Federal Reserve, Hayes and Coombs of the FRBNY, Cromer and Preston of the Bank of England, and Sir Denis Rickett of the British Treasury.[51] Minutes show that Cromer began the discussion by complaining that the 'secondary effects' of the US payments deficit were causing the UK 'some concern and difficulties'; for the dollar outflow was affecting the 'Euro-dollar market which … was not in a particularly healthy state'. Replying, Roosa 'agreed that the Euro-dollars presented problems, both statistically and as to their significance', because they 'involved dubious pyramiding of inter-related credits … the classical case of the sort of pyramiding which preceded the 1929 collapse'. Here he confirmed, was 'the same pack of cards structure', a matter for 'serious concern'. Roosa also admitted there 'were differences of view on the US side as to what action we should take'. He concluded by saying 'he would welcome any thoughts from the British side as to what could be done'. Cromer replied that 'they were in no position to give any, but that they were looking into the problem, and would discuss it with [them] later if they found anything of interest to the US'. He concluded by stressing that finding a solution to the problem of the Eurodollar market 'was important to all of us'.

It is almost certain that the meeting of 8 March 1962 witnessed the first detailed discussion the US and British monetary authorities had had on the Eurodollar, because minutes of that meeting also reveal the subject had only been 'briefly discussed at earlier meetings'. Yet the minutes of such an earlier meeting, one held on 5 January 1962, not only make no direct reference to the Eurodollar market, they also show far less awareness of the problematic being created by its existence, with Roosa referring to the 'rather odd nature' of capital movements in the fourth quarter of 1961.[52] Thus, while he paid 'particular attention' to these movements, referring to the 'substantial shifts in bank balances from some large banks in New York to Canadian agency banks in

New York reflecting interest rate regulations', he made no mention of the Cano-dollar phenomenon, nor any reference to the pyramiding of credit, which seemed so important at the discussions two months later.

The following year, on 9 April 1963, at another meeting between US and UK representatives, it was acknowledged that the Eurodollar market 'certainly had become an important element in international liquidity and very responsive to changes in comparative interest rates'. The British were asked if they 'had any new information on the Euro-dollar market'. Roosa remarked again that the market 'was potentially a vehicle for instability' and 'not completely welcome', although, he added, it is 'also an important part of liquidity' and 'could not be done way with now'. However, Roosa was quickly becoming frustrated with the attitude of the British, as the minutes of a Treasury meeting held just one week later make clear. Emile Van Lennep, Chairman of the Working Party, 'commenting on the degree to which Britain had benefited from the operations of the Euro-dollar market, noted that inflows of dollar deposits helped the British reserve position'. Roosa then observed that 'the Euro-dollar market had now become more active in London than the ordinary money market, so that London had become an international financial center of a new type'. John E. Smith *of Societe Generale* commenting on these Washington meetings, where he saw the US and UK 'entirely at cross purposes', claimed the British viewed 'dollar weakness as a sterling advantage', and had a 'large vested interest' in a higher price for gold – developments which flowed naturally from the growth of the Eurodollar market.[53]

Roosa made his impatience with the British clear at the beginning of May 1963, when he arrived at the Bank of England and announced that the US was 'increasingly worried about the Euro-dollar market'. He explained that he had discussed the problem with the US banking community and suggested they 'ask themselves whether they are serving the national interest by participating in this sort of activity which adds to the volume of short-term capital outlay from the US'. Although, he added, he was not 'optimistic about the outcome'. This visit came just three months after Cromer had informed Sir Charles Hambro that Eurodollar business was 'par excellence an example of the kind of business which London ought to be able to do both well and profitably' and that the Bank did not believe 'the existence of risks provided any reasons for our seeking to restrict the development of this market'. Roosa was now of a different mind. He informed the Bank that he felt 'that [their] attitude to the Eurodollar market and Eurocurrency markets generally, needs to be considered further'. In July, Cromer attempted to re-assure the FRBNY, which was becoming increasingly concerned that the newly formed Eurobond market was encouraging holders of dollars to avoid the recently enacted IET. He wrote to Hayes,

> It would seem to me that operations of this character, in so far as they provide useful employment of existing externally held dollars, are, if anything, a stabilising factor in the Euro-dollar market. If, on the other hand, they were to attract new funds from the US, then clearly this would be something which would only aggravate your own position. My feeling, therefore, is that we should watch these operations carefully, and providing one can accept the assurances of the sponsors that the funds are being found form externally held dollar resources, then we should do nothing to discourage. I think it unlikely that the volume of this type of operation will grow to any very great extent, and it should be well within the means of the existing Euro-dollar market to take this sort of operation in its stride.

Hayes responded by phoning Cromer and pointing out that while, 'in general', the FRBNY agreed they 'could afford to stand aside and observe developments, especially as to the source of the dollars used to take up these issues, he 'would be reluctant to see a sudden burgeoning of such issues under present circumstances'. Cromer assured him that 'he fully understood this attitude and would make a careful note of this aspect'. Yet, surprisingly, the US Treasury left it until as late as December 1963 to ask the Bank of England to clarify the UK's 'rules and practices as regards the transactions ... [UK] banks might undertake in U.S. dollars'. The Bank replied in writing: 'Lending by Authorised banks against Euro-dollar deposits ... is not controlled, as regards amount, nature or tenor. Though cases like Ira Haupt might give us pause, reliance is placed on the commercial prudence of the lenders.'[54] If the US were looking to London to find a way of restricting the Eurodollar market they were to be disappointed, for when the US Comptroller of the Currency took up residence in London in order to inspect American banks, he got no support from the Bank of England, with the Bank's James Keogh saying, 'It doesn't matter to me, whether Citibank is evading American regulations in London. I wouldn't particularly want to know' (cited in Mayer, 1976: 454).

With the establishment of the Eurobond market and the utilisation of dollar capital to fund European investment, another, more prosaic, problem began to occupy US thinking. Where previously US investment houses had made easy commissions from bonds issued in New York on behalf of European clients, now they were being issued in Europe and

US banks were losing out. By April 1964 the Bank of England had been informed that 'the US Treasury would wish that in all future issues in this market denominated in dollars a New York house should be included amongst the list of underwriters'. In fact they 'further expressed the view that it would be appropriate that a New York house should take a leading participation in any such underwriting'. The Bank's reaction was to make sure that the US Treasury understood that this was not possible. To do this Cromer sent Hayes at the FRBNY a copy of a letter he had sent to the Issuing Houses Committee which makes the Bank's view clear that 'in a London issue the leader of the syndicate must, in our view, be a London house'.[55]

Coming late to the feast

In August 1963, in the immediate aftermath of the introduction of IET, the *Banker* published an article entitled 'America Tackles its Deficit', from which the popular view that the US Monetary Authorities actively supported the early development of the Eurodollar market, can be easily derived. It states,

> Until a few months ago, the Fed looked kindly upon the Euro-dollar market as providing a useful employment for non-resident dollar balances – and thus a useful incentive to hold them. The signs that an increasing volume of American-owned dollars were finding their way into the market, however, have caused the Fed to take a less benevolent view. For where the dollar balances are American-owned their employment in the market swells the balance of payments deficit, as officially computed.[56]

Any antagonism the Fed might have had towards the Eurodollar market after 1963 is not then an issue, and, in fact, was confirmed by Hayes when he told the President of the Federal Reserve Bank of Cleveland, in April 1964, that 'the Treasury and the Federal Reserve System ... have been concerned over the growth of the Euro-dollar market and the questions this has raised as to unsound banking practices in certain areas'. But when did the US monetary authorities actually began to take 'a less benevolent view' of this market? If the *Banker* is correct, this implies that the Federal Reserve – given their concern as to the suscepti-bility of both foreign, and domestic-owned dollar deposits to short-term interest rate movements and the potential impact on the US short-term capital position and its gold stock – did not understand how the

Eurodollar market operated until the middle of 1963. Yet, while the Fed certainly appears to have woken up late to the existence and true nature of the Eurodollar market, as it did from 1960 onwards, it was not entirely sanguine over what it saw happening, which is why in January 1962, FRBNY officials discussed what could be done to prevent the capital outflows resulting from New York corporations transferring their deposits to Canadian banks, via the banks' New York agencies, and suggested that 'the Superintendent of Banks of New York should make sure that the Canadian agencies in New York are not accepting deposits'.[57] Although, it has to be said, as this chapter has demonstrated, it seems that the FRBNY was not entirely aware of what was happening with these dollar transfers in the first place. Did they, in fact, know, that in transferring these dollars to Canadian banks to get round Regulation Q, the US banks had tapped directly into the 'Eurodollar transmission belt'? But, either way, clearly, from 1960 onwards the Federal Reserve became increasingly critical of the operation of the market. In fact, it could only 'look kindly' at the Eurodollar phenomenon so long as it did not fully comprehend how the market operated. For, at the point where it understood the nature of this financial innovation it, necessarily, had to take a much 'less benevolent' view. To argue that the Fed supported the development of the Eurodollar market is, then, to argue that it did not know what it was doing.

What of the US Treasury's view of the Eurodollar market? From the evidence set out in this chapter it appears, at worst, that little was known or understood in Washington about the market until 1962; at best, that it was thought to be of no great importance anyway. But this history is somewhat clouded by the fact that because the Treasury was concerned to encourage European countries to develop their own long-term capital markets, it is assumed to have promoted the establishment of the Eurobond market, and by extension, the Eurodollar market, given the general inability to distinguish between these two distinct institutions. The fact that once up and running, the Treasury welcomed the Eurobond market as a mechanism for mopping up footloose Eurodollars and keeping them out of official reserves, does not constitute evidence that it supported its creation and development. The US Treasury wanted Europe to utilise its own capital, and the Eurobond market was again a market in dollar capital. Indeed, as a Treasury report analysing European capital markets, written in 1963, reiterated, 'the City should not delude itself that in arranging such lending it is responding to Mr Dillon's pleas that Europe should assist the dollar by liberalising its capital market'.[58]

Yet, given that the Treasury had in Robert Roosa a central banker who had moved from the FRBNY in 1961 to work for Kennedy, someone who, according to Douglas Dillon, was 'considered by market experts at the time to be the most knowledgeable person in the US regarding financial markets, foreign and domestic', is to imply that the Treasury must have been kept up to date with any innovatory developments in international finance, although much evidence suggests otherwise. And while Dillon says of Roosa that he 'cannot conceive that he did not understand the Eurodollar market as it existed at that time', he adds that 'it is perfectly possible that he did not foresee the extent of its future development'.[59] To that end he would have expected to rely on support from the Treasury research staff. However, according to Roosa himself, their 'capacity for creative contribution to the economic policy of the country was rather limited'. For, as he explained, while Harry Dexter White had in the 1940s 'created a division of monetary research ... which had attracted some of the ablest economists, at least on the financial broad world economic side', George Humphrey, Secretary for the Treasury under Eisenhower, had 'cleaned them out ... simply dissolved the unit' out of a paranoid fear that they were tainted with communism, and a feeling that 'every hangover from the Democratic administration was probably a sinister agent of a foreign power'. Roosa believed this action had 'blighted the Treasury for a long time'. He concluded that even as late as 1972 the Treasury had yet to be restored 'to the position of assured staff confidence that it had during W.W. 2'.[60] Not surprisingly then, in 1976 the Congressional House Committee on Banking produced a report which expressed amazement that the growth of the Eurodollar market had passed by almost unnoticed. It stated, '[its] growth has been encouraged by the absence of regulatory restraints and perpetuated by bank regulators who know too little to be able to determine whether and what form of regulation will be beneficial'.[61]

Given, that as the US payments deficit got larger, so did the Eurodollar market, then as the US Monetary Authorities got more concerned about the problem of the former, it became more pertinent that they became more aware of the danger of the latter. Until this time, the US Treasury showed little urgency in understanding the particular nature and character of this parallel international money market, creator of private international liquidity and pathway into an *offshore* world, which ultimately could not be controlled by any number of 'swap' arrangements, central bank cooperation, or by any existing mechanism for controlling speculative capital flows. Indeed, Roosa himself, who had little to say about the Eurodollar up to 1962, summed up its significance in 1967, as having 'greatly enlarged the scale' of speculative capital flows, 'in magnitudes much larger than anything experienced in the past, massive movements' (Roosa 1967: 56).

While, with hindsight, the importance of the creation of the Eurodollar market is clear, could it be argued that up until the middle of the late 1960s it was largely insignificant in terms of the volume of capital passing through it, so that the US monetary authorities could not have been expected to pay much attention to its evolution. Not really, as by late 1959 it seems over \$1 billion worth of funds were already passing through the Eurodollar market – more than total foreign bank time deposits, bankers' acceptances and the Treasury bill holdings of European banks in the US. In addition, by then, the Eurodollar market had already become the most important depository for European commercial banks to place their surplus funds (Holmes and Klopstock, 1960a: 8).

What is not under question here, is that one of the greatest problems faced by the Kennedy Administration was the growing US payments deficit and the threat this represented to US gold stocks. This resulted in the eventual stiffening of US interest rates that had long been called for by the US financial community. It may also explain why John Saxon, Kennedy's appointee as Comptroller of the Currency, might have taken 'an extremely lenient approach to banking regulations', as De Cecco (1976: 390) claims, and allowed the First National City Bank to launch the negotiable Certificate of Deposit (CD) – a 'very permissive view' that was extended to the big banks' other new service activities. These measures, which the American banking community exploited to the full, certainly, in themselves, made a large contribution to the re-structuring of the international financial system into one more responsive to private speculative capital flows, and hence more unstable. They also led to a strengthening of the Eurodollar market. Yet, these measures were simply taken as inducements thought necessary by the Kennedy Administration to reverse short-term capital outflows, especially of US-owned capital. There is no evidence that either the Kennedy Administration (1961–63) or the previous Eisenhower Administration (1953–61) acted intentionally to promote the development of the Eurodollar or Eurobond markets. In fact, during this period, especially the early part, as has been demonstrated in this chapter, the Federal Reserve Board, the FRBNY, the US Treasury, the President and President's Office, the New York banks and the wider US banking community, were all very late in realising the significance of the Euromarket phenomenon, and when they did they were all somewhat ambivalent as to its merits.

7
Public accountability v. private interest government

When Sir George Bolton, matter-of-factly described the creation of the Eurodollar market as the cobbling together of 'the bits and pieces that were floating about', he was alluding to the harnessing of the mighty greenback to the 'historical mechanisms' inherited from the old London Bill market and the *free* international financial system of the nineteenth century. Once he and his merchant banking chums in the City had substituted a dysfunctional sterling with the large quantity of dollars that had been circulating outside of the US – and for all intents and purposes outside its monetary control – since the late 1940s, it was possible for an unregulated money market to be reconvened – a system free from capital, credit and ratio controls. The 'private exercise of monetary authority' was back on track. In this way, a new global money medium evolved, anchored in an old institutional framework. A parallel international money market was created, able to operate effectively outside of British banking regulation but within British sovereignty: an *onshore external market* trading in Eurodollars, otherwise and most commonly described as *offshore*.

The evolution of the Euromarkets poses then important questions with regard to the structure and behaviour of the British state. The institution of the Bank of England and its relationship with the City is particularly significant. For the Bank is the proverbial 'poacher turned gamekeeper' – a private bank until nationalisation, yet regarded as having become a *de facto* state institution long before that, as it had slowly acquired central bank responsibilities in the eighteenth and nineteenth centuries. Yet, even when it eventually became a bona fide state institution, there seems little dispute that not much actually changed, its institutional autonomy remaining virtually intact into the 1970s. How then is the Bank of England of the late 1950s and early

1960s to be regarded – as a public or a private institution? Or is this perhaps a somewhat misleading distinction? Could the position of the Bank in Britain's body politic during this period be better considered in terms of the notions of 'public accountability' on the one hand and 'public interest' on the other, as well as 'governance', or, more specifically, the 'governance of regulatory space', concepts that transgress the discrete public/private, state v. market divide.

The Bank of England and public accountability

The 1946 Bank of England Act which brought the Bank formally into the state sector, is, as Fforde (1992: 13) points out, 'devoid of any reference to the wider purposes and responsibilities of central banking'. While, for example, Australia's central bank is statutorily responsible for carrying out monetary and banking policy to 'the greatest advantage of the Australian people in such a manner as will … best contribute to the stability of the currency of Australia, the maintenance of full employment and economic prosperity and welfare', no such formal requirement defines the Bank of England's responsibilities. When, in preparing for nationalisation in 1945, the Bank's Humphrey Mynors submitted a brief on this matter, including a legal formulation, it simply stated, 'The objects of the Bank will be within the limits of its power and in accordance with the policy of HMG from time to time to control the currency credit and banking system of the UK and to maintain and protect the value of the pound sterling'. Yet even this half-hearted requirement is missing from the final Bill.

The subject came up again a little later in relation to the Canadian banking system, where the system of 'joint responsibility' for monetary policy, shared by the Federal Government and the Bank of Canada, 'ensured that major differences of opinion were brought to the attention of Parliament and public'. However, the Bank of England had never accepted the notion of 'public accountability' (Sampson, 1965: 407; Fforde, 1992: 14). Thus, at this juncture it showed no inclination to want to assume statutory responsibility for monetary policy. While it fought successfully to remain operationally and institutionally distinct from government, it was happy to let government take full responsibility for policy and remain, to paraphrase Montagu Norman, 'an instrument of the Treasury'. In this way, it was actually offloading what responsibility it had unwittingly assumed over the centuries as a private central bank, and which had brought it much criticism and condemnation, particularly during the inter-war years. It neither wanted to become a government department, nor to take responsibility for its actions. Nationalisation gave the Bank authority without responsibility. However, though the Bank has no constitutional notion of 'public accountability', clause 4(3) of the 1946 Act does require it to regulate commercial banks in the 'public interest', a notion that in practice seems invariably to revolve around the totem of sterling. It is no coincidence, of course, that behind the apparently apolitical, neutral but nationalist symbol of monetary sovereignty that is sterling, lies a set of private interests which, over the years, have acted in such a way as to expose the artifice of the state v. market, public/private dichotomy and reveal the incestuous relationship that for so long existed between the Bank and the City, specifically, between the Bank's executive members, made up of Bank officials and non-executive directors, the most influential of whom were traditionally drawn from the City's merchant banking community.

In 1969, in what would be a last hurrah in the Labour Party's long struggle to open up the Bank to democratic scrutiny and control, Governor O'Brien used the notion of 'national interest' to clarify to the Select Committee on Nationalised Industries, the Bank's view of its role as an intermediary between the state and the market. Noting that the Bank was 'an arm of Government in the City', O'Brien also thought it fair 'to claim that the Bank has an understanding of the legitimate interests and needs of City institutions'. He qualified this statement by concluding, 'If, however I think that what they are asking for is contrary to the national interest I will tell them to go away and think again. I am not then the representative of the City but I do represent City interests where I think it is right and proper to do so'.[1] While this may appear perfectly reasonable, to repute any suggestion that the Bank is an instrument in the hands of City interests, it was not enough for O'Brien to claim that proof of the Bank's autonomy from the City could be found at the point where the Bank's concepts of 'right' and 'proper' did not coincide with the interests of the City, if that point itself can not be located. In other words, he needed to show where he thought it was *not* right and proper for the Bank to represent City interests.

For example, with regard to the City's sponsorship of the Eurodollar market in the 1950s and 1960s, this would be where the Bank's view of its supervisory role came into conflict with the merchant and overseas banks' view of how they should be supervised. But, in practice, these views appeared to coincide in the main, as did their views on broader financial and economic policy matters, the pursuance of which they believed, unquestionably, to be correct, regardless of whether they might, in reality, have been contrary to government policy. Lord Cromer's confrontation with the Wilson Government in the 1960s demonstrated this. Suggesting that in 'matters of high finance ... the small circle of institutions' domiciled in the City, who were believed to posses 'an intuitive understanding of the "national interest" ' in the nineteenth century', as Cain and Hopkins (1987: 6) put it, remained hegemonic, that, in fact, Pollard's tiny section, concerned with international finance – the Inner City – was still able 'to present policies favourable to itself' as policies benefiting the British people. Yet perhaps it just too easy to jump to these conclusions, when what is needed is to examine the workings of the Bank of England at the time the Eurodollar market was established, if, that is, the problem of the Bank's institutional obsession with secrecy can be overcome.

Until the recent Freedom of Information Act, most state papers were closed for a minimum of 30 years. Not only that, but sensitive documents were, and still are, often 'weeded out', or kept closed indefinitely. The Bank, however, is not even obliged to open its papers, given its special status. A problem compounded by the fact that at an executive level, the Bank was traditionally very anti-bureaucratic, meaning, at least until the 1960s, that meetings were mostly conducted informally and little was ever committed to paper. Court proceedings were more like family gatherings, and the taking of minutes was, according to Henry Gillett, the present Bank archivist, perfunctory, if done at all. As for how the Bank interacted with Government, in relation to Britain's monetary and wider financial policy, custom dictated that this be done at meetings between the Governor and the Prime Minister, and, more recently, the Chancellor of the Exchequer, with no other persons present. We are therefore mostly denied the knowledge necessary to fully understand how and why decisions were made. However, coincidentally and fortuitously, at the very point in history which saw the creation of the Eurodollar market, an opportunity was provided, through the Parker Tribunal, to open the inner workings of the Bank's executive to public scrutiny. What was revealed challenged the commonly held belief of the time, that nationalisation had replaced the Inner City and its closed caste of City bankers, with a more representative and pluralist Bank Court (Davenport, 1974: 162; Daunton, 1992a: 124). Instead, it exposed the 'behind-the-scenes' policy making of the City's merchant banking community, largely hidden within the institutional structure of the British state, and confirmed, in the process, the survival and continuity of the Bank's historical role (van der Pijl, 1984: 192).[2]

The Parker Tribunal, or Bank Rate Tribunal, was set up in 1957 to examine whether Lord Kindersley and Sir William Keswick, Chairman of

Lazard Brothers and Director of Mathesons, respectively, had gained any pecuniary benefit from having had prior knowledge of a rise in Bank rate [coincidentally, the same increase that had stimulated the creation of the Eurodollar market] as non-executive Directors of the Bank Court. And although such providential use of insider information was not an unusual event in the 1920s and early 1930s, in this instance, after a vigorous campaign by the HM Opposition, especially the Shadow Chancellor, Harold Wilson, the government set up a public tribunal, under the chairmanship of Judge Parker to investigate these allegations.[3] Up until 1959, it was the long established custom for the Governor to discuss Bank rate with the Directors of the Court, who were therefore privy to any changes before they were announced. In 1957 these included, aside from Lord Kindersley – also a Director of BOLSA – and Sir William Keswick, Cobbold's uncle and Chairman of Hambro's Bank, Sir Charles Hambro, Lord Bicester of Morgan Grenfell, and once again, Sir George Bolton, who was also a part-time director of the Committee of Treasury, which was responsible for recommending any change of Bank rate to the Court.

The Tribunal was a whitewash. It duly established that the merchant banks in question had sold gilt-edged the day before the rate was raised from 5 to 7 per cent – as they had before Bank Rate increases in 1951 and 1955 – and that Kindersley and Keswick, 'both with some foreknowledge of the rate change, were directly involved'. But, it concluded, 'there had been no leak' (Fforde, 1992: 700). Interestingly, those Directors of the Court who Cobbold thought it important to consult, were those he thought, 'particularly qualified to give [him] an opinion about the likely effect of a 7 per cent Bank rate on sterling'.[4] This meant those directors involved in the foreign exchange market, that is the merchant bankers, and not those, such as Mr. Cadbury, Sir Alf Roberts and Sir Harry Pilkington who would have been more concerned about the effects of such a dramatic rate rise on industry (Devons, 1959: 9). Cobbold did not even consult the Chief Economic Advisor to the Treasury, Robert Hall, nor the Cabinet. But then, Bank Rate, as the Chancellor explained to the Parker Tribunal, was not a matter for Cabinet decision, the 1946 Act being interpreted, as having given the Treasury, and therefore the Chancellor, rather than the Government, power to issue directives to the Bank. In this instance, as already detailed in Chapter 4, the Chancellor and the Prime Minister were very reluctant to accept the Governor's recommendation to increase Bank rate, preferring instead to deflate the domestic economy by calling on the clearing banks to reduce their lending by 5 per cent. But finally, they had no alternative, as

Cobbold refused to give the banks such a direction.[5] Cobbold had demonstrated the Bank's essential operating independence. Yet this was mainly derived from a coterie of City merchant bankers who, as part of a closed kinship group on the Bank Court, took, as Cobbold told the Tribunal, an 'active and continuous part in forming policy'.[6] But the Tribunal took this to represent a potential conflict of interest, suggesting that remnants of the Bank's 'institutional schizophrenia', that is, the conflict of interest which had existed in the nineteenth century between the Bank's private and public role, was still evident in 1957. The issue, however, was even more contentious, as Cobbold was unwilling to even recognise that private interest could in any way conflict with the Bank's public responsibilities. He continued to call for retention of the *status quo*, going as far as submitting a special additional statement to the Tribunal to this end, 'on the grounds firstly that prior consultation ... was both useful and necessary, given the Court's responsibility for agreeing a change in the rate, and secondly that the integrity and *savoir-faire* of Directors was beyond question' (Fforde, 1992: 701–2). Mr Pitman, MP and former Bank Director, perfectly articulated the Bank's view during a debate in Parliament, when he argued that there could be no conflict of interest, because there was 'an identity of interest between such directors and the national interest', and that was in maintaining a stable pound (quoted in Hanham, 1959: 20).

Here we see that the instinctive notion of 'public interest' is one which has been conveniently used as a substitute for the lack of a constitutional commitment to 'public accountability' in the 1946 Act. This, in turn, allowed the maintenance of what was, in effect, an overvalued pound – maintained so, in continuance of its international role, through which the City could do business – to be presented as both economically rational and politically neutral, even while the effect of this policy was, once again, to debilitate Britain's manufacturing base and ultimately undermine the currency itself. For, largely as a result of the Bank of England's determined effort under Cobbold's leadership, sterling had remained a potent symbol and measure of both economic certitude and achievement, and national pride and sovereignty. Pitman's view was not, therefore, uncommon, pointing to the fact that even as late as 1957 the City was still able to have its private, pecuniary interests interpreted by the state – and even the wider public – as being identical to the wider public interest, by virtue of the fact that they converged around the almost totemic symbol of 'sterling'.

This mutual supportive concept pervaded the Bank's view of how control of the banking sector was to be enforced. In the 'absence of legislative sanction', the Bank of England, in the main, had always exercised its power in a 'highly arbitrary way'. This meant that banks would often have to have, as McRae and Cairncross (1973: 213–15) put it, a *'tête-à-tête'* with the Governor or the Chief Cashier to ascertain what was acceptable to the Bank.[7] While even top merchant or clearing banks were loath to risk presenting the Bank with a *fait accompli* in relation to their impending plans, US, and other foreign-owned banks, who relied on the Bank's goodwill to maintain their position in the City, had to be even more circumspect. Yet the City's banking community was reluctant to call for 'more specific guidelines' regarding what banks could and could not do, as this could only disturb the delicate balancing act which maintained the Bank's duel role as both *policeman of* and *spokesman for* the City. For, under this institutional arrangement, the Bank oversaw a financial system whereby it guarded its control over the British banking system from other state institutions, especially the Treasury – and from Keynesian-minded governments – as it had done so zealously since 1946, only to then delegate much of this authority, in turn, via 'representative associations', to the City's banks; enabling them to operate, to a great extent, on a self-regulating basis.[8]

When the institution of the Bank and the evolution of its supervisory role are viewed within the context of the City–Bank–Treasury nexus and Britain's wider historical state structure, which, as Moran (1984: 18) puts it, 'drew regulation away from the politics of Parliament and Whitehall, and into the City', this does not in any way seem incongruous. For the Bank of England, which until 1931 effectively controlled 'the financial policy of Great Britain', was not only an executive institution in which the government had 'no voice', as the Bank officially stated before the First World War, it was at the same time, according to the Macmillan Committee, 'a private institution practically independent of any form of legal control'. In the words of the then Deputy Governor, Sir Ernest Harvey, the Bank was 'practically free to do whatever it like[d]'.[9] While it lost some of its powers in 1931, it remained a private bank until February 1946, the same powerful 'pre-state institution' that had been founded in 1694 by the Protestant, Whig merchants and bankers who ran the City after the Glorious Revolution of 1688 had redefined 'the relationship of King, Parliament and the people' and with it, 'the political basis of public credit'.[10] The Bill of Rights that followed the deposition of the pro-French Catholic James II, not only ending the monarchy's absolutist tendency, but also allowing a 'financial revolution' to take place that established the institutional basis for the modern capital market, both public and private, with the Bank at its centre.

But its more immediate effect was to make available a financial fund sufficient to allow the incoming Protestant William III to successfully prosecute the Nine Year War against the French and turn England into the powerful 'fiscal-military state' that grew to dominate Europe in the eighteenth century. This was something that further embedded the Whig oligarchy – the 'financial interest' as it increasingly became – in the institutions of government, the City's financiers becoming prosperous and powerful as a consequence of their role as 'middlemen and brokers between the state and the public' (Brewer, 1990: 206).

The Bank of England then, was created to stand between the state and the market, as Gladstone put it, to 'induce moneyed men to be lenders' to the Crown, at a time when they would not otherwise have been willing to do so, the City having come to regard the Stuarts, as being 'justly in ill odour as a fraudulent bankrupt'. This had had the effect of not only bringing the financial absolutism of the monarchy to an end, but also of constraining Parliament, to the extent that, from this point onwards, the English state, as Gladstone wrote, 'came forward under the countenance of the Bank as its sponsor' and hence was forced to adopt a 'position of subserviency which it became the interest of the Bank and the City to prolong'. That is, in return for 'accommodating measures towards the government ... the government itself was not to be a substantive power in matters of finance, but was to leave the money power supreme and unquestioned',[11] the money power being the powerful Whig oligarchy, which consequently was able to withstand any encroachment upon its private business, preventing the English state 'from developing a major regulatory and control function' (Braun, 1975). In this way, the constitutional and institutional framework which emerged out of the Glorious Revolution allowed the City to operate, for the most part, outside the reach of government authority. In relation to the state, it existed, in modern parlance, *offshore* – a self-governing enclave, almost a sovereign state in its own right, the 'Vatican of the financial world', with the Governor assuming the role of the City Pope – a situation which flowed symbolically from the fact that the City of London was deemed never to have been conquered by William of Normandy. It therefore had its own troop of guards and the monarch was not even allowed into the Square Mile without permission of the Lord Mayor. This ancient right being, as Daunton (1989: 154) put it, 'inherited by the commercial and financial institutions of the City'.

This 'financial revolution' gave the City control of the financial market, because, in future, all loans to the state would go through the Bank of England, creating a new instrument – the national debt.

Most importantly, this arrangement, by ensuring property rights for private money interests, removed the danger of confiscation by the crown, bringing much needed security and stability, that had the effect of unleashing a large capital fund and laying the institutional foundations of modern self-governing capital markets in the City, the institutions evolving out of the establishment of a stable market for public debt providing the wherewithal for 'the parallel development of a market for private debt', with the Bank intermediating in both. In this way the 'gentlemanly revolution of 1688' cleared the path for a 'money ruling-class' to emerge, with the Bank of England at its head, that would become increasingly rich and powerful.[12] Braithwaite and Drahos (2000: 480) argue that the Bank's status as a 'pre-state institution' ended finally with nationalisation in 1946. Yet, from the evidence of Chapter 4, it would appear that to a great extent, it survived into the 1960s. Suggesting that the antecedents of the offshore market in foreign-owned dollars that emerged in the City in 1957, can still be found in this private fiefdom created in 1689, which managed to withstand the transfer of sovereignty to the British people that had begun the previous year.

The City and private interest government

When the City's merchant and overseas bankers happened upon a fund of foreign-owned dollars languishing in West European banks, and began using them for their burgeoning acceptance business in the late 1950s, it was only as a temporary replacement for sterling. They would continue to call for a strong and free pound and work towards the full re-establishment of its international role for the next ten years, no matter what the damage to Britain's manufacturing base. Yet, once liberated from dysfunctional sterling, while not a case of 'with one-bound-the-City-was-free', the effect of the Eurodollar market was to loosen the Keynesian straight jacket and make it possible for the City to find a way back to the future. As the 1960s and 1970s progressed, global capital gradually re-emerged and London again became home to the world's foremost international financial center, just as Britain's regard as an industrialised nation fell ever further into disrepute. But who would have predicted this in 1945, after Labour's landslide victory and the Attleeite settlement?

But while the advent of the Euromarkets might have acted as the proverbial philosophers' stone in the recovery of the City's glorious heritage, to most bystanders it fell almost unbeckoned into play, like a gift from the gods, as the long and ultimately futile battle to re-establish sterling's international role waged on – the defining project of Britain's post-war economic policy, led by a central bank determined to re-establish the liberal state, while a Keynesian-minded Treasury sat by, bemused. Once again the City had been successful in having its own private interests interpreted by the state as being identical to the national interest, if even by default. But how was this achieved? Longstreth (1979) answered in orthodox Marxist terms, suggesting that the City had 'penetrated' the state, through the medium of the Bank. But this explanation appears to pose a problem for Marxist theorists, in that it pre-supposes a confrontation between different capital fractions, *manufacturing* and *financial*, (or *financial/commercial*), quite contrary to the Marxist concept of 'finance capital', that fuses banking and industrial capital. However, for some, this apparent paradox was overcome by reference to the wider debate between the instrumentalist and the structuralist theories of the state, with the latter explaining that the state was 'relatively' autonomous, which allowed it to oppose the interests of individual capitalists when necessary, in order to sustain the capitalist system itself, as a whole. Yet, taking Trimberger's (1978: 4) criteria for 'autonomy', that the state apparatus is autonomous when state managers are neither recruited from, nor form close working relationships with, the dominant classes, it seems that the British state, in relation to the City, was far from 'autonomous'.

Ingham (1984) rejects Longstreth's instrumentalism for a different reason. He claims that rather than the Bank and the Treasury acting as passive 'instruments' doing the City's bidding, there has been a 'coincidence of interests' – centred around their mutual desire to maintain stable money – creating 'institutional relations of autonomy and interdependence', where policies which have benefited the City, have also suited the Bank and the Treasury for their own independent reasons.[13] However, while Ingham draws a more complex and realistic description of City–Bank–Treasury relations, their 'coincidence of interests' and structural and institutional inter-dependencies, can the unity he imposes on these relations be applied wholly to all policy areas, at all times? (Stones, 1988). Does Ingham's view of how the City influences policy fully explain the Euromarkets? Or even negate the broad thrust of Longstreth 'instrumentalism'? What is not in dispute is that the Bank saw no reason to break with the custom of self-regulation and hinder the development of the new market, despite the risks to Britain's gold and sterling reserves, and the potential difficulties the market posed in relation to monetary policy. It relied entirely on the competence and integrity of the bankers to conduct their business safely and prevent a repeat of the 1920s. That this group of men were their friends, colleagues or relatives was the only assurance the Bank's Governors needed. They all belonged to the small merchant banking community. The Treasury, meanwhile, continued to leave technical and monetary matters to the Bank, in keeping with the Norman/Snowdon compact of 1929, if not the 1689 Financial Revolution. In addition, relations between the Treasury and the Bank, at that time, were bad and communication poor, to the point that the Bank deliberately kept the Treasury in the dark about the new market until as late as 1963. Nevertheless, it should be said, the Treasury would almost certainly have supported any device which took the pressure off sterling. That the City had found an alternative money medium for its commercial and banking activities would therefore not have been wholly unwelcome news.

Perhaps 'capture' theory, which implies a view of the state as, less a unified cohesive actor with a universalistic rationality, and more a collection of agencies permeated by private actors pursuing particular interests, might better explain City–Bank relations. Yet without a concept of 'power' can it demonstrate how interests are translated into outcomes? How in fact does 'capture' occur? Power is certainly not missing from Cerny's (1993b: 164) explanation. He defines a hegemonic 'power nexus' which 'manifested itself not in the British state *per se*, but in the transnational network of *haute finance* with the City of London at its core'. Yet, while he explains where hegemonic power lies, in a 'civil society' dominated by 'socio-economic interests rather than an autonomous and politic-bureaucratic elite', how is this nexus able to operate so as to be hegemonic? Perhaps it would be useful to take one step back and look at the matter through the prism of a dynamic theory of how institutions like the City–Bank–Treasury nexus are created and how they evolve and change. Coates (2000: 176) points the way, explaining that 'behind' Britain's institutional structure lies a particular relationship between her financial and industrial fractions; between 'money' capital and 'productive' capital. In other words, the institutional structure originates in the realm of the accumulation process itself. Overbeek (1990: 25) explains that the interdependence of circulation and production 'is not confined by spatial limits ... [and] can take place in quite distinct geographical locations'. So the owners and agents of financial capital need not rely on domestic industry for accumulation to occur. However, because financial capital is ultimately 'abstract', there is an even more fundamental potential dislocation between these capital fractions, in the sense that it is not only 'spatially indifferent', but can be employed 'without specific commitments to concrete production'.

For the *owners and agents* of money/commercial capital need have nothing directly to do with the *employers* of capital and the productive process – wherever in the world that might be taking place – so long as they are able to 'absorb' a share of the eventual surplus. Something they do through commercial and financial intermediation, in the form of commissions, fees or arbitrage profit, which is precisely what the City's bankers have been doing with such aplomb since the 1870s. (Harvey, 1982: 257–67; Ticktin, 1983: 36; Lash and Urry, 1987: 85).

The 'circulation or the exchange of commodites creates no value' in themselves, as Marx (1976: 331) explained. Neither does the financing of these 'commercial' activites. However, while it is therefore impossible for capitalism as a whole to replace production with trade and commerce – M-C-M' with M-M' – it is perfectly logical for an individual or group of indivuduals to do so. If, in addition, they can become hegemonic within a particular state, as the City of London merchant banking community was able to be in Britain, then the institutional structure necessary to support and perpetuate such a form of tangential accumulation will itself become dominant. As the logic of accumulation is such that it determines the evolution of an institutional structure necessary for a particular form of accumulation to take place – what Screpanti (1999) calls an 'accumulation governance structure' (AGS). The essential institutional uniqueness of Britain's capitalist model is then rooted in the particularity of her form of accumulation, or AGS. It is this which determines the particular relationship each nation's banking sector has with her indigenous industrial base. But once again something is missing. In 1945 the City's hegemony was challenged by socialism and national capitalism, resulting in the Keynesian Compromise and an 'institutional stalemate'. It took 34 years for the City to fully recover its hegemonic role. Something that was not possible so long as the City was constrained by the demands of domestic production and national capitalism from opening up the international realm (Burn, 2002). It was only with the creation of the Euromarkets and the re-establishment of the power of global capital, that Britain's dominant capital fraction was able to re-impose fully a tangential form of AGS on the state. To explain this, it is necessary to replace the concept of the 'state' with that of 'governance' or the 'governance of regulatory space', whether by the state or the market. Then a more realistic model of a societal/state structure, which moves beyond the artificial divisions of 'state/market' or 'public/private,' can be drawn upon to explain events. For, by examining which actors, at any one time, occupy and control regulatory space that power can be located (Hancher and Moran, 1989: 277).

In relation to City–state relations described in this book, private City interests saw no reason to seek control of the state so long as the state assured the unfettered operation of the market and let them go about their business unimpeded. Sovereignty was in private hands and remained so. The City had, therefore, no need for a formal interest intermediation system to achieve its political goals (Moran, 1983: 51). Up until 1914 governance in the City was, for the most part, conducted in and by the market. The market was sovereign and not the state. The Bank of England had been established to intermediate between lenders and one borrower, the Crown. Owned and controlled by the City's merchant banking community, it remained more an institution for arranging credit for the British state, when it was not conducting commercial business on its own account. It was only after 1918, when the City elite needed the Bank to act as its 'Praetorian Guard', in the face of a potentially democratic state, that the Bank began to evolve into Montagu Norman's powerful institution. Under Norman, the Bank was able to resist statutory control. Defensively, he introduced a network of meso-corporatist associations within which the City could police itself. An 'enclosed regulatory community' that shielded it 'from the attention of democratic politics' (Zysman, 1984: 200; Hancher and Moran, 1989: 283). Offensively, he promoted the return to 'normalcy' and the self-regulating mechanism of the gold standard, thought necessary to keep the state permanently out of regulatory space. But while this did eventually take place in 1925, its inability to function without requiring tremendous sacrifice from Britain's industrial sector and its people, created the opposite effect. So that economic relations became increasingly politicised, even before the fall from gold in 1931. They remained so right through to Bretton Woods and the Keynesian settlement, which gave the state formal responsibility for managing the economy really for the first time, an event symbolised in the City by the nationalisation of the Bank. However, although the Bank became a *de jure* state institution, in essence it continued to function well into the 1960s, more as the City's 'peak association' or, as a form of 'private interest government'.

While this concept was used by Streeck and Schmitter (1985) to describe a social order that has evolved since the late 1970s, as states began to withdraw from direct regulation and devolve public responsibility and governance to private group interests – in the process transforming pluralist pressure groups into private interest government – I am using it here to describe the Bank, as it evolved in the inter-war years in order protect the market from being 'captured' by the state. In both instances 'private interest government' denotes an institutional order created to stand between the market and the state, just as the Bank of England had been established to do, in 1694. While Streeck and Schmitter apply this concept to a historical period that is experiencing, the supposed, withering away of the state, I am applying it to a period that saw the ascendance of the state. The Eurodollar market evolved within this social order, but operated in opposition to it, becoming ultimately a new self-regulating mechanism, drawing governance away from the state arena and back to the market, in accordance with City tradition. Although, ironically, while, Streeck and Schmitter's concept of private interest government has evolved out of the supposed withering away of the state, the same process with regard to the City has resulted in the British state intervening to replace Norman's highly restrictive, meso-corporatist system with a more codified, statute-based system of regulation, to break the barriers to price competition in order to safeguard the City's position as an international financial centre.[14]

To sum up. The City's survival as a self-governing enclave depended on its ability to maintain control of regulatory space and keep government out. But the collapse of the international economy in 1931 and the end of the gold standard, and then the outbreak of war, drew the state into this arena (Moran, 1983: 53). It was also to some extent, circumscribed both legally, by the control of sterling which flowed from the Exchange Control Act of 1947, and politically, as the pre-war primacy of currency stability in the setting of Britain's economic policy was joined by a commitment to full employment and building a 'national economy'. This was preventing the final piece in the nineteenth-century institutional framework for the organising of global credit from being put back in place, so that normal business could be resumed. Sterling was the final piece. While its former status as an international vehicle and reserve currency would never be re-created, and needed to be substituted with the Eurodollar before the old framework was complete, this was not without a struggle – one that lasted over 20 years.

In this way, the offshore Eurodollar market was created and developed in what remained of the City's free international financial regime, in the late 1950s and early 1960s, by market operators, some of whom were also Directors of the Court of the Bank of England, and by Bank officials whose careers flowed effortlessly from the *City* to the *Bank* and back again, Sir George Bolton falling into both these categories. The Bank, unlike any other central bank, had 'its roots deep in the financial structure', and had become part of the informal British 'constitution' long before it had become an official state institution. Regulation was conducted privately, within the 'enclosed regulatory communit[y]' that resided in the City (Pringle, 1973: 14; Hancher and Moran, 1989: 283). This, in turn, assured that the re-assertion of a nineteenth-century institutional framework for the organisation of global credit would be re-convened outside the control of the quasi-public monetary order established at Bretton Woods, once sterling had been replaced with a more robust world money medium. The advent of the Eurodollar market finally allowed the City to regain its autonomy, lost in 1931. British financial elites re-established control of regulatory space and re-imposed 'a regulatory order largely separate from the central institution of the state' (Clarke 1986: 19; Moran, 1991: 16). Something welcomed by the American banking community, given that the US would remain tied up in New Deal regulation until Reagan arrived in the White House, by which time there would be more American banks in London than in New York and the rise of global capitalism would be prising open the City oyster. First the British merchant banks lost control of the Eurodollar market. Thirty years later they were gone.

Musings, questions and conclusions

The Bank of England believed that it was 'an entirely natural development' that London came to dominate the Eurodollar market. But why with an alternative money medium in place did it take until 1969 for the Bank of England and the City finally to give up on sterling? Sir George Bolton had understood as early as 1957 – as had the Radcliffe Committee in 1959 – that it mattered less which currency financed international trade, than that it be carried out through London. Then why struggle on with sterling for another decade? There are different views on this. Cassis (1990: 16) believes this was because Britain's 'ruling elite' regarded sterling as a 'major symbol' of Britain's status as a world power, which it was determined to maintain – The one opportunity that remained for the 'elites of a declining power, now without a hinterland ... to play a leading international role'. It was their only chance, agrees Moran (1991), 'to retain a place at the very top'. This was perhaps why Cromer and even Bolton and Warburg, did not, in Kynaston's (2002: 270) opinion, '*wholly*' appreciate that the 'City's destiny' lay aside from sterling. Others see things more prosaically. Jones (1993: 246–8) believes that it was not until the 1967 devaluation that the British establishment was finally forced to accept that sterling's international role was over. Certainly, with the City reeling from the news that its beloved currency had been brought so low, the *Banker* thought it necessary to reassure the nation that, at least, the City 'will survive the devaluation of sterling'.[15]

If prior to 1967 the City still continued to hanker after a sterling renaissance, then devaluation came as an awakening. Of course, without sterling to worry about, the Eurodollar market would be left free to draw governance back to the market. So, in the future, there would be less not more regulation in the City. Not only because the Eurodollar phenomenon led to offshore finance and the eventual globalisation and de-regulation of financial markets, but also because domestically it had already played a considerable part in destroying 'national capitalism'. First, as Denizet argues in *Inflation, Dollar, Euro-dollar* (1971: 67–8), when it was used as a base from which to mount the sterling crisis that began when Labour returned to power in 1964. While this might have ended in the sorrow of devaluation that finally destroyed sterling's international role, it also effectively killed off the Wilson Government's 'National Plan' and the hopes of the modernisation movement.[16] Then, again in 1971, it precipitated the Bank of England policy, Competition and Credit Control (CCC), which not only set the clearing banks free to join the merchant and overseas banks in the Euromarket casino, but also handed control of credit creation to the market, in the process, dismantling a large part of the mechanism that controlled Britain's money supply. With a Keynesian minded government reluctant to raise interest rates in the face of rising unemployment, it resulted in the most astonishing period of credit expansion Britain had ever experienced, feeding into a boom in commodity prices, that accelerated the politicising and radicalising of industrial relations that ultimately undermined the Keynesian settlement.

The demise of Keynesian hegemony signalled, as Longstreth (1979: 139) explains, 'the resurrection of an ideological equivalent of the gold standard' – monetarism. Eradicating inflation supplanted full employment as the central aim of government, to be achieved by what, on the face of it, was a totally illogical policy mix – by controlling the money supply and deregulating financial markets. For in carrying out the latter it would become increasingly difficult to achieve the former. Nevertheless, on 23 October 1979, Sir Geoffrey Howe, Chancellor of the Exchequer in the first Thatcher Government, finally announced the suspension of those dreaded 'exchange controls' that the Bank of England, especially Governors Cobbold and Cromer had worked so hard and long to destroy. Finally, the 'compartmentalisation' of the British economy into the domestic and international realms was at an end. Such was the delight at the Bank that it commemorated the event with a special neck tie adorned with the Bank's crest and the inscription: 'EC 1939-79', which it presented to Howe as a token of gratitude. The dividing line which had separated the two 'Cities' was erased and full global capital mobility restored (Bonnetti and Cobham, 1992: 7; Lawson, 1992: 40).

If the Eurodollar phenomenon had a devastating impact on the City and the British state, on an international level it played an even more dramatic role, quickening the demise of the quasi-public Dollar–Gold standard in 1971 and the Bretton Woods system itself in 1973. And as Plender and Wallace (1985: 13) point out, this 'proved a boon to London's foreign exchange market – if to no one much else', as the change from fixed to floating exchange rates created much greater instability with regard to foreign exchange values, requiring companies and banks to provide a hedge against potential loss by moving their funds across foreign exchanges in anticipation of changes in currency rates. It also, by definition, increased the likelihood of currency speculation, as ever larger Eurodollar funds, far in excess of the gold and dollar reserves held by governments and the IMF, became increasingly powerful as 'market makers', taking on and winning against national central banks, while, in the process, becoming indispensable as privately owned and controlled disequilibrating international liquidity.

It would be difficult then to disagree with Van Dormael (1997: 9) who described the Eurodollar as 'the most significant monetary development since the banknote'. Yet, why then has so little historical research been conducted on its creation and early evolution? Hitherto, analysis has been based largely on anecdotal evidence and folklore. Nevertheless this has not been regarded as a barrier to truth. The Euromarkets have been explained as the consequence of new technological developments, or legal changes, or the quixotic actions of individuals developing innovative financial instruments to overcome friction in the market created by states, or the active and conscious creation of the realm of offshore. Yet, while, for the most part, these explanations see the creation of the Euromarkets as a consequence of 'discontinuity' in one form or another, it would seem the opposite is true, that, in fact, 'continuity' abounds in this history, because the institutional framework which underpinned the Eurodollar market was one that had been borrowed from the Victorian London bill market, by City traders, like Sir George Bolton. They were precisely the same people who had been employed in a similar capacity going as far back as the 1920s, arranging acceptance credit business denominated in sterling, in the London Discount Market. Even the activity of combining the currency of one country with the banking regulation of another had been taking place in London up until the standstill of 1931. But then offshore was not a new phenomenon either. For, it was not *offshore* that had been created, but *onshore*. Offshore evolved in what remained of the free international currency market, after dealing in sterling was regulated in 1939.

As for the newly nationalised Bank of England of 1946, this was essentially the same institution that had controlled British economic policy in the 1920s; with no greater commitment to public accountability than before, and ruled by the same elite group of merchant banking families who had owned it in the glorious days of the *Pax Britannica* of the late nineteenth century. Not surprisingly then, up until the 1970s the Governors of the Bank, without exception, were either merchant bankers or the former favourites of Montagu Norman. Finally, the supposed radical changes taken by the Bank of England in the 1950s, that some consider to have encouraged the Euromarkets to develop, were, in fact, the re-imposition of structures and techniques that had evolved in the nineteenth century. The creation of the Euromarkets and an unregulated international financial structure was simply the re-assertion of the interests of financial, as opposed to manufacturing, capital. That these events took place in the City, a self-regulatory financial enclave that owed its existence to decisions taken in 1689, is not accidental.

Yet, if continuity is the overriding observation of this book, why did it take until the late 1950s for an unregulated international financial market to be re-convened? The accepted explanation is that it was only then that both the demand and supply streams for foreign dollar credits began to interact at any great intensity. This, of course, brings me back to the question: did the re-assertion of a nineteenth-century institutional structure for the organising of global credit bring about the re-assertion of the power of the City and the re-assertion of a *free* international financial structure? Or, does the causal relationship run the other way? For then, as Michie (1992: 145) claims, it was the global economy's need for an effective system for providing and distributing international liquidity, that called forth an institutional structure for organising global credit, which only London could provide. Yet, the Eurodollar market had been created 15 months before the Bretton Woods system was first put into operation. In effect, then, even before this monetary system was up and running, an international financial structure had been created which would ultimately render it inoperable. However, I do not want to read into this fact more than what is there. Essentially, I agree that this is an example of the market overcoming friction, as the expansion of international trade in the 1950s bid up the price of international credit above the rate ceilings pertaining in the US and began to divert dollars away from the US money market into the new foreign dollar market. Of course, if the acceptance of foreign dollar deposits had been restricted by banking regulation in the other PFCs, especially London, a new private monetary order would surely have been impossible to create in this way.

Another factor to consider, although it did not really come into play until the middle of 1959, was that the inherent inability of the Dollar–Gold standard to function as the Bretton Woods system intended, necessitated the creation of a private international mechanism for holding foreign-owned dollars and keeping them out of official reserves. Otherwise, everything else being equal, the creation of international liquidity necessary for the expansion of the international trading system in the 1960s would have resulted in a much more rapid run-down of US gold stocks and systemic collapse. However, the existence of the Eurodollar market did not alter the fact that using the dollar as both a domestic and an international reserve and vehicle currency linked to gold at a fixed price, meant that as international liquidity expanded, by definition, its ability to function as a money medium was debased, making the operation of the Eurodollar market an increasingly volatile factor in the functioning of the international monetary system as the 1960s wore on and the Eurodollar deposits grew larger. Sir George Bolton pointed out that it was the inability to create public international liquidity that made the provision of private international liquidity essential for the functioning of the multilateral international trading system created after the Second World War. However, it should not be forgotten, that it was precisely the actions of powerful international banking interests, especially in the US, which had prevented a system being created at Bretton Woods which would have provided this.

Yet an awareness in the US of the dangers of the Eurodollar market, even when it did emerge, had little, or nothing to do with the distinction Keynes and White made between the freedom of international trade and capital flows. Rather, it had everything to do with the dangers this new institution might create for the US economy. And although these dangers were inseparable from those affecting the wider global economy, concerns for the international financial system came a distant second. It is possible to argue, therefore, that during the late period of the Eisenhower Administration and through the Kennedy Administration, the US supported the creation of an international financial system controlled by a private monetary order, by default – as a direct consequence of a neglect to regulate the international financial market effectively. Yet, the contradictions in the operation of the Bretton Woods system would not have been easily solved without creating both an alternative form of public global liquidity that could have replaced the dollar, and a powerful international regulatory agency with which to control it. If then complicity is to be located for the failure of Bretton Woods it is, perhaps, with those who were able to prevent the vision of Keynes from being properly realised in the first place, at a time when it was possibly, just possibly, a politically viable project. I am, perhaps, being a little romantic in suggesting that without Roosevelt's untimely death, Morgenthau's and White's consequent fall from power, and the return to prominence of the internationalist US State Department, US banking interests, might not have been able to, as Gill (1993b: 249) makes clear, 'resist the imposition of stricter state controls and a more rigorous system of international economic co-operation'.

However, while US internationalist interests were successful in defeating the *national capitalists* at Bretton Woods and while the US, certainly, used its hegemonic power to promote the deregulation of the international financial system from the beginning of the 1970s onwards, it would be wrong to assume that the creation and development of the Eurodollar was part of the same US-inspired internationalist project. Peter Gowan (1999: 22) makes an interesting observation, that 'the Nixon Administration was able to exploit a breach in the Bretton Woods system that had already existed since the 1950s'. This breach had taken place in the City of London and, apart from utilising their currency, had little to do with the US. Gowan, however, explains this as a consequence of action taken by the British Government. Yet, it had little to do with our elected representatives. They, whatever their political hue, were almost entirely ignorant of the fact that City merchant and overseas bankers were able to re-assert an institutional structure for organising global credit and operate it within a type of parallel universe, free from almost any constraint that had been applied at Bretton Woods or by British Parliament.

In 1976 the US Congressional House Committee on Banking expressed both bewilderment, that the development of the Eurodollar market had been able to escape regulatory scrutiny, and incongruity 'that such a small sector of the banking system has been permitted/encouraged to assume quasi-government functions'.[17] In regard to the market's origins and early development (1957–63), whilst they might not have known it, they could only have been referring to that *remarkably small section* of the City, concerned with international finance, 'for whose sake all the sacrifices' had always been made. For, entwined and bound up, as it was, with Britain's enduring historical–structural integration with the international economy, an unorganised and undetermined market in foreign-owned dollars, re-possessed and re-defined by the City's Victorian institutions, became the fast-track offshore and led, in the process, to the complete reconstruction of the global financial economy.

The Eurodollar market, it seems, is another great British invention. With it in place, the British ruling class could finally get back to its 'international financial vocation'. The City could start operating on a global basis again, and the liberal internationalism and *laissez-faire* order of the private and central bankers that ended in 1931, if not in 1914, could be gradually re-convened. The restrictive international monetary system that the architects of the Bretton Woods system which underpinned the 'Golden Age' had been concerned to create after the Second World War, would soon be history.

Notes

1 Introduction

1. Economic Report of the President (1969), cited in Galbraith (1987: 255).
2. See Gill (1993a: 92); Helleiner (1991: 60) and Van Dormael (1978: 10, 33), who quote from FO371/28899, Keynes undated amendment to memo of 13 Jan. 1941 and T177/57, Keynes to Waley and Hopkins, 7 April 1941.
3. Evans (1994) claims that this figure reached $5 trillion a day at its apex in 1994 – over 450 times the daily value of international trade (cited in Palan and Abbott, 1996: 22). See Cohen (1986: 19) and Loriaux (1997b: 7–8).
4. Cited in Channon (1988: 8).
5. See Loriaux (1997b: 9) for a short summary of the market v. state theses.
6. Important exceptions being, Ingham (1984, 1988), Burk (1992b) and Schenk (1998).
7. Also described by Newton and Porter (1988) as 'an entrenched authority of the core institutional nexus at the heart of British capitalism'. See also Cain and Hopkins (1986, 1987).
8. See Ingham (1984: 226).
9. The term 'historic mechanism' is borrowed from Forsyth (1987: 147).
10. Mayne, cited in Braudel (1994: p. xxiv).

2 The evolution of the Euromarkets

1. Pollard (1982); Ingham (1984, 1988); Hall (1986); Leys (1986); Anderson (1987); Barratt Brown (1988); Newton and Porter (1988); Overbeek (1990); Green (1992); Cain and Hopkins (1993a, b).
2. Clarke (1965); Wechsberg (1966); Strange (1971); Kerr (1984); Holmes and Green (1986); Chernow (1993).
3. Hirsh (1967); Swoboda (1968); Friedman (1969); Machlup (1970); De Cecco (1976); Kelly (1976), Block (1977); Clarke (1979); Mendolsohn (1980); Versluysen (1981); Born (1983); Strange (1986); Collins (1988); Wachtel (1990); Helleiner (1991, 1992, 1993, 1994a, b); Cerny (1993a); Hampton (1996); Van Dormael (1997).
4. Holmes and Klopstock (1960a, b); Johnson (1964); Einzig (1964a, 1965a, 1965b, 1971, 1972); Clendenning (1969, 1970); Friedman (1969); Davis (1976); McKenzie (1976); McKinnon (1977); Einzig and Quinn (1977); Dufey and Giddy (1978); Hogan and Pearce (1982); Kerr (1984); Davis (1992); Dosso (1992); Giddy (1994); Grabbe (1996); Schenk (1998).
5. Which is why, in Nov. 1979, the US was able legally to block Iran's dollar holdings deposited with non-US banks outside the US.
6. Being issued, both, outside the authority of the state in which the purchasers are domiciled, and in 'bearer' not 'registered' form, guarantees the owner total anonymity, allowing interest to be collected on Eurobonds without incurring

withholding tax. A Eurobond is, in fact, an alternative to the foreign bond as the prime method of international investment and borrowing in fixed income securities. However, whereas the foreign issues market comes under the regulatory control of the issuing country and is therefore very likely to be dictated by the broader aims in its government's monetary or fiscal policy, the Eurobond market is not, and is free from direct control and not subject to withholding tax. For a history of the Eurobond see Kerr (1984).

7. Because of its links with the pre-1931 era of international finance, a motion to abolish the BIS was passed at Bretton Woods in 1944. It survived and remains, as Hirsch (1967: 239) says: 'a link between the old financial world and the new'.

8. An ironic codicil to this history was the fact that after the Cuban missile crisis the US began to fear that the Soviet Union might use the Eurodollar market to engineer a major global financial crisis, by calling in all their substantial short-term Eurodollar deposits and, having done that, then blocking their own Eurodollar loans (BoE, C20/5, 8 June 1963).

9. BoE, EID10/19, 23 July 1960; G3/136, June 1963.

10. See Struthers and Speight (1986: 124); Holmes and Klopstock (1960a: 13); Robbie (1975/76: 27).

11. Other countries not party to this agreement have continued to convert dollar surpluses into Eurodollars; OPEC countries, after the great rise in their oil revenues consequent to the oil price increases of 1973 and 1979, being a good example. See Mendolsohn (1980: 26) and Struthers and Speight (1986: 124). See also *American Banker*, 24 April 1970: 6; *Wall Street Journal*, 15 June 1971: 12; *New York Times*, 17 March 1973: 41.

12. Einzig (1960: 23); Scott-Quinn (1975: 35); McKenzie (1976: 88). See also Gibson (1989: 10) who claims European banks reinvested their dollar deposits in US until 1957.

13. Regulation Q evolved out of authority given to the Federal Reserve Board in 1933 to prescribe the maximum rates of interest paid by US banks on time deposits. Changes in Reg. Q were made in Jan. 1962, July 1963 and Nov. 1964 which allowed small increases to interest rates on time deposits and savings accounts. Yet, the prime lending rate from Aug. 1960 to Dec. 1964 was officially 4.5 per cent, though with borrowers having to maintain between 10 and 20 per cent of their loans on deposit, the real cost of borrowing was between 5 and 5.5 per cent. Thus, without Reg. Q the margins for profitable arbitrage in the Eurodollar market from using dollar deposits would have been greatly reduced and hence this market would certainly not have evolved the way it did. See Bell (1973: 9), Pillbeam (1998: 314), Tew (1985: 141) and Wojnilower (1987: 18).

14. See Johns (1983: 23). Permission had been given by the Treasury while the BoE worried about 'the very dangerous position which might arise if these short-term lendings were substantially recalled by the bankers'. It also appears the BoE was not sure what was going on, as Cobbold mentions *hearing* of 'people seeking deposits in order to re-lend to local authorities' (BoE, G3/76, 16 August 1957). According to *The Times*, 6 March 1961, Dawney Urban District Council borrowed £232,000 from the Moscow Narodny Bank, to finance their housing programme. See also Altman (1961: 320); Grady and Weale (1986:114–16); Tether (1961: 402).

15. BoE, 23 July 1956.
16. Legal in England from 1697, though not defined as such until Bills of Exchange Act 1882. Used to finance domestic trade until 1857 financial crisis ended the country banks' practice of rediscounting, and the development of branch banking offered a more efficient means of equalising balances around the country. Its importance for financing international trade occurred in second half of nineteenth century when, with the BoE standing behind them as lender of last resort, the City's merchant banks could guarantee their bills, which they did by simply writing 'accepted' across their face. The Bill on London was effectively a risk-free IOU which could be discounted for slightly less than face value and turned into cash. Providing exporters with immediate payment and importers with three months credit.
17. Estimates vary considerably. I have taken the figure provided by future Governor of the BoE, Lord Cromer (Baring, 1966: 35).
18. Rather, the clearing banks provided funds to the dealers in the money market. These were then made available to only a privileged few merchant banks and overseas banks (only British or Commonwealth), via a discounting system using Bills of Exchange, with the BoE, at its hub, effectively acting as guarantor. When in 1981 the BoE extended this privilege to other banks and thereby abolished this cartel, Chips Keswick of Hambros Bank said: 'We all lived like fat cats on it for donkey's years. ... It was one of those gloriously English institutions which grew from power and privilege. I'm all in favour of monopolies. It was amazing it lasted until 1981.' See also Clarke (1965: 20).
19. PRO, T236/5677, 16 Oct. 1957.
20. PRO, T231/1034, 12 Aug. 1968.
21. As BoE Director, Tony Coleby, explained: 'not all in the Bank and City were enthusiastic about the Eurodollar and Eurobond markets in the beginning, as they held out the hope that sterling could fulfil that role; a view they held until the 1964–67 problems with sterling' (Coleby, 1997).
22. First National Bank of Chicago in 1959; Chemical Bank in 1960; Continental Illinois in 1962; six more in 1963–66; twenty more in 1968–70. According to Dufey and Giddy (1978), by 1974, 331 foreign banks (including 97 of the top 100), had an office in London (161 more than in New York). The assets belonging to London's foreign banking community came to about 53 per cent of the total UK banking sector. Almost 50 per cent of total foreign transactions made by US banks were channelled via their London branches.
23. First issued in New York in 1961, the advantage of a 'certificate of deposit' was that it certified that the original holder had made a deposit of cash for a fixed period. This gave banks security that this money could not be withdrawn until the fixed maturity date while the certificate itself could be traded on a secondary CD market. An example of consortia banking was Chase Manhattan, Nat West, Westdeutsche Landesbank Girozentral, Credit Italiano, Royal Bank of Canada and Nikko Securities of Japan forming a consortium named Orion Bank (Davies, 2002: 419).
24. Also in units of $25,000; $100,000; $500,000 and $1 million (Einzig and Quinn, 1977: 28). CDs had been available in New York since 1961. The First National City Bank of New York was first to issue securities of this type in the City (Einzig and Quinn, 1977: 26; Attali, 1992: 238).

25. Signatories to the agreement were Prof. Ezio Donatoni and Dr Carlo Obber for the IRI; Gert Whitman and Ian Fraser for Warburg, the lead managers; Alexandre Lamfalussy for the Banque Bruxelles; Dr Paul Krebe and Dr Kurt Stahl for Deutsche Bank AG; and F. Hoogendijk for Rotterdamsche Bank, the co-managers, who shared with Warburgs a 3.5 per cent commission. The solicitors to the issue were Allen and Overy. Two London stockbrokers, Strauss, Turnbull & Co and L. Messel & Co. were appointed to arrange for the issue to be listed on the London Stock Exchange.

26. The OECD records over $200 million of Eurobond issues made between 1958 and 1962. The World Bank lists 22 issues placed between 1957 and 1962. Mendolsohn (1980: 136) claims the 'rudiments of a Eurobond market' had existed before 1963, when 'experimental' dollar bond issues were made on behalf of international borrowers crowded out of New York. Steinberg (1976: 150) claims 'the Swiss invented the 'Eurobond' in the 1960s. Jonckheere suggests they were first issued in 1949 and 1951 in Amsterdam, by Philips NV for $25 million (Kerr, 1994: 11). Damien Wigny of Kredietbank in Luxembourg says that the first issue was a 17-year bond made for Sociedade Anonima Concessionaria de Refinacao de Petroleos em Portugal (SACOR), on 23 January 1961, denominated in European Units of Account (EUA) for $5 million. Christian Hemain agrees the SACOR issue is 'a true original Eurobond' issue, as it fulfils all necessary criteria. Hayes and Hubbard (1990: 30) refer to 'a climate of experimentation' resulting in issues denominated in EUAs and 'offered outside home jurisdictions' in 1961 and 1962, principally those made by the Kredietbank in Brussels to clients in Benelux countries.

27. See Hayes and Hubbard, 1990: 28, Leyshon and Thrift, 1997: 76 and Roberts and Kynaston, 1995: 183. Leslie O'Brien (1969: 74), Gov. of the BoE, in speech to the Overseas Bankers Club, 3 Feb. 1969.

28. Strange claims the BoE virtually *guaranteed* profitable arbitrage to the lenders by keeping UK Bank Rate above Eurodollar and comparable rates in Europe, and by offering very cheap forward cover to insure against exchange rate changes when switching sterling back into dollars. However, while these actions encouraged the growth of the Eurodollar market, they had been taken to support the price of sterling in the foreign exchange market, that is, an attractive interest rate combined with cheap insurance against any sterling devaluation were inducements to market operators to hold sterling at a time when they would otherwise have preferred to sell.

29. Nevertheless Chalmers (1969: 92) says the BoE did not start to pursue this policy until 1964 and ended it in 1967. See also Sayers (1967: 322–7); Strange (1976); Hall (1986b: 77).

30. I spoke with Peter Gowan regarding this question, by phone, 24 Aug. 2000.

31. In 1986 the total average daily turnover of the big three foreign exchanges, London, New York and Tokyo stood at $200 billion, of which London claimed $90 billion, New York $50 billion and Tokyo $48 billion (BIS 57th Annual Report, cited in Davies (1994: 447). By 1992 this lead had been extended with London's daily turnover rising to $300 billion compared with $192 in NY and $128 in Tokyo (BEQB Nov. 1992, cited in Davies, 1994: 451).

32. Even as late as the 1980s, while 75 per cent of bank deposits in Britain were owned by overseas residents, in the US this figure was only 10.4 per cent and

in Japan, less than 7 per cent (Forsyth, 1987: 146). In the Mundell–Fleming trade-off each state must make, between exchange rate stability, capital mobility and national monetary autonomy, the City's rational choice is clear.

3 Sterling and the City–Bank–Treasury nexus

1. Britain was on a *de facto* gold standard between 1717 and 1797, when it was suspended after a fall in gold reserves brought on by the cost of the Napoleonic Wars. Officially adopted in 1821, it was an automatic system for balancing international payments. As gold flowed into and out of a country as a consequence of trading surpluses and deficits, so that country's domestic money supply, tied as it was to its internal stock of gold, was supposed to expand and contract accordingly, raising and lowering domestic prices and costs, which, in turn, had the effect of altering demand for exports and imports so as to keep the international economy in balance. In practice, however, as the nineteenth century progressed, this adjustment mechanism was increasingly supplemented by one using interest rate changes to induce short-term capital flows to maintain external balance.
2. Scammell (1968: 166) citing Clapham.
3. See Fetter (1965) for evolution of BoE's role and development of British monetary orthodoxy. See also Collins (1988: 192) and Eichengreen (1990: 133).
4. With the Committee of Treasury the main policy-making body within the Court.
5. I say effectively, because while the gold standard had not been operating since the outbreak of war in 1914, it was not formally suspended until 1919, a situation that was deemed to end in 1925.
6. Cited in Adams Brown Jr (1970: 64); in Boyce (1987: 76).
7. Newton and Porter (1988: 43); Cain and Hopkins (1993b: 55).
8. PRO, T176/5. Cited in Boyce (1987: 65–6).
9. The Chamberlain/Bradbury Committee was constituted ostensibly to consider the amalgamation of the two note issues, the BoE and Treasury notes, but this was inseparable from the issue of a return to gold. See Boyce (1987: 66) and Kynaston (1999: 108).
10. PRO, T160/197, F7528/01/1. Cited in Boyce (1987: 68) and Moggridge (1969: 26).
11. The Committee of National Expenditure, was set up in March 1931 under Sir George May, to recommend budget proposals to the Labour Government.
12. While remaining the responsibility of the Treasury, management of the EEA was later taken over by the Bank, although as Hirsch (1965: 138) writes, 'no one quite knows how or why'.
13. Sterling's more competitive rate, together with protective trade measures and the 'cheap money' policy which was eventually followed, set the foundation for an industrial recovery well ahead of the other major industrial nations.
14. In fact output was at an all-time historically high level. See Ham (1981: 58).
15. PRO, CAB 24/273, 25 Nov. 1937 (cited in Ham, 1981: 58).
16. Between 1929 and 1933 the number of trade bills declined by more than 50 per cent, and the period 1933–39 saw only a small recovery (Scammell, 1968: 32). See also Overbeek (1993: 112).

17. Countries within the British Empire were 'obliged' to use sterling (or local currencies linked to sterling) as their 'legal monetary medium' (Strange, 1971: 44). This bloc was strengthened by the 1932 Ottawa Agreements Act, which gave Imperial Preference formal legality. The act demarcated a free trade area, made up of Britain and the countries of the Empire. It was in other words, 'trade discrimination in favour of the Empire' (Cairncross and Eichengreen, 1983: 19).
18. The 1939 Defence (Finance) Regulation (reaffirmed by 1947 Exchange Control Act).
19. See also Howson (1993: 31) and Gardner (1969: p. lvii).

4 Restoring sterling after 1945

1. In Aug. 1945 UK reserves were £610 million, 30 per cent of one year's imports (Howson, 1993: 2).
2. Cited in Howson (1993: 54). For details of British opposition to Article VII, see Van Dormael (1978).
3. PRO, T160/1281/F18885/7, 19 Jan. 1944.
4. Telegram from Winant, 12 April 1944, *White Papers*. Cited in Gardner (1969: 123). See also Strange (1971: 57).
5. This decision was taken at a meeting between BoE and Treasury officials on 17 Dec. 1954 (BoE, ADB14/39). See Gardner (1969: 30).
6. Moreau bitterly opposed this idea and thought Norman 'an agent of British imperialism' (Boyce, 1987: 24). See also Strange (1971: 50) and Kunz (1987: 11). Memo, 1 March 1961, on US Treasury visit to London money market, Jan. 1961 (RUSIMA, RG 56). Sir Ernest Musgrave Harvey's (Dep. Gov. of BoE) evidence to Macmillan Committee, Dayer (1988: 174). BoE, G15/19. Dalton's evidence to Radcliffe Committee, 1959: 864. Snowden, 14 May; (HC, Deb. 5s, 217, col. 706). *Economist* (1945: 513). PRO, T233/1205, Sept. 1955. See also Chapman (1968: 72); Hall (1986b: 66); Davenport (1974: 161); Daunton (1993). Roseveare (1969: 321); Davenport (1974: 17); Sampson (1965: 442); Wechsberg (1966: 69) and Macrae (1955: 193).
7. BoE, G15/19.
8. BoE, G15/19. PRO, T233/1664. Catto requested the phrase 'after consultation with the Governor ...' be added to clause 4(1) in a debate in the HoL, 22 Jan. 1946.
9. BoE, G13/1, 27 Feb. 1946; G15/19.
10. BoE, G15/19.
11. Such as the right to be represented on various committees at which Government economic policy is decided. See Brittan (1964: 101); Sayers (1976) and Keegan and Pennant-Rea (1979: 99).
12. BoE, G15/9. PRO, T176/13, cited in Kynaston (1995a: 25).
13. PRO, PREM11/3756, 3 Aug 1960.
14. BoE, EC4/414, 7 April 1943. See also Howson (1993: 55). PRO, T236/3940, 30 March 1948. Britain's gold and foreign currency reserves dropped from $503 million in 1939 to £71 million in 1941, prior to the introduction of Lend–Lease (Howson 1993: 31).
15. While it can be argued that Britain benefited from acting as banker for the Sterling Area, because most of official Sterling Area balances were held in

London, it made sterling more vulnerable to market volatility. In addition, one advantage for Sterling Area countries of this arrangement was, to some extent, being given special access to the London capital market and British investment funding, which not only increased the likelihood of capital export but strengthened the BoE's argument against exchange controls (Hirsch, 1965: 40).

16. High interest conflicted with the commitment to full employment, hence the 'frequent oscillation in economic policy. ... Britain's infamous and literally exceptional "stop-go policy" '. This curbed industrial investment and undermined any plans productive capital had for long-term growth. Britain's consequent poor industrial performance resulted in payments deficits, increasing the economy's reliance on attracting short-term capital flows, or 'hot money', to balance the books. This, in turn, made sterling even more vulnerable to speculation and perpetuated the need for maintaining a high interest regime.

17. BoE, EC4/414, 7 July 1943. Sir George Bolton's Personal File.

18. PRO, CAB134/225: EPC(50)28. Cited in Plowden (1989: 82).

19. As Davenport (1974) explains:, 'naturally, the first action taken by the restoration of the old moneyed ruling clique was to restore freedom to the money market and the bond market'. Scammell (1968: 242) regards the whole period 1945–59, as having seen 'the restoration of the Bank ... to full power as controller of the monetary system ... the restoration of monetary policy with the Bank at its centre'.

20. There is a large literature on ROBOT. See Cairncross (1985: ch.9); Newton (1986); Procter (1993); Schenk (1992); Plowden (1989); Birkenhead (1961:284); Butler (1973:160); BoE Archive.

21. PRO, PREM 11/137, 18 March 1952.

22. Mansion House Speech, 7 Oct. 1952; 14 Oct. 1953.

23. PRO, PREM11/655, 17 March 1954. Fforde (1992: ch.7).

24. BoE, ADM14/40, 23 Feb. 1955.

25. BoE, OV44/65, 7 Feb. 1956. PRO, T236/5678, 18 May 1956. Mansion House Speech, 9 Oct. 1956.

26. PRO, T236/5678, 14 Oct. 1958. BoE, ADB14/49, 26 June 1957. G3/76, 3 Sept. 1957. PRO, T233/1664, 5 Sept., 15 June 1957. BoE, G3/76, 10 Sept. 1957. Letter from Mynors to Thorneycroft. G3/76, 16 Sept.–9 Oct. 1957. Letters from Cobbold to Thorneycroft.

27. Speech at IMF, Washington, 24 Sept. 1957; cited by Brittan (1964: 187). Speech at Lord Major's Banquet, cited in Davenport (1974: 189).

28. PRO, T236/5677, 12 Dec. 1957.

29. BoE, C160/55.

30. BoE, OV44/12, 1 June 1959. G3/22, 25 Nov. 1959.

31. BoE, C160/55, 10 Nov. 1959.

32. BoE, G3/93, 31 Oct. 1961. PRO, PREM11/3758, 19 Dec. 1960.

33. BoE, EID10/19, 4–8 Nov. 1960. This is, however, a complex issue, as the German authorities were also encouraging development of the Eurodollar market, by using it as a home for surplus dollars earned running a trade surplus with the US, rather than allowing an expansion of their domestic money supply.

34. PRO, PREM11/3758, 16 June 1961. BoE, ADM/13/6, 12 July 1961.

35. The Institute of Bankers (1961: 158). BoE, C160/154. OV44/12, 27 Sept. 1961. EC5/118, 2 Oct. 1961. EID10/19, 19 Oct. 1961.EC5/118, 1–16 Nov. 1961.
36. BoE, EC5/604, 5 Jan. 1962. G3/93, 18 Jan. 1962. EC5/604, 30 Jan. 1962.
37. RUSIMA, RG 56, 22 March 1962. BoE, EID10/21, 27 April 1962.
38. JFKL, Box 89, 12 March 1962. BoE, OV44/12, 26 April 1962. C91; OV44/12, 1 June 1962.
39. PRO, T 295/9, 22 Oct. 1962. Cited in Kynaston (2002: 271). BoE ADM13/5, 5 Dec. 1962. Memo from Parsons to Cromer.
40. For more details see Ch. 6.
41. RUSIMA, RG 56, 6 Nov. 1962; 2 July 1963. BoE, G3/135, 8 Feb. 1963. G3/135, 6 March 1963. G3/241, 30 April 1963. G3/136 & ADM 13/6, 30 April 1963. Cited in Kynaston (2001: 273). ADM13/6, 22 Nov. 1963.
42. Cited in Ponting (1989: 65) and Wilson (1974: 27).
43. PRO, PREM13/237, 21 Dec. 1964. See also Wilson (1971: 37). Mansion House Speech, 21 Oct. 1965.
44. Cited in Morgan (1997: 246) and Brittan (1971: 331).
45. BoE, C20/5, 4 Dec. 1967. Committee on Invisible Exports. *Britain's invisible earnings* (Clarke Report). London, British National Export Council, 1967. Cited in Strange (1971: 234).
46. The Institute of Bankers (1961: 158).

5   The state, the City and the Euromarkets

1. These syndication techniques created in London during this earlier period were more efficient and superior to the 'consortium' banks formed in the City in the 1960s for the same purpose (Forsyth, 1987: 148).
2. Back-to-back loans were a way companies could get round exchange control regulations in the UK and obtain cheaper finance abroad, by utilising the comparative advantages of their own national credit markets. Swap agreements extended this concept into a single transaction.
3. Robert Blomquist, vice-president of Chase Manhattan said that US banks chose London as their base because 'the government is stable and there is a similar culture and language to the US' (cited in Spiegelberg, 1973: 98). See also Davis (1992: 112).
4. Little, 1985: 54. Alec Cairns, Ernest Ingold and George Mallinckrodt and Gordon Richardson developed Schroder Wagg's early Eurocurrency business (Roberts, 1992: 417, 442).
5. *Bank of England Quarterly, 1891–1944, Vol 2* (1976); Davenport (1964: 116); *The Banker* (1958; vol. 108: 167). Sampson (1981: 110); Mendelsohn (1980: 20). National Archives, FCO 59/1255, 1974. Fry (1970: 27).
6. While it may be common practice for BoE officials to move to the City, it was, nevertheless, still a sensitive issue. Thus, when Standard Bank wrote to ask for Hamilton's early release, Cromer replied, 'I assume there will be some suitable lapse of time between Mr Hamilton's retirement and his taking up his new duties. You will, I am sure, wish to do everything to minimise the likelihood of possible criticism' (BoE, G/135, 25 Jan. 1963).
7. BoE, C48/156, 29 Sept. 1948, memo from Cobbold. C48/156, 15 Jan. 1957, Cobbold's hand-written note. G3/9, 19 Jan. 1957, entry in Governor's diary.

See also, note from Cobbold to Chief Cashier, Sir Kenneth Peppiatt, 28 March 1949; memo to Cobbold, 29 Jan. 1952; Cobbold's note, 5 July 1955. FRBNY, C.261; see correspondence between Bolton and Hayes, 7–11 Jan. 1957.

8. BoE, C160/55. See Bolton's speeches, 19 May and 10 Nov. 1959. Lloyds Bank Archives, F2/D/COM.4; F2/D/REP.8. See also the *Banker*, April 1963: 222.

9. BOLSA: A Short History 1862–1970. See also Spiegelberg (1973: 131). Cited in Ferris (1968: 34–5). The *FT*, 27 July 1962, includes a description of the development of the Eurodollar market by Bolton. BoE, C160/154. EID3/335, 10 Jan. 1964.

10. This power was delegated to the BoE by the Treasury in accordance with the Exchange Control Act 1947 (Section 14, pt 1, par. 1(1). BoE, EID16/7, 10 Feb. 1965).

11. M. J. Babington Smith, Director (BoE) did, however, suggest that Section 34 of the Exchange Control Act could be used to apply quantitative controls on the taking of dollar deposits (BoE, EC5/561, 30 March 1962). BoE, C20/5(10), 30 March 1965.

12. Mansion House Speech, 3 Oct. 1962.

13. See also Cairncross (1995: 206); Pringle (1973: 10–13).

14. BoE, EC5/561, 19 March 1962. EC5/561, 20 March 1962.

15. Cooper (1968: 117); Shaw (1975: 121); Struthers and Speight (1986: ch. 6). In 1975 the BIS agreed that parent banks should be responsible for all overseas banking operations in which they have a direct stake, supported by adequate last resort finance made available by their respective central banks (Struthres and Speight, 1986: 131). However, Versluysen (1981: 17) for one, is doubtful these facilities are enough to protect this vast offshore market.

16. In 1977 it was estimated that of the $55 billion worth of Eurobonds that had been issued approximately 60 per cent were held by persons, 15 per cent by banks and 25 per cent by institutions (Struthers and Speight, 1986: 123).

17. The Bank of France misunderstood the implications of an entrepôt role for Paris and how the Eurodollar market worked, and worried about the exchange problems for the franc (Atalli, 1986: 224). It placed obstacles in the way of issuing a foreign currency bond that were not overcome until Nov. 1963, by which time, as Welsh (1986: 45) writes, 'Warburg had put themselves firmly in the lead'.

18. JFKL, Box 89, 10 April 1962. Letter from Dillon to author, 2 March 2000. RUSIMA, RG 56, 17 May 1962.

19. See press release of Dillon's speech at 9th Annual Monetary Conference of ABA in Rome, Italy, Friday, 18 May 1962. Treasury Department, D-493. Although newly issued Eurobonds could not be sold in the US, trading in the secondary market was allowed 90 days after issue. These restrictions did not apply to foreign buyers outside the US, although until 1964 US investment banks were not allowed to distribute Eurobonds, even to non-US nationals (Evans, 1992: 44).

20. Letter from Dillon to author, 2 March 2000.

21. BoE, C160/173, cited in Kynaston (2001: 276). The *Banker*, Aug. 1963: 518. New foreign bond issues in the US fell from $369 in 1962 to $191 in 1964 (Dosso, 1992: 14). Capital raised for foreign portfolio investment in under-developed countries was excluded from IET. See Carl Reich (1980); cited in Attali (1986: 226–7) Fraser (1999: 259–62); cited in Kynaston (2001: 277).

22. Interview with Henry Grunfeld, 7 April 1997. Grunfeld, whom Warburg met in June 1935, became Warburg's partner in August 1937 and remained 'his alter ego for nearly fifty years'. Paul Haas said, 'Nobody else has the same status ... in Siegmund's entourage' (Attali, 1986: 128). Interview with Peter Spira, formerly of Warburgs Bank, 24 June 1997. Spira said that he and Ian Fraser 'spent a lot of time in meetings ... at the Bank of England working out all the technicalities ... supported by Geoffrey Salmons', of Allen & Overy. In June 1963 an article entitled 'On London as a Commercial Centre' appeared in the *Bank of England Quarterly Bulletin* developing this theme further.

23. BoE, C160/154. C160/154, 12 Feb. 1962. G3/93, 18 Jan. 1962. EC5/604.G3/93, 21 June 1962. C160/154, 6 June 1962.

24. BoE, G3/95 and C160/154, 14 June 1962. C160/154, 11 July, 1962. *The Banker*, Aug. 1963: 518. BoE, C160/154 and G3/96, 23 July 1962. Mansion House Speech, 3 Oct. 1962.

25. BoE, EC5/397, 17 June 1955. C160/155, 10 Aug. 1959.

26. *Committee on the Working of the Monetary System, Report* (1959).

27. BoE, ADM13/6, 22 Nov. 1963. G3/135, 29 and 31 Jan. 1963, C40/1213, 30 Jan. 1963, G3/135/136/241 and C160/154, 19 March, 11 April 1963 and 17 April 1963. The guest list also included William Armstrong, W.J. Keswick, E. G. Kleinwort, Kenneth Keith, the Earl of Inchcape and J. F. Prideaux. Announcement made in the Chancellor's Budget, 3 April 1963.

28. BoE, EID10/21, 16 June 1961. C40/773, 25 Jan. 1963, cited in Schenk (1998: 232). BoE, C43/676, 7 Dec. 1964. Letter from Rawlinson (Treasury) to Leigh at BoE.

29. Ham (1981: 34) maintains that this characterised relations between the BoE and the Treasury until at least as late as 1976.

30. Brittan (1964: 58, 65) writes that the 'Treasury's main links with the BoE are through the Finance group', which communicated the Bank's views to Government. As such it was 'inevitably infected with the Bank's approach', which explained 'the group's conservatism'. BoE, G15/19.

31. BoE, EID3/335, 31 March 1959. EC5/561, 6 July 1962. G3/151; BoE EID10/22. G3/136. On 20 June, Cromer sent Armstrong [head of Treasury's 'Finance group'] a general background note on the Eurocurrency market. RUSIMA, RG 56, 23 July 1963, letter from Cairncross to Dr Sachs.

32. BoE, EC5/561, 27 Feb. 1962.

33. BoE, C43/113, 29 Sept. 1959.

34. BoE, EC5/561, 27 Feb. 1962. C43/113, 29 Sept. 1959. EC5/561. EC5/326, 3 Oct. 1960. Bankers' Sub-Committee made up of representatives from the clearing banks, the Accepting Houses, American banks, British Overseas banks, continental banks and the BoE. BoE, EC5/326, 5 Dec. 1960. BoE, EC5/561, 19 March 1962. 'Memorandum to Authorised Dealers in Foreign Exchange', Sept. 1939. BoE, EC5/561, 27 Feb. 1962.

35. Both Bruder and Muûl are cited in Kynaston (2001: 442).

36. Letter from Sir George Blunden to author, 11 April 1997. BoE, EC5/561, 19 March 1962. EID16/7, 17 Feb. 1965. EC5/561, 20 March 1962. EC5/561, 8 March 1962.

37. BoE, EID16/7, 17 Feb. 1965. See Giddens (1990: 165), Ingham (1984: 231) and Leyshon and Thrift (1997: 60, 76). Schenk (1998) cites BoE, C43/111,

28 June 1955. BoE EC5/561, 19 March 1962. EID3/335, C43/113, 19 Sept. 1959. EID10/19, 20 April 1961.

38. RUSIMA, RG 56, 1 March 1961. BoE, G3/94, 28 Feb. 1962. EID10/21, 5 May 1962.

39. BoE, EC5/561, 13 Dec. 1962. EC5/561, 25 Sept. 1963. EC5/561, 30 March 1962. EID10/21, 7 Aug. 1962. EID10/21, 20 March 1962.

40. BoE EID10/22, 28 Nov 1962. EID10/22, 29 Jan. 1963. The *Economist*, 26 May 1962: 821. BoE, G3/136.

41. BoE, EID10/22; EID10/21, 15 May 1962. Tether cited in Kynaston (2001: 283). BoE, EID10/22. EID10/21, 5 Dec. 1963. Cited in Schenk (1998: 236). BoE, C20/5(7), 16 March 1964.

42. BoE, EID10/21, EID10/22, 5, 6 Dec. 1963. Cited in Schenk (1998: 236). BoE, EID10/22, 6 Nov. 1963. EID3/335, 10 Jan. 1964.

43. BoE, EID16/7, 18 Feb. 1965. EID16/7, 10 Feb. 1965. EID16/7, 17 Feb. 1965.

6   America and the Euromarkets

1. During the 1950s only one-third of the expansion of world trade (excluding communist bloc countries) was accompanied by an increase in gold reserves, the remaining increase in international liquidity being met by the deficit in the US balance of payments. Of the $14 billion that was fed to the rest of the world from US reserves during this period, $4 billion was in the form of gold, the other $10 billion represented by an increase in foreign dollar holdings (Gardner, 1960: 434; Anderson, 1960: 426).

2. RUSIMA, RG 56. As Frazer B. Wilde, chairman of the Connecticut Life Assurance Association, explained at an LIAA meeting of 13 Dec. 1961: 'Exchange controls are, of course, obnoxious and are not desirable for a great nation trying to lead in greater world freedom of trade. Revaluation of our dollar in terms of gold is even worse. Our world prestige would be shaken. Whatever propaganda advantage the Russians have gained over us by their space exploits would be nothing were they able to say that the greatest capitalist nation of the world has gone bankrupt and has had to revalue its money' (RUSIMA, RG 56).

3. By 'gold traditions' is meant those institutional factors by which, historically, each nation/state's central bank defines the 'gold to dollar' ratio of its reserves.

4. BoE, EID10/21, 4 Oct. 1962. Schenk (1998: 232), however, claims that by the end of 1962 New York banks were more innovative in developing new facilities in the Eurodollar market than their British counterparts, who were mainly using dollar deposits for switching into sterling. RUSIMA, RG 56, 19 Aug. 1963. RG 56, Dec. 1961. RG 56, 26 April 1963.

5. RUSIMA, RG 56, 1 March 1961.

6. FRBNY, C.260.4, 28 Nov. 1958.

7. RUSIMA, RG 56, 25 March 1960.

8. FRBNY, C.260, 20 Sept. 1960.

9. FRBNY, C.260.4, 3 June 1960. C.260.4, 14 June 1960. C. 260, 13 May 1960. C.260.4, 23 Jan. 1962. BoE ADM 13/4, 14 April 1961, cited in Kynaston (2001: 269).

10. RUSIMA, RG 56, 25 March 1960; 14 Feb. 1962.

11. 2 May 1962, Treasury Department, D-95.
12. RUSIMA, RG 56, 28 Feb. 1961.
13. RUSIMA, RG 56, 22 June 1960.
14. RUSIMA, RG 56, 6 April 1961.
15. *Banker*, August (1963: 525).
16. Meier (1982: 97); McKenzie (1976: 9); Altman (1960–61: 325, 1962: 301).
17. RUSIMA, RG 56, 7 Feb. 1962.
18. JFKL, Box 89, 12 March 1961.
19. RUSIMA, RG 56, 17 May 1962.
20. RUSIMA, RG 56, 15 Feb. 1962. RG 56, 17 May 1962; JFKL, Box 89, 10 April 1962.
21. 18 May 1962. Treasury Department, D-493. See the the *Banker*, June 1962: 346. 25 Sept. 1962. Treasury Department, D-617. JFKL, Box 89a, 21 Aug. 1962.
22. RUSIMA, RG 56, 17 May 1962.
23. The *Banker*, Feb. 1963; 123; April 1963: 276.
24. JFKL, Box 90, 4 Feb., 2 March, 10, 17, 20 April 1963. Treasury Department, D-8607, May 1963.
25. JFKL, Box 90, 14 May 1963.
26. RUSIMA, RG 56, 29 May, 2, 19, 22, 25 July 1963.
27. RUSIMA, RG 56, 2 July 1963.
28. RUSIMA, RG 56, 2 July, 26 April 1963.
29. RUSIMA, RG 56, 30 Aug., 1 March 1961, 7 Feb. 1962. JFKL, Box 89, 18 Jan. 1962.
30. Remarks of Dillon, 30 Jan. 1962. Treasury Department, D-376.
31 After Oct. 1962 US banks were allowed to pay higher rates on time deposits, and then just to foreign official institutions. Regulation. Q ceilings on 3–6 month deposits were raised to 4 per cent for all depositors in July 1963 and to 4.5 per cent in Nov. 1964, when ceilings on time deposits of less than 90 days were also increased from 1 per cent to 4 per cent. In Dec. 1965 these were raised to 5.5 per cent and lowered again to 5 per cent in Sept. 1966.
32. Although, when a dollar deposit moves from one foreign bank to another foreign bank, say from a bank in London to a bank in Paris, even if ownership belongs to a US resident, or when a non-US resident transfers a dollar deposit from the US to any other financial centre in the world, this has no effect on the US balance of payments, as ownership has already moved outside of the US. *First National City Bank Monthly Economic Letter*, Nov. 1970; cited in Meier (1982: 97).
33. 7 Feb. 1962.
34. 'Short-term Capital Outflow & US Balance of Payments', 12 Feb. 1962. RUSIMA, RG 56.
35. During 1960/61 the total increase in recorded short-term claims on foreigners, payable in foreign currencies reported by banks was $370 million (RUSIMA, RG 56, 12 Feb. 1962).
36. RUSIMA, RG 56, 14 Feb., 9 March, 15 Feb. 1962.
37. RUSIMA, RG 56, 4 June 1962.
38. RUSIMA, RG 56, 7 July, 4 Sept., 3 Oct. 1962.
39. RUSIMA, RG 56, 16 Oct. 1962.
40. RUSIMA, RG 56, 16 Oct. 1962.
41. RUSIMA, RG 56, 8, 16 Nov 1962; Kenen (1962); Bell (1962); Cohen (1963).
42. RUSIMA, RG 56, 17, 26 April 1963. JFKL, Box 90, 9 May 1963.

43. RUSIMA, RG 56, 22 April, 3 June 1963.

44. RUSIMA, RG 56, 5 July 1963. Treasury Department, D-8988, July 1963.

45. JFKL, Box 90, 16 July 1963. *The Times*, 20 July 1963; the *Banker*, Aug 1963, 520–523. See Kynaston (2001: 280).

46. RUSIMA, RG 56, 15, 16, 21 Oct. 1963.

47. RUSIMA, RG 56, 23 Oct. 1963.

48. RUSIMA, RG 56, Oct., 21 Nov. 1963.

49. JFKL, Box 89, 12 March 1962.

50. BoE, ADM 13/4, 14, 20 April 1961. Cited in Kynaston (2001: 269).

51. RUSIMA, RG 56, 8 March 1962.

52. RUSIMA, RG 56, 5 Jan. 1962.

53. RUSIMA, RG 56, 9, 17 April,16 Oct. 1962.

54. BoE, EID10/20, 1 May 1963. FRBNY, C.260.4, 8 July 1963; C.261, 23 July 1963 BoE, EID3/335, 10 Jan. 1964.

55. FRBNY, C.260.4, 23 April 1964.

56. The *Banker*, Aug. 1963: 524.

57. FRBNY, C.260.4, 13 April 1964, 28 April 1960, 23 Jan. 1962.

58. US Congress (1964: 221), cited in the *Banker* June 1963: 377.

59. Letter from Dillon to author, 2 March 2000.

60. Roosa (1972: 62–66). Interestingly, Roosa believed that 'there had been a few rotten apples in the Treasury, Harry White being the principal one'. Also Harris (1964: 21).

61. The Congressional House Committee on Banking Report 'FINE' (1976).

7   Public accountability v. private interest government

1. See Governor's statement before the Select Committee on Nationalised Industries, (1970: 273–4). Cited in Kynaston (1995a: 52). Re-iterated by Sir George Blunden (Solomon, 1995: 33).

2. See also Lupton and Wilson (1959), Lisle-Williams (1984b) and Rubinstein (1993).

3. The *Banker* (Vol. 108, 1959: 27). *Proceedings of the Tribunal Appointed to Inquire into Allegations that Information about the Raising of the Bank Rate was Improperly Disclosed.* Cmnd 350. London: HMSO (1957). Presented to Parliament Jan. 1958.

4. According to Radcliffe Committee 'the Committee of the Treasury can be treated without qualification as the voice of the Court.' Cited in Chapman (1968: 72).

5. Hall (1991: 21, 126–7). FRBNY, C.261, 3 Feb. 1958: 15. See also Brittan (1964: 60) and Hanham (1959: 18).

6. Cited in Aaronovitch (1961: 151). See also Chapman (1968: 92).

7. BoE, EC5/561, 13 Dec. 1962.

8. London Discount Market Association; Accepting Houses Committee; Committee of London Clearing Bankers; Issuing Houses Committee; Foreign Exchange & Currency Deposit Brokers Association (FECDBA). See Moran (1984); Moran (1981: 387); Hancher and Moran (1989: 283); and Mitnick (1980).

9. Cited in Chapman, (1968: 72); Cairncross (1995: 62); PRO, T175/11, 9 May 1927; Hinton (1987: 104–5); Boyce (1987: 280).
10. Wilson quoted in Hill (1984: 231). Braithwaite and Drahos (2000: 480).
11. Cain and Hopkins (1993a: 63). Gladstone quoted in Kynaston (1995a: 19–20). Brenner, (1993: 716); North and Weingast (1989: 821). See also Plender and Wallace (1985: 4) and Dickson (1967).
12. Davenport (1974: 162); North and Weingast (1989: 825); Elgie and Thompson (1998: 36); Cain and Hopkins (1993a: 60).
13. In the case of the Bank, to retain control of the monetary system and the financial sector, and for the Treasury, to retain its control over the apparatus of state.
14. The Banking Act, 1979; the Financial Services Act, 1986.
15. The *Banker* (1967: 1031).
16. Denizet accused the Euromarket of creating the 1966 and 1967 sterling crises, and 1967 sterling devaluation (Bourguinat *et al.*, 1971); cited in Higonnet (1985: 35–6). See also Newton and Porter (1988).
17. US Congress (1976).

Bibliography

Printed Books

Aaronovitch, S. (1961), *The Ruling Class*. Westport (U.S.A.): Lawrence & Wishart.

Adams Brown Jr, W. (1970), 'The Conflict of Opinion and Economic Interest in England', in S. Pollard (ed.), *The Gold Standard and Employment Policies Between the Wars*. London: Methuen.

Aglietta, M. (1985), 'The Creation of International Liquidity', in L. Tsoukalis (ed.), *The Political Economy of International Money*. London: Sage.

Altman, O. L. (1969), 'Euro-dollars', in E. Chalmers (ed.), *Readings in the Euro-dollar*. London: W.P. Griffith.

Artis, M. J. (1965), *Foundations of British Monetary Policy*. Oxford: Basil Blackwell.

Attali, J. (1986), *A Man of Influence: Sir Siegmund Warburg 1902–82*. London: Weidenfeld & Nicolson.

Bagehot, W. (1906), *Lombard Street: A Description of the Money Market*. London: Kegan, Trench & Trubner.

Bank of England (1984), *The Development & Operation of Monetary Policy 1960–1983*. Oxford: Clarendon Press.

Bank of England Quarterly 1891–1944, vol. 2 (1976). Cambridge: Cambridge University Press.

Bank of London & South America (1970), *The Bank of London & South America: A Short History, 1962–1970*. London: Bank of London & South America.

Bareau, P. (1979), 'The International Money & Capital Markets', in E. V. Morgan, R. A. Brealey, B. S. Yamey and P. Bareau (eds), *City Lights*. London: The Inst. of Economic Affairs.

Baring, G. R. (Earl of Cromer) (1966), *Speeches, 1959–1966*. Debden (Essex): Gordon Chalmers.

—— (1976), 'Foreword', in C. J. J. Clay and B. S. Wheble (eds), *Modern Merchant Banking*. London: Woodhead-Faulkner.

Barnet, R. J. and Muller, R. E. (1975), *Global Reach*. London: Jonathon Cape.

Bell, G. (1973), *The Euro-dollar Market & the International Financial System*. London: Macmillan.

Bell, G. L. (1969), 'Credit Creation through Euro-Dollars?', in E. Chalmers (ed.), *Readings in the Euro-Dollar*. London: Griffith & Sons.

Best, M. H. and Humphries, J. (1986) 'The City & Industrial Decline', in B. Elbaum and W. Lazonick (eds), *The Decline of the British Economy*. Oxford: Oxford University Press.

Birkenhead, Lord (1961), *The Prof in Two Worlds: The Official Life of Professor Lindemann, Viscount Cherwell*. London: Collins.

Block, F. (1977), *The Origins of International Economic Disorder*. Berkeley, LA: University of California.

Bolton, G. (Sir) (1970), 'Background and Emergence of the Eurodollar Market', in H. V. Prochnow (ed.), *The Eurodollar Market*. Chicago: Rand McNally.

Bonetti, S. and Cobham, D. (1992), 'Financial Markets and the City of London', in D. Cobham (ed.), *Markets & Dealers: The Economics of the London Financial Markets*. London: Longham.

Born, K. (1983), *International Banking in the 19th and 20th Century*. Leamington Spa: Berg Publishers.

Boyce, R. W. D. (1987), *British Capitalism at the Crossroads 1912–1932*. Cambridge: Cambridge University Press.

Braithwaite, J. and Drahos, P. (2000), *Global Business Regulation*. Cambridge: Cambridge University Press.

Braudel, F. (1981), *On History*. London: Weidenfeld.

—— (1994), *A History of Civilisations*. New York: Allen Lane.

Braun, R. (1975), 'Taxation, Sociopolitical Structure and State-Building: Great Britain and Brandenburg-Prussia', in C. Tilly (ed.), *Formation of Nation States in Western Europe*. Princeton, NJ: Princeton University Press.

Brenner, R. (1993), *Merchants and Revolution*. Princeton, NJ: Princeton University Press.

Brewer, J. (1990), *The Sinews of Power: War, Money and the English State, 1688–1783*. Cambridge, MA: Harvard University Press.

Bridges, Lord (1964), *The Treasury*. London: Allen & Unwin.

Brittan, S. (1964), *The Treasury Under the Tories 1951–1964*. Harmondsworth: Penguin.

—— (1971), *Steering the Economy*. Harmondsworth: Penguin.

Burk, K. (1992a), 'Money and Power: The Shift from Great Britain to the United States', in Y. Cassis (ed.), *Finance & Financiers in European History*. Cambridge: Cambridge University Press.

Burn, G. (2002), 'Germany Unlocked? Globalising Capital and the Logic of Accumulation', in J. Abbott (ed.), *Critical Perspectives on International Political Economy*. London: Palgrave.

Burnham, P. (1990), *The Political Economy of Postwar Reconstruction*. London: Macmillan.

Butler, R. A. (1971), *The Art of the Possible*. London: Hamish Hamilton.

Byng, G. (1901), *Protection: The Views of a Manufacturer*. London: Eyre & Spottiswoode.

Cain, P. J. and Hopkins, A. G. (1993a), *British Imperialism: Innovation and Expansion 1688–1914*. London: Longman.

—— (1993b), *British Imperialism: Crisis and Decontruction 1914–1990*. London: Longman.

Cairncross, A. K. (1985), *Years of Recovery: British Economic Policy. 1945–51*. London: Methuen.

—— (1988), 'The Bank of England: Relationships with the Government, the Civil Service, and Parliament', in G. Toniolo (ed.), *Central Banks' Independence in Historical Perspective*. Berlin: de Gruyter.

—— (1995), 'The Bank and the British Economy', in R. Roberts and D. Kynaston (eds), *The Bank of England 1694–1994*. Oxford: Clarendon Press.

Cairncross, A. and Eichengreen, B. (1983), *Sterling in Decline*. Oxford: Blackwell.

Calleo, D. P. (1982), *The Imperious Economy*. London: Harvard University Press.

Cassis, Y. (1990), 'British Finance: Success and Controversy', in J. J. Van Helten and Y. Cassis (eds), *Capitalism in a Mature Economy*. Aldershot, Hants: Edward Elgar.

Cerny, P. G. (1993a), 'The Deregulation and Re-regulation of Financial Markets in a More Open World', in P. G. Cerny (ed.), *Finance and World Politics: Markets, Regimes, and States in the Posthegemonic Era*. Aldershot: Edward Elgar.

—— (1993b), 'American Decline and Embedded Financial Orthodoxy', in P. G. Cerny (ed.), *Finance and World Politics: Markets, Regimes, and States in the Post-hegemonic Era*. Aldershot: Edward Elgar.

Chalmers, E. B. (1969), 'Monetary Policy Aspects of the Euro-Dollar', in E. B. Chalmers (ed.), *Readings in the Euro-Dollar*. London: Griffith & Son.

Channon, D. F. (1988), *Global Banking Strategy*. New York: John Wiley & Son.

Chapman, R. A. (1968), *Decision Making*. London: Routledge.

Chernow, R. (1993), *The Warburgs: A Family Saga*. London: Chatto & Windus.

Clapham, J. (Sir) (1944), *The Bank of England, Volume II, 1797–1914*. Cambridge: Cambridge University Press.

Clarke, M. (1986), *Regulating the City*. Oxford: Oxford University Press.

Clarke, S. (1998), *Keynesianism, Monetarism and the Crisis of the State*. London: Edward Elgar.

Clarke, W. M. (1965), *The City in the World Economy*. London: The Institute of Economic Affairs.

—— (1979), *Inside the City*. London: Allen & Inwin.

Clendenning, E. W. (1969), 'Euro-dollars: The Problem of Control', in E. B. Chalmers (ed.), *Readings in the Euro-Dollar*. London: Griffith & Son.

—— (1970), *The Eurodollar Market*. Oxford: Oxford University Press.

Coakley, J. (1988), 'The Internationalisation of Bank Capital', in L. Harris, J. Coakley, M. Croasdale and T. Evans (eds), *New Perspectives on the Financial System*. USA: Croom Helm.

Coakley, J. and Harris, L. (1983), *City of Capital*. Oxford: Basil Blackwell.

Coates, D. (2000), *Models of Capitalism: Growth & Stagnation in the Modern Era*. Cambridge: Polity Press.

Cohen, B. J. (1986), *In Whose Interest? International Banking and American Foreign Policy*. New Haven, CT: Yale University Press.

Collins, M. (1988), *Money and Banking in the U.K.: A History*. London: Croom Helm.

Cooper, R. N. (1968), *The Economics of Interdependence: Economic Policy in the Atlantic Community*. New York: Columbia University Press.

Cottrell, P. L. (1995), 'The Bank of England in Its International Setting, 1918–1972', in R. Roberts and D. Kynaston (eds), *The Bank of England, 1694–1994*. Oxford: Clarendon Press.

Cox, A. (1986), 'The State, Finance & Industry Relationship in Comparative Perspective', in A. Cox (ed.), *State, Finance & Industry*. London: Harvestor Wheatsheaf.

Dalton, H. (1962), *High Tide and After: Memoirs 1945–1960*. London: Jonathon Cape.

Daunton, M. J. (1992a), 'Financial Elites & British Society, 1880–1950' in Y. Cassis (ed.), *Finance & Financiers in European History*. Cambridge: Cambridge University Press.

—— (1992b), 'Finance and Politics: Comments', in Y. Cassis (ed.), *Finance & Financiers in European History*. Cambridge: Cambridge University Press.

Davenport, N. (1964), *The Split Society*. London: Victor Gollancz.

—— (1974), *Memoirs of a City Radical*. London: Weidenfeld & Nicolson.

Davies, G. (1994), *A History of Money: From Ancient Times to the Present Day*. Cardiff: University of Wales Press.

Davis, P. (1992), 'The Eurobond Market', in D. Cobham (ed.), *Markets & Dealers: the Economics of the London Financial Markets*. London: Longham.

Davis, S. I. (1976), *The Euro-Bank*. London: Macmillan.

Dayer, R. A. (1988), *Finance & Empire: Sir Charles Addis, 1861–1945*. London: Macmillan.

De Cecco, M. (1974), *Money and Empire: The International Gold Standard, 1890–1914*. Oxford: Blackwell.

—— (1987), 'Financial Innovations and Monetary Theory', in M. de Cecco (ed.), *Changing Money: Financial Innovation in Developed Countries*. Oxford: Blackwell.

Denizet, J. (1971), in Bourguinat, H., Denizet J. and Perroux, F. *Inflation, Dollar, Euro-dollar*. Paris: NRF Gallimard.

Dickson, P. G. M. (1967), *The Financial Revolution in England: A Study in the Development of Public Credit, 1688–1756*. London: Macmillan.

Dosso, G. (1992), *The Eurobond Market*. London: Woodhead-Faulkner.

Dufey, G. and Giddy, I. H. (1978), *The International Money Market*. New York: Prentice-Hall.

Durham, K. (1992), *The New City*. London: Macmillan.

Eichengreen, B. (1990), *Elusive Stability: Essays in the History of International Finance, 1919–1939*. Cambridge: Cambridge University Press.

Einzig, P. (1964), *The Euro-dollar System*. London: Macmillan.

—— (1965a), *Foreign Dollar Loans in Europe*. London: Macmillan.

—— (1965b), *The Euro-bond Market*. London: Macmillan.

—— (1971), *Parallel Money Markets vol. 1: The New Markets in London*. London: Macmillan.

—— (1972), *Parallel Money Markets vol. 2: Overseas Markets*. London: Macmillan.

Einzig, P. and Quinn, B. S. (1977), *The Euro-dollar System*. London: Macmillan.

Elgie, R. and Thompson, H. (1998), *The Politics of Central Banking*. London: Routledge.

Evans, J. S. (1992), *International Finance: A Markets Approach*. Orlando, FL: The Dryden Press.

Fay, S. (1988), *Portrait of an Old Lady*. London: Penguin Books.

Ferris, P. (1968), *Men and Money*. London: Hutchinson.

—— (1984), *Gentlemen of Fortune: The World's Merchant & Investment Bankers*. London: Weidenfeld & Nicholson.

Fetter, F. W. (1965), *Development of British Monetary Orthodoxy*. Cambridge, MA: Harvard University Press.

Fforde, J. (1992), *The Bank of England and Public Policy 1941–1958*. Cambridge: Cambridge University Press.

Forsyth, J. H. (1987), 'Financial Innovation in Britain', in M. de Cecco (ed.), *Changing Money: Financial Innovation in Developed Countries*. Oxford: Blackwell.

Fraser, I (1999), *The High Road to England*. Norwich: Michael Russell.

Fry, R. (ed.) (1970), *A Banker's World – The Revival of the City 1957–1970*. London: Hutchinson.

Galbraith, J. K. (1987), *A History of Economics*. Harmondsworth: Penguin Books.

Gardner, R. N. (1956), *Sterling-Dollar Diplomacy in Perspective*. Oxford: Oxford University Press.

—— (1969), *Sterling-Dollar Diplomacy in Current Perspective: The Origins and the Prospects of Our International Economic Order*. New York: McGraw-Hill Book Co.

Geddes, P. (1987), *Inside the Bank of England*. London: Boxtree.

Germain, R. D. (1997), *The International Organization of Credit: States and Global Finance in the World Economy*. Cambridge: Cambridge University Press.

Gerschenkron, A. (1962), *Economic Backwardness in Historical Perspective*. Cambridge, MA: Harvard University Press.

Gibson, H. D. (1989), *The Euromarkets: Domestic Financial Policy and International Instability*. London: Macmillan.

Giddens, A. (1990), *Consequences of Modernity*. Cambridge: Polity Press.

Giddy, I. H. (1994), *Global Financial Markets*. Toronto: D.C. Heath.

Gill, S. R. (1993a), 'Global Finance, Monetary Policy and Cooperation Among the Group of Seven, 1944–92', in P. G. Cerny (ed.), *Finance and World Politics: Markets, Regimes, and States in the Post-hegemonic Era*. Aldershot: Edward Elgar.

—— (1993b), 'Neo-Liberalism & the Shift Towards a US-Centred Transnational Hegemony', in H. Overbeek (ed.), *Restructuring Hegemony in the Global Political Economy*. London: Routledge.

Gowan, P. (1999), *The Global Gamble: Washington's Faustian Bid for World Dominance*. London: Verso.

Grabbe, J. O. (1996), *International Financial Markets*. Englewood, NJ: Prentice-Hall.

Grady, J. and Weale, M. (1986), *British Banking, 1960–85*. London: Macmillan.

Green, E. H. H. (1992), 'The Influence of The City over British Economic Policy, 1880–1960', in Y. Cassis (ed.), *Finance & Financiers in European History*. Cambridge: Cambridge University Press.

Giuseppi, J. (1966), *The Bank of England: A History from its Foundation in 1694*. London: Evans Bros.

Hall, P. A. (1986a), 'The State & Economic Decline' in B. Elbaum and W. Lazonick (eds), *The Decline of the British Economy*. Oxford: Clarendon Press.

—— (1986b), *Governing the Economy*. Cambridge: Polity Press.

Hall, R. L. (1991), *The Robert Hall Diaries 1954–1961* (ed. A. Cairncross). London: Unwin Hyman.

Ham, A. (1981), *Treasury Rules*. London: Quartet.

Hampton, M. (1996), *The Offshore Interface: Tax Havens in the Global Economy*. New York: St. Martins Press.

Hancher, L. and Moran, M. (1989), 'Organising Regulatory Space', in L. Hancher and M. Moran (eds), *Capitalism, Culture and Economic Regulation*. Oxford: Clarendon Press.

Harris, L., Coakley, J., Croasdale, M. and Evans, T. (eds) (1988), *New Perspectives on the Financial System*. USA: Croom Helm.

Harris, N. (1972), *Competition and the Corporate State*. London: Methuen.

Harris, S. E. (1964), *Economics of the Kennedy Years*. London: Harper & Row.

Harvey, D. (1982), *The Limits to Capital*. Oxford: Basil Blackwell.

Hawley, J. (1987), *Dollars and Borders: US Government Attempts to Restrict Capital Flows, 1960–1980*. New York: M.E. Sharpe Inc.

Hayes, S. L. and Hubbard, P. M. (1990), *Investment Banking: A Tale of Three Cities*. Boston: Harvard Business School Press.

Helleiner, E. (1991), *American Hegemony and Global Economic Structure: From Closed to Open Financial Relations in the Postwar World*. Ph. D. dissertation, London School of Economics, (unpublished).

Helleiner, E. (1993), 'When Finance was the Servant: International Capital Movements in the Bretton Woods Order', in P. G. Cerny (ed.), *Finance and World Politics: Markets, Regimes and States in the Post-Hegemonic Era*. Aldershot: Elgar.

—— (1994a), *States & the Reemergence of Global Fanance*. New York: Cornell University Press.

—— (1994b), 'From Bretton Woods to Global Finance: A World Turned Upside Down', in R. Stubbs and G. R. D. Underhill (eds), *Political Economy and the Changing Global Order*. London: Macmillan.

Higonnet, R. (1985), 'Eurobanks, Eurodollars and International Debt', in P. Savona and G. Sutija (eds) (1985), *Euro-dollars and International Banking*. London: Macmillan.

Hill, C. (1984), *The Century of Revolution, 1603–1714*. Wokingham: Van Nostrand Reinhold.

Hinton, A. (1987), *City within a State: A Portrait of Britain's Financial World*. London: Tauris.

Hirsch, F. (1965), *The Pound Sterling*. London: Victor Gollancz.

—— (1967), *Money International*. London: Penguin.

Hogan, W. P. and Pearce, I. F. (1982), *The Incredible Euro-dollar*. London: Allen & Unwin.

Holmes, A. R. and Green, E. (1986), *Midland: 150 Years of Banking Business*. London: B.T. Batsford.

Howson, S. (1975), *Domestic Money Management in Britain 1919–1938*. Cambridge: Cambridge University Press.

—— (1993), *British Monetary Policy 1945–1951*. Oxford: Clarendon Press.

Ingham, G. (1982), 'Divisions within the Dominant Class and British "Exceptionalism" ', in A. Giddens and G. McKensie (eds), *Social Class & the Division of Labour*. Cambridge: Cambridge University Press.

—— (1984), *Capitalism Divided? The City & Industry in British Social Development*. London: Macmillan.

Institute of Bankers (1961), *The City of London as a Centre of International Trade & Finance*. London: Institute of Bankers.

Johns, R. A. (1983), *Tax Havens and Offshore Finance: A Study in Transnational Economic Development*. London: Pinter.

Johns, R. A. and Le Marchant, C. M. (1993), *Finance Centres: British Isle Offshore Development Since 1979*. London: Pinter.

Jones, G. (1993), *British Multinational Banking*. Oxford: Oxford University Press.

—— (1998), 'Banking after the Second World War', in S. Kinsey (ed.), *International Banking in an Age of Transition*. Aldershot: Ashgate.

Keegan, W. and Pennant-Rea, R. (1979), *Who Runs the Economy?* London: Maurice Temple Smith.

Kellett, R. (1967), *The Merchant Banking Arena*. London: Macmillan.

Kelly, J. (1976), *Bankers & Borders*. Cambridge, MA: Ballinger.

Kerr, I. M. (1984), *A History of the Eurobond Market: The First 21 Years*. London: Euromoney Publications.

Keynes, J. M. (1970), 'The Economic Consequences of Mr Churchill', in S. Pollard (ed.), *The Gold Standard & Employment Policies Between the Wars*. London: Methuen.

Kolko, J. and Kolko, G. (1972), *The Limits of Power: The World and United States Foreign Policy, 1945–54*. NY: Harper & Row.

Kunz, D. (1987), *The Battle for Britain's Gold Standard in 1931*. London: Croom Helm.

Kynaston, D. (1994), *The City of London: A World of its Own, 1815–90*. London: Chatto & Windus.

—— (1995a), 'The Bank and the Government', in R. Roberts and D. Kynaston (eds), *The Bank of England, 1694–1994*. Oxford: Clarendon Press.

—— (1995b), *The City of London: Golden Years, 1890–1914*. London: Chatto & Windus.

—— (1999), *The City of London: Illusions of Gold, 1914–1945*. London: Chatto & Windus.

—— (2002), *The City of London: A Club No More, 1945–2000*. London: Pimlico.

Lash, S. and Urry, J. (1987), *The End of Organized Capitalism*. Cambridge: Polity Press.

Lawson, N. (1992), *The View from No. 11: Memoirs of a Tory Radical*. London: Bantam Press.

Lazar, D. (1990), *Markets & Ideology in the City of London*. London: Macmillan.

Leyshon, A. and Thrift, N. (1997), *Money/Space: Geographies of Monetary Transformation*. London: Routledge.

Little, J. S. (1985), 'Comment' on R. Higonnet, 'Eurobanks, Eurodollars and International Debt', in P. Savona and G. Sutija (eds), *Euro-dollars and International Banking*. London: Macmillan.

Longstreth, F. (1979), 'The City, Industry & the State', in C. Crouch (ed.), *State & the Economy in Contemporary Capitalism*. London: Croom Helm.

Loriaux, M. (1997a), 'Capital, the State, and Uneven Growth', in M. Loriaux *et al. (eds), Capital Ungoverned: Liberalizing Finance in Interventionist States*. Ithaca, NY: Cornell University Press.

—— (1997b), 'The End of Credit Activism in Interventionist States', in M. Loriaux *et al. (eds), Capital Ungoverned: Liberalizing Finance in Interventionist States*. Ithaca, NY: Cornell University Press.

Macrae, N. (1955), *The London Capital Market*. London: Staples Press.

Marx, K. (1976), *Capital, Vol. 1*. Harmondsworth: Penguin.

Mason, S. (1976), *The Flow of Funds in Britain: An Introduction to Financial Markets*. London: Paul Elek.

Mayer, M. (1976), *The Bankers*. London: W.H. Allen.

Mayhew, N. (1999), *Sterling: The Rise and Fall of a Currency*. London: Allen Lane, the Penguin Press.

McKenzie, G. W. (1976), *The Economics of the Euro-Currency System*. London: Macmillan.

McRae, H. and Caincross, F. (1973), *Capital City*. London: Eyre Methuen.

Meier, G. M. (1982), *Problems of a World Monetary Order*. New York: Oxford University Press.

Mendelsohn, M. S. (1980), *Money on the Move. The Modern International Capital Market*. New York: McGraw-Hill.

Michie, R. C. (1992), *The City of London: Continuity and Change, 1850–1990*. London: Macmillan.

Mikesell, R. F. and Furth, J. H. (1974), *Foreign Dollar Balances and the International Role of the Dollar*. New York: National Bureau of Economic Research.

Milward, A. S. (1992), *The European Rescue of the Nation-State*. London: Routledge.

Mints, L. W. (1946), *A History of Banking Theory in Great Britain and the United States*. Chicago: University of Chicago.

Mitnick, B. M. (1980), *The Political Economy of Regulation.* New York: Columbia University Press.

Moggridge, D. E. (1969), *The Return to Gold.* Cambridge: Cambridge University Press.

Moran, M. (1983), 'Power, Policy & the City of London', in R. King (ed.), *Capital & Politics.* London: Routledge.

—— (1984), *The Politics of Banking.* London: Macmillan.

—— (1991), *The Politics of the Financial Services Revolution.* London: Macmillan.

Morgan, K. O. (1997), *Callaghan: A Life.* Oxford: Oxford University Press.

Nau, N. (1990), *The Myth of America's Decline.* New York: Oxford University Press.

Newton, S. and Porter, D. (1988), *Modernisation Frustrated: The Politics of Industrial Decline in Britain Since 1900.* London: Unwin Hyman.

Overbeek, H. (1990), *Global Capitalism & National Decline.* London: Unwin Hyman.

—— (1993), 'Atlanticism & Europeanism in British Foreign Policy', in H. Overbeek (ed.), *Restructuring Hegemony in the Global Political Economy.* London: Routledge.

Palan, R. and Abbott, J. (1996), *State Strategies in the Global Political Economy.* London: Pinter.

van der Pijl, K. (1984), *The Making of an Atlantic Ruling Class.* London: Verso.

Pilbeam, K. (1998), *International Finance.* London: Macmillan.

Pimlott, B. (1992), *Harold Wilson.* London: Harper Collins.

Plender, J. and Wallace, P. (1985), *The Square Mile.* London: Century Hutchinson.

Plowden, E. (1989), *An Industrialist in the Treasury.* London: Andre Deutsch.

Pollard, S. (1970), 'Editor's Introduction', in S. Pollard (ed.), *The Gold Standard & Employment Policies Between the Wars.* London: Methuen.

—— (1979), 'The Nationalisation of the Banks: The Chequered History of a Socialist Proposal', in D. Martin and D. Rubinstein (eds), *Ideology & the Labour Movement.* London: Croom Helm.

—— (1982), *The Wasting of the British Economy: British Economic Policy, 1945 to the Present.* London: Croom Helm.

—— (1992), *The Development of the British Economy, 1914–1990,* 4th edn. London: Edward Arnold.

Ponting, C. (1989), *Breach of Promise.* London: Hamish Hamilton.

Porter, T. (1993), *States, Markets and Regimes in Global Finance.* New York: St. Martin's Press.

Powell, J. (1988), *The Gnomes of Tokyo.* New York: Amacom.

Pressnell, L. S. (1986), *External Economic Policy Since the War: Vol. 1, The Post-War Financial Settlement.* London: Her Majesty's Stationery Office.

Pringle, R. (1973), *Banking in Britain.* London: Charles Knight.

Przeworski, A. (1990), *The State and the Economy under Capitalism.* London: Harwood.

Ramsay, R. (1998), *Prawn Cocktail Party.* London: Vision Paperbacks.

Reading, B. (1969), 'Euro-Dollars-Tonic or Toxic?', in E. Chalmers (ed.), *Readings in the Euro-Dollar.* London: Griffith & Sons.

Reid, M. (1988), *All Change in the City.* London: Macmillan.

Roberts, R. (1992), *Schroders: Merchants and Bankers.* London: Macmillan.

—— (1995), 'The Bank and the City', in R. Roberts and D. Kynaston (eds), *The Bank of England, 1694–1994.* Oxford: Clarendon Press.

Roberts, R. and Kynaston, D. (eds) (1995), *The Bank of England, 1694–1994*. Oxford: Clarendon Press.

Roosa, R. V. (1967), 'Second Lecture', in M. Friedman and R. V. Roosa, *The Balance of Payments: Free Versus Fixed Exchange Rates*. Washington, D.C.: American Enterprise Institute for Public Policy Research.

Roseveare, H. (1969), *The Treasury: The Evolution of a British Institution*. London: Allen Lane.

Rubinstein, W. D. (1993), *Capitalism, Culture & Decline in Britain*. London: Routledge.

Sampson, A. (1965), *Anatomy of Britain Today*. London: Hodder & Stoughton.

—— (1981), *The Moneylenders*. London: Hodder & Stoughton.

Sarver, E. (1988), *The Eurocurrency Handbook*. New York: Prentice-Hall.

Savona, P and Sutija, G. (eds) (1985), *Eurodollars & International Banking*. Basingstoke: Macmillan, in association with International Banking Center, Florida International University.

Sayers, R. S. (1967), Modern Banking. Oxford: Clarendon Press.

—— (1976), *The Bank of England, 1891–1944. Vol. 1*. London: Cambridge University Press.

Scammell, W. M. (1968), *The London Discount Market*. London: Elek Books.

Schonfield, A. (1958), *British Economic Policy Since the War*. Harmondsworth: Penguin.

Scott-Quinn, B. (1975), *The New Euromarkets*. London: Macmillan .

Shaw, E. R. (1975), *The London Market*. London: Heineman.

Smith, A. (1982), *Paper Money*. London: Macdonald.

Snooks, G. D. (1998), *The Laws of History*. London: Routledge.

Solomon, S. (1995), *The Confidence Game: How Unelected Central Bankers are Governing the Changed Global Economy*. New York: Simon & Schuster.

Spiegelberg, R. (1973), *The City: Power without Accountability*. London: Quartet.

Steinberg, J. (1976), *Why Switzerland?* Cambridge: Cambridge University Press.

Stewart, M. (1967), *Keynes and After*. Harmondsworth: Pelican Books.

Stigum, M. (1978), *The Money Market*. Homewood, IL: Dow Jones-Irwin.

Stones, R. (1988), *State-Finance Relations in Britain 1964–70: A Relational Approach to Contemporary History. Essex Papers in Politics*. University of Essex: Dept. of Government.

Strange, S. (1971), *Sterling & British Policy: A Political Study of an International Currency in Decline*. London: Oxford University Press.

—— (1976), 'International Monetary Relations', in A. Shonfield (ed.), *International Economic Relations of the Western World, 1959–1971*. Oxford: Oxford University Press.

—— (1986), *Casino Capitalism*. Oxford: Blackwell.

Streeck, W. and Schmitter, P. C. (1985), 'Commnuity, Market, State and Associations? The Prospective Contribution of Interest Governance to Social Order', in W. Streeck and P. C. Schmitter (eds), *Private Interest Government: Beyond Market and State*. London: Sage.

Struthers J. and Speight, H. (1986), *Money: Institutions, Theory & Policy*. London: Longman.

Tew, B. (1985), *The Evolution of the International Monetary System, 1945–1985*. London: Hutchinson.

Trimberger, E. K. (1978), *Revolution from Above: Military Bureaucrats and Development in Japan, Turkey, Egypt and Peru*. New Brunswick, NJ: Transaction Books.

Tuma, E. H. (1971), *Economic History and the Social Sciences: Problems of Methodology*. Berkeley, CA and Los Angeles: University of California Press.

Van Dormael, A. (1978), *Bretton Woods: Birth of a Monetary System*. London: Macmillan.
—— (1997), *The Power of Money*. London: Macmillan.
Versluysen, E. L. (1981), *The Political Economy of International Finance*. Farnborough: Gower.
Wachtel, H. M. (1990), *The Money Mandarins*. London: Pluto Press.
Wechsberg, J. (1966), *The Merchant Bankers*. London: Weidenfeld & Nicholson.
Welsh, F. (1986), *Uneasy City: An Insider's View of the City of London*. London: Weidenfeld & Nicholson.
Widlake, B. (1986), *In the City*. London: Faber & Faber.
Williamson, P. (1984), 'Financiers, The Gold Standard and British politics, 1925–1931', in Turner, J. (ed.), *Business and Politics*. London: Heinemann.
Wilson, C. (1965), *England's Apprenticeship, 1603–1763*. London: Longman.
Wilson, H. (1971), *The Labour Government 1964–1970*. London: Weidenfeld & Nicolson.
—— (1974), *The Labour Government 1964–1970*. Harmondsworth: Pelican Books.
Winton, J. R. (1969), *Lloyds Bank 1918–1969*. Oxford: Oxford University Press.
Wojnilower, A. M. (1987), 'Financial Change in the United States', in M. de Cecco (ed.), *Changing Money: Financial Innovation in Developed Countries*. Oxford: Blackwell.
Wootton, G. (1980), 'The Impact of Organised Interests', in, W. B. Gwyn and R. Rose (eds), *Britain: Progress & Decline*. London: Macmillan.
Young, G. K. (1966), *Merchant Banking: Practice and Prospects*. London: Weidenfeld & Nicholson.
Zysman, J. (1984), *Governments, Markets and Growth: Financial systems and the Politics of Industrial change*. London: Cornell University Press.

Articles, essays, pamphlets, papers and electronic texts

Altman, O. L. (1961), 'Foreign Markets for Dollars, Sterling & Other Currencies', *I.M.F. Staff Papers*, Vol. 8: 313–352.
—— (1962), 'Canadian Markets for U.S. Dollars', *I.M.F. Staff Papers*, Vol. 9: 297–316.
Anderson, P. (1987), 'The Figures of Descent', *New Left Review*, 161 (January—February): 20–77.
Anderson, R. B. (1960), 'The Balance of Payments Problem', *Foreign Affairs*, Vol. 38: 419–432.
Bank of England (1963), 'On London as a Commercial Centre', *B.E.Q.B.* (June): 346–349.
—— (1964), 'U.K. Banks' External Liabilities and Claims in Foreign Currencies, *B.E.Q.B.* (June): 100–108.
—— (1967), 'The U.K. Exchange Control: A Short History', *B.E.Q.B.* (September): 245–260.
—— (1968), 'The Exchange Equalisation Account: Its Origins and Development', *B.E.Q.B.*, Vol. 8, No. 4 (December): 377–387.
—— (1972), *B.E.Q.B.* (June).
Banker (1958), Vol. CVIII: 171.
—— (1959), Vol. CVIV: 27.
—— (1960), 'Change at the Bank', Vol. CX: 775–778.

—— (1962), 'Economizing America's Gold', Vol. CXII (June): 346.

—— (1963), 'More Euro-dollars for BOLSA', Vol. CXIII (April): 222.

—— (1963), Vol. CXII (June): 377.

—— (1963), 'Euro-dollars for Highways', Vol. CXIII (August): 518.

—— (1963), 'America Tackles its Deficit', Vol. CXIII (August): 519–526.

—— (1967), Vol. CXVII: 1030.

—— (1969), 'The Euro-Dollar Market: What it Means for London', Vol. CXIX: 773–781.

Barratt Brown, M. B. (1988), 'Away with all the Great Arches: Anderson's History of British Capitalism', *New Left Review*, 167: 22–51.

Blank, S. (1997), 'Britain: The politics of Foreign Economic Policy, the Domestic Economy, and the Problem of Pluralistic Stagnation', *International Organization*, Vol. 31: 673–721.

Bloomfield, A. L. (1946), 'Postwar Control of International Capital Movements', *American Economic Review*, Vol. 36 (March–May): 687–709.

Blunden, G. (1975), 'The Supervision of the UK Banking System', *Bank of England Quarterly Bulletin*, Vol. 15: 188–195.

Bolton. G. (Sir) (1963), 'International Money Markets', *Bank of London & South America Quarterly Review* (July): 113–119.

—— (1967a), 'Review of the Year', *BOLSA Review:* 118–126.

—— (1967b), 'Devaluation', *BOLSA Review*; 470–475.

—— (1970a), 'What the Bank of England is', *Banker*, Vol. 120 (August): 820–825.

Burk, K. (ed.) (1992b), 'Witness Seminar on the Origins and Early Development of the Eurobond Market', *Contemporary European History*, Vol. 1, part 1: 65–87.

Burn, G. (1999), 'The State, the City and the Euromarkets', *Review of International Political Economy*, Vol. 6, No. 2 (Summer): 225–261.

—— (2000), 'La Naissance des Eurodollars', *Alternatives Economiques*, No. 182 (June): 60–63.

Cain, P. J. and Hopkins, A. G. (1986), 'Gentlemanly Capitalism & British Expansion Overseas, Vol. I: The Old Colonial System 1688–1850', *Economic History Review*, 2nd ser. XXXIX, 4: 501–525.

—— (1987), 'Gentlemanly Capitalism & British Expansion Overseas, Vol. II: New Imperialism 1850–1945', *Economic History Review*, 2nd ser. XL, 1: 1–26.

Clarke, W. M. (1968), 'Bolsa and the City's Overseas Earnings', *BOLSA Review*, Vol. 2: 15–19.

Crick, W. F. (1967), 'The City and the Pound; Yesterday, Today and Tomorrow', *Banker*, Vol. 117: 700–707.

Daunton, M. J. (1989), ' "Gentlemanly Capitalism" and British Industry', *Past and Present*, No. 122 (February): 119–158.

—— (1993), 'Inside the Bank of England', *Twentieth Century British History*, Vol. 4, No. 2, 197–200.

De Cecco, M. (1976), 'International Financial Markets and US Domestic Policy Since 1945', *International Affairs*, Vol. 52: 381–399.

Devons, E. (1959), 'An Economist's View of the Bank Rate Tribunal Evidence; The Bank Rate Tribunal Evidence: a Symposium', *The Manchester School of Economic & Social Studies*, Vol. XXVII, No. 1 (January): 1–17.

The Economist (1944), 'Government in the City', Vol. CXLVI (1 January): 17–18.

The Economist (1945), Vol. CXLVII: 513.

—— (1959), 'Dollar Deposits in London' (11 July): 109–110.

Einzig, P. (1960), 'Dollar Deposits in London', *Banker*, Vol. CX (January): 23–27.

—— (1962), 'The Relations Between Practice and Theory of Forward Exchange', *Banca Nazionale del Lavoro*, Vol. 15, No. 62 (September): 227–239.

—— (1964b), 'European Capital Markets', *National Banking Review*, 569–576.

Evans, J. (1994), 'Currency Trading Hits New Heights', *The European*, (13–19 May).

Friedman, M. (1969), 'The Euro-dollar Market: Some First Principles', *The Morgan Guaranty Survey* (October).

Gardner, R. N. (1960), 'Strategy for the Dollar', *Foreign Affairs*, Vol. 36: 434.

Glyn, A. (1986), 'Capital Flight and Exchange Controls', *New Left Review*, No. 155 (January/February): 37–49.

Grabbe, J. O. (1995), *The End of Ordinary Money, Part II: Money Laundering, Electronic Cash, and Cryptological Anonymity* (May). Web page: http://www.ci.net/kalliste/.

Green, E. H. H. (1988), 'Rentiers Versus Producers? The Political Economy of the Bimetallic Controversy', *English History Review* (July): 588–612.

Hanham, H. J. (1959), 'A Political Scientist's View; The Bank Rate Tribunal Evidence: a Symposium', *The Manchester School of Economic & Social Studies*, Vol. XXVII, No. 1 (January): 17–29.

Helleiner, E. (1992), 'States and the Future of Global Finance', *Review of International Studies*, No. 18: 31–49.

Hirsch, F. (1962), 'Expedients for the Exchanges: The American Initiative', *Banker*, Vol. CXII (May): 292–300.

Holmes, A. R. and Klopstock, F. H. (1960b), 'The Market for Dollar Deposits in Europe', *Federal Reserve Bank of New York Monthly Review* (November): 197–202.

Howson, S. (1988), ' "Socialist" Monetary Policy: Monetary Thought in the Labour Party in the 1940s', *History of Political Economy*, Vol. 20, No. 4: 543–564.

—— (1991), 'The Problem of Monetary Control in Britain, 1948–51', *The Journal of European Economic History*, Vol. 20, No. 1 (Spring).

Ingham, G. (1988), 'Commercial Capital and British Development: A Reply to Michael Barratt Brown', *New Left Review*, No. 172: 45–65.

Johnson, N. O. (1964), 'Eurodollars in the New International Money Market', *First National City Bank*, 6–7.

Leys, C. (1986), 'The Formation of British Capital', *New Left Review*, 160 (November–December): 114–120.

Lisle-Williams, M. (1984a), 'Beyond the Market: the Survival of Family Capitalism in the English Merchant Banks', *The British Journal of Sociology*, Vol. XXXV, No. 2 (June): 241–271.

—— (1984b), 'Merchant Banking Dynasties in the English Class Structure: Ownership, Solidarity Kinship in the City of London, 1850–1960', *The British Journal of Sociology*, Vol. XXXV, No. 3 (September): 333–362.

Lupton, T. and Wilson, C. S. (1959), 'The Social Background & Conections of "Top Decision Makers"; The Bank Rate Tribunal Evidence: A Symposium', *The Manchester School of Economic & Social Studies*, Vol. XXVII, No. 1 (January): 30–51.

Machlup, F. (1970), 'Eurodollar Creation: A Mystery Story', *Banca Nazionale Del Lavaro Quarterly Review*, Vol. 23 (September): 219–260.

McKinnon, R. I. (1977), 'The Eurodollar Market', *Essays in International Finance*, No. 125 (December), Princeton, NJ: International Finance Section, Dept. of Economics, Princeton University.

McMahon, C. (1964), 'Sterling in the Sixties', *Chatham House Essay*: 4. Oxford: Oxford University Press.

Moran, M. (1981), 'Finance Capital and Pressure-Group Politics', *British Journal of Political Science*, Vol. 11: 384–404.

—— (1988), 'The City of London as a Pressure Group Since 1945', *Contemporary Record*, Vol. 2 (Summer): 29–30.

Newton, C. C. S. (1986), 'Operation Robot and the Political Economy of Sterling Convertibility, 1951–1952', *EUI Working Paper no. 86/256*. Florence: European University Institute.

Nobay, A. R. (1973), 'The Bank of England, Monetary Policy & Monetary Theory in the UK, 1951–1971', *The Manchester School of Economic & Social Studies*, Vol. 41.

North, D. C. and Weingast, B. R. (1989), 'Constitutions and Commitment: The Evolution of Institutions Governing Public Choice in Seventeenth-Century England', *The Journal of Economic History*, Vol. 89 (December): 803–832.

Palan, R. (1998), 'Trying to Have Your Cake and Eating it: How and Why the State System has Created Offshore', *International Studies Quarterly*, Vol. 42: 625–644.

Peters, J. (1993), 'The British Government and the City–Industry Divide: The Case of the 1914 Financial Crisis', *Twentieth Century British History*, Vol. 4, No. 2, 126–48.

Pressnell, L. S. (1978), '1925: The Burden of Sterling', *Economic History Review*, 2nd Series, Vol. 31: 67–88.

Procter, S. J. (1993), 'Floating Convertibility: The Emergence of the Robot Plan, 1951–52', *Contemporary Record*, Vol. 7, No.1 (Summer).

Reich, C. (1980), 'The Confessions of Siegmund Warburg', *Institutional Investor*, (March).

Richardson, G. (1966), 'The Organisation and Practice of Investment and Merchant Banking', Paper No. 361 which Richardson introduced at a seminar on *Problems in Industrial Administration 1965/66*, on 25 January, at the London School of Economics & Political Science.

Robbie, K. J. H. (1975/76), 'Socialist Banks and the Origins of the Euro-currency Markets', *Moscow Narodny Bank Quarterly Review* (Winter): 21–36.

Roberts, R. (1993a), 'Birthday of the Bond', *The Times* (14 January): 27.

Roosa, R. V. (1963), 'Reforming the International Monetary System', *Foreign Affairs*, No. 42 (October): 107–122.

Roosa, R. V. and Hirsch, F. (1966), 'Reserves, Reserve Currencies, and Vehicle Currencies: An Argument', *Essays in International Finance*, No. 54 (May).

Rubinstein, W. D. (1977), 'Wealth, Elites, & the Class Structure of Modern Britain', *Past & Present*, Vol. 76: 99–26.

Schenk, C. R. (1998), 'The Origins of the Eurodollar Market in London: 1955–63', *Explorations in Economic History*, Vol. 35: 221–238.

—— (1992), 'The Sterling Area and the British policy Alternatives in the 1950s', *Contemporary Record*, Vol. 6, No. 2 (Autumn): 266–286.

Screpanti, E. (1999), 'Capitalist Forms and the Essence of Capitalism', *Review of International Political Economy*, Vol. 6, No. 1 (Spring): 1–26.

Swoboda, A. K. (1968), 'The Euro-Dollar Market: An Interpretation', *Essays in International Finance*, Princeton, NJ: International Finance Section, Dept. of Economics, Princeton University.

Tether, C. G. (1961), 'Dollars- Hard, Soft and Euro', *Banker*, Vol. CXI, No. 400 (June): 395–404.

Ticktin, H. (1983), 'The Transitional Epoch, Finance Capital and Britain', *Critique*, No. 16: 23–42.

Tomlinson, J. (1989), 'Labour's Management of the National Economy 1945–51: Survey and Speculations', *Economy and Society*, Vol. 18: 1–24.

Wriston, W. (1988), 'Technology and Sovereignty', *Foreign Affairs*, Vol. 67: 63–75.

Reports

Bell, P. W. (1962), 'Private Capital Movements and the US Balance of Payments Position', *Factors Affecting the US Balance of Payments*, prepared for the Subcommittee on International Exchange and Payments of the Joint Economic Committee: Washington: 395–482.

B.I.S. (1960), 'The Market for Dollar Deposits in Europe', *B.I.S. 30th Annual Report*.

—— (1964), *34th Annual Report*.

Cohen, B. J. (1963), 'The Interest Sensitivity of Certain Capital Movements in the US Balance of Payments', Report written for *FRBNY* (29 January).

—— (1963), 'A Survey of Capital Movements and Findings Regarding their Interest Sensitivity', *FRBNY* (5 July).

Committee on Finance and Industry (1931), *Report* Cmnd. 3897 (Macmillan Committee Report).

Committee on the Working of the Monetary System (1959), *Report* Cmnd. 827. (Radcliffe Committee Report) London: H.M.S.O.

Committee on Invisible Exports (1967), *Report* 'Britain's Invisible Earnings'. (Clarke Report) London: British National Export Council.

Holmes, A. R. and Klopstock, F. H. (1960a), 'The Continental Dollar Market', A Report Based on Visits to European Banks in June 1960 for the US Commission on Money and Credit, *FRBNY*, 26 August. Unpublished.

Kenen, P. B. (1962), 'Short-term Capital Investments and the US Balance of Payments'. Report written for the US Treasury (October).

New York Clearing House Association (1960), *A Study of Regulation Q as It Applies to Foreign Time Deposits* (July). The New York Clearing House Association.

Proceedings of the Tribunal Appointed to Inquire into Allegations that Information about the Raising of the Bank Rate was Improperly Disclosed, Report (1957), Cmnd. 350. London: H.M.S.O.

US Congress (1964), 'A Description and Analysis of Certain European Capital Markets, Paper No. 3 of Economic Policies and Practices'. *Materials Prepared for the Joint Economic Committee, Congress of the United States, 88th Congress, 2nd Session*, Washington, DC: U.S. Government Printing Office: pp. xii and 280.

US Congress (1976), The Congressional House Committee on Banking, Report. 'FINE'.

Letters

Sir George Blunden, 11 April 1997.
A. L. Coleby, 17 July 1997.
Douglas Dillon, 2 March 2000.
Richard Fry, 12 April 1997.
Henry Gillett, 24 December 1999.

Interviews

Cobbold, D., Lord (1997), 'Interview with David Cobbold', by Gary Burn (March).
Coleby, T. (1997), 'Interview with Tony Coleby', by Gary Burn (March).
Grunfeld, H. (1997), 'Interview with Henry Grunfeld', by Gary Burn (7 April).
Roosa, R. (1972), 'Interview with Robert Roosa', by John Richards, 17 November, Columbia Oral History, New York.
Spira, P. (1997), 'Interview with Peter Spira', by Gary Burn (24 June).

Speeches, lectures and conference presentations

Baring, G. R. (Earl of Cromer) (1962), 'Speech by the Governor of the Bank of England to the Bankers and Merchants of the City of London', 3 October, *Bank of England Quarterly Bulletin* (December): 263–265.
—— (1964), 'Speech by the Governor of the Bank of England to the Bankers and Merchants of the City of London on 3 November', *Bank of England Quarterly Bulletin* (December): 287–290.
—— (1965), 'Speech by the Governor of the Bank of England to the Bankers and Merchants of the City of London', 21 October, *Bank of England Quarterly Bulletin* (December): 346–349.
Bolton, G. (Sir) (1967), 'The International Money Market', in *The European Capital Market*, Report of Proceedings of Conference organised by the Federal Trust for Education. London: Federal Trust for Education & Research.
Cobbold, C. (1952), 'Speech by the Governor of the Bank of England to the Bankers and Merchants of the City of London', 7 October, 1952, *Bank of England Quarterly Bulletin* (December).
—— (1953), 'Speech by the Governor of the Bank of England to the Bankers and Merchants of the City of London', 14 October 1953, *Bank of England Quarterly Bulletin* (December).
—— (1956), 'Speech by the Governor of the Bank of England to the Bankers and Merchants of the City of London', 9 October 1956, *Bank of England Quarterly Bulletin* (December).
Dillon, D. (1962), 'Speech at 9th Annual Monetary Conference of the American Bankers Association', Rome, Italy (18 May).
Keynes, J. M. (1944), 'Speech in House of Lords in the debate on the Foundation of the IMF', 23 May 1944.

O'Brien, L. (1966), 'Speech by the Governor of the Bank of England to the Bankers and Merchants of the City of London', 20 October 1966, *Bank of England Quarterly Bulletin* (December): 352–355.

O'Brien, L. (1969), 'Speech by the Governor of the Bank of England to the Overseas Bankers Club', 3 February 1969, *Bank of England Quarterly Bulletin* (March): 74–76.

Roosa, R. V. (1967), 'Second Lecture', in M. Friedman and R.V. Roosa (eds), *The Balance of Payments: Free Versus Fixed Exchange Rates*. Washington, DC: American Enterprise Institute for Public Policy Research.

Index